IS PSYCHOLOGY FOR THEM?

A Guide to Undergraduate Advising

Paul J. Woods, editor

**American
Psychological
Association**

Library of Congress Cataloging-in-Publication Data

Is psychology for them?

Bibliography: p.
1. Psychology—Vocational Guidance—United
States. 2. Psychology—Study and teaching—United
States.
I. Woods, Paul J., 1930-
BF76.I76   1988   150′.23′73   88-3341
ISBN 1-55798-019-5

Copies may be ordered from:
Order Department
P.O. Box 2710
Hyattsville, MD 20784

Published by the
American Psychological Association
1200 Seventeenth Street, N.W.
Washington, DC 20036

Printed in the United States of America

Contents

Part **5**   **Preparing the psychology major for specific careers**

Part **6**   **Issues of interest to specific groups**

Preface

Faculty and staff members who help students select their courses of study and decide on majors know that some students have made clear, carefully considered decisions about their degree and career goals before they come to college—and that many students make those decisions (or change their initial decisions, sometimes more than once) after coming to college. Providing students with the help they need in making such decisions is one of those "miscellaneous" tasks to be performed—and it is not an easy one.

The faculty adviser is, in effect, a facilitator or guide who provides the student with basic information about a particular school's academic requirements and about the professions for which a particular degree provides a foundation. It is the faculty adviser's responsibility to know and understand the resources needed by the student and, as part of a department and school, help assemble those resources in a way that makes them useful to students. This task is complicated not only by changes occurring within a department and school and limitations on facilities and resources, but also by changes that may be occurring in a field of study and the discipline it represents. While coping with these changes, the faculty adviser has the weighty responsibility of conveying to students the philosophy of a profession, the knowledge base and tools needed to understand and function as a professional, the relationship of the individual professional to his or her colleagues, and the nature and requirements of professional practice in a variety of settings.

This volume, *Is Psychology for Them? A Guide to Undergraduate Advising,* and its companion student volume, *Is Psychology the Major for You? Planning for Your Undergraduate Years,* are designed to provide faculty advisers (and students) with the support they need as students decide on their major fields of study.

One only needs to review the content of these two volumes to see the widely divergent areas into which psychologists are moving.

The influence of psychology and psychologists extends far beyond the traditional arenas of the classroom, the laboratory, the clinic, and the personnel office. Indeed, it appears that there is virtually no area of human endeavor to which those trained in the content and methodology of psychology could not make a creative and valuable contribution. It is also clear that changes in what society will demand of psychologists in the future will occur. Futurists predict that as many as 80% of the jobs that will exist at the end of this century do not exist today. It is likely that this will be true as well in the applications of psychology and roles of psychologists.

Thus, today's students, as well as tomorrow's, are faced with the need to lay a foundation for career development that enables them to adapt to changing career directions. They will be unable to rely on specific sets of skills or plan for work in restricted career areas. What will be most valuable to them is a liberal education, one that provides a strong knowledge base in not only their area of specialization but also in other areas, as well as developing general skills in critical thinking, problem solving strategies, verbal ability, creative application of scientific methodology (both generally and specifically to psychology) to new areas, and so forth. The content of both *Is Psychology for You?* and *Is Psychology for Them?* is a useful resource for this kind of development.

Moreover, although the two volumes are directed toward answering the needs of the field of psychology, much of the information and, certainly, the approach advocated in the volumes can be used by other disciplines. Why? Because students and their advisers in all fields of study share a common need—to understand the relationship of individual abilities and goals and the requirements and benefits of work in a given profession.

Paul J. Woods
Hollins College

A word on how this volume was written

In 1984, a group of psychologists, some of whom contributed to the 1979 edition of *The Psychology Major: Training and Employment Strategies,* were asked to participate in a revision of that volume. All shared a common interest in helping students better prepare themselves to pursue a degree in psychology. Once the manuscripts were received and comments were provided by other psychologists and educators, it was recognized by all that what was really needed and, indeed, what was actually in hand, were two separate books— one for students and one for advisers. The decision was made to develop the two books separately, beginning with the student volume, now called *Is Psychology the Major for You? Planning for Your Undergraduate Years.* The student volume was published in the fall of 1987. As in the student's volume, the adviser's volume, *Is Psychology for Them? A Guide to Undergraduate Advising,* contains carefully selected and edited chapters drawn from the manuscripts originally developed for the revision of *The Psychology Major.*

Acknowledgement

A special thanks to the production staff at the American Psychological Association, especially to Brenda Bryant, who supervised the project and whose ideas and guidance were invaluable in the organization of both the student and advisers volume, and to Donna Stewart and Julia Frank-McNeil for their expert editing and restructuring of the book.

How to use this book

This volume provides basic information of use to those who must advise students. Used in conjunction with *Is Psychology the Major for You?*, the student handbook, this book will enable advisers to

- methodically assess student interest in the discipline of psychology;

- provide a foundation for the student's understanding of the discipline and requirements of psychology;

- understand the nature of good advisement;

- assess how the department's advising program and resources might be improved; and

- of course, become a more effective adviser.

Although the adviser and student volumes share some of the same content, the student edition contains only information that is considered useful to and understandable by the student. This adviser's edition contains greater detail about some matters (e.g., surveys), as well as selections that may help the adviser communicate with the student and other members of the faculty. The adviser's volume is both a resource and a functional tool, just as the student volume is.

Is Psychology for Them? has 35 chapters in six sections, a resource chapter, and two appendixes. It will be useful for the adviser to work through both volumes in order to understand what the student will be told and the exercises he or she will be doing, as well as to gain an understanding of how the adviser's volume can be used to enhance the student's understanding. The adviser and student volumes provide essential information but should be supplemented (see chapter 36, Resources,

and the resource list in the student edition) with other materials. The parts of this volume are described below.

Part 1, Is Psychology the Major for Them?, emphasizes student self-analysis of interests, the decision-making process that should be followed by the student (and supported by the adviser), what psychology offers the student, and what students should know before deciding on psychology as a major.

Part 2, Surveys of the Psychology Major, provides information on the application of psychology degrees to the world of work—the relationship between study and work, employer needs, and how people viewed their psychology degrees after graduation. The chapters emphasize both the general value of a psychology degree in many fields as well as the specific value of a psychology degree in psychology-related occupations.

Part 3, Advising the Psychology Major, reports on career preparation, counseling, and development options. It includes information on field experience and development of job-search skills.

Part 4, Psychology Majors in the Workplace and School, concerns the differences between preparing to seek work immediately on graduation and going on to graduate school.

Part 5, Preparing the Psychology Major for Specific Careers, provides information on what a psychology degree can mean to work in a variety of settings (and expands much of the information provided in part 3 of the student volume).

Part 6, Issues of Interest to Specific Groups, expands on part 6 of the student edition, providing information on special concerns of women, cultural groups, and older men and women returning to school or changing careers.

The Resources chapter lists publications, organizations, and other resources of use to both the adviser and the student.

The Appendixes include Appendix A, Titles of Jobs in Human Services for Students with a Bachelor's Degree in Psychology, and Appendix B, Guidelines for Preparing a Student Advisement Handbook.

The emphasis of both this volume and the student volume is that education, and learning to use one's education after one's school years have ended, is a growth process. For the student, that process involves learning more and more about himself or herself as a person and understanding what he or she can expect to face and to contribute as a professional. For the adviser, that process involves understanding the needs and expectations of not only the student but also of the school and the discipline of psychology, and, at least to some degree, of the work settings in which the skills and knowledge the school and the discipline of psychology have brought to the student.

As you, the adviser, work with students while using both of these volumes, you may find that additional information would be helpful. Please forward any suggestions in care of the Communications Office of the American Psychological Association, so that with *your advice*, we can better advise you in the future!

PART 1

Is psychology the major for them?

Initiating goal assessment

Chapter 1

Helping students choose careers in psychology

Paula Sachs Wise, Western Illinois University

I would like to begin by making two statements. First, I believe that any decisions about majors, minors, and careers are the primary responsibility of individual students. Parents, peers, and professors may serve as consultants and facilitators in the decision-making process, but they should not be making these important decisions for the students.

My second statement is that there are right reasons and wrong reasons for choosing a major, a minor, and a career. In my mind, the right reasons include interest, commitment, and satisfaction while the wrong reasons include almost everything else. I cannot imagine spending time, effort, and money preparing for a career in which I have little or no interest, but for which the employment opportunities appear to be good.

Admittedly, both of these statements are opinions. Yet, I believe that they merit careful consideration when one is faced with decisions which may have a tremendous impact on the course of one's life. Many students seem merely to follow the crowd to whatever major seems to provide the best job prospects at a particular time, regardless of whether they have the aptitude for or interest in that field.

I urge students to take the initiative in planning their careers. They should read all available material; ask questions; seek out individuals employed in occupations of interest to them; volunteer their services; and of course, get to know themselves.

In an attempt to assist in career exploration endeavors, I have prepared a list of questions that students should begin to answer before they can make a final decision. Ask students:

- Why did you decide to major in psychology?

- Does it seem as though you made the right decision? Why or why not?

- What options are available for psychology majors?

- Can you really do anything remotely resembling the activities of a psychologist with an undergraduate degree?

- Are you willing and able to attend a graduate or professional program to attain your occupational goals?

- What would you like to be doing 5 years after you graduate? 10 years? 25 years?

- What are your own strengths and weaknesses, likes and dislikes? How do they match with individuals in your preferred occupation?

- How committed are you to learning about prospective careers? Are you willing to seek out answers to your questions?

- Are you willing to try out various careers through volunteer work, field experience courses, seminars, or practicum experiences?

Of course there are no right or wrong answers to these questions. Still, I believe they are questions which must be addressed by students interested in career exploration.

Chapter 2

How to help students decide if psychology is the major for them

Patricia W. Lunneborg, University of Washington

This chapter is to help you advise students who want to choose their college major so that it will be the first step in a career. In career decision making, people typically go through a process of gathering information and mulling it over before making a choice. This process usually involves a succession of stages, proceeding from the exploration stage to the crystallization stage, to the choice stage, and finally to the clarification stage. This process does not follow a straight line and is not necessarily rational or even conscious. Furthermore, it can be so frightening that people would rather put it off.

If the student is just beginning the process of deciding a major, he or she will probably explore and crystallize (or more clearly define) his or her goals for about 2 years before choosing a major and clarifying that choice. Most students select their major by their junior year, after much weighing and rejecting of alternatives.

- Do some fieldwork.

- Take part in extracurricular activities.

- Get paid work experience.

- Talk to people about their occupations.

- Get to know your interests, values, and aptitudes.

- Prepare a resume and keep it up to date.

- Read career planning guides.

By taking advantage of the resources at hand, students can explore their course and career options. To help students crystallize what it is they really want to do, we suggest that you give them the following exercises. They can bring back the completed exercises, and you will have an excellent means to initiate a counselling session.

What to do for students at the exploration and crystallization stages

College is the students' first big step on the road to the future. From the start they must take advantage of all the resources around them. The following is a checklist of suggestions for students to use as they decide what they want to do.

- Gather information about careers.

- Take a variety of courses.

What to do for students at the choice stage

When students reach the choice stage, they will probably have experienced a change in outlook. They will feel more certain about the kind of work they want to do and clearer about the major they want to pursue. They should have a clearer idea of what major requirements are and what is left to be done. To help students choose a major, I suggest that you give them the following exercises. They can bring their results back to you for a counselling appointment.

The Learning Goal Exercise

The exercise of picking a learning goal has three steps.

Step 1. Go through the following list and check the three top learning goals that you think other students have. Think of other students you know and why you think they are in college. How do you believe they would finish the sentence, "I really want to learn. . . ."?

I really want to learn . . .

___ How to be more creative

___ How to change society

___ How to continue to learn

___ How to state hypotheses and test them

___ How to think logically

___ How to write well

___ How to speak effectively to others

___ How to be more confident socially

___ More about the arts

___ More about myself

___ More about values and ideas

___ New fields of knowledge

___ New modes of problem solving

___ Practical skills and knowledge

___ How to get along with all kinds of people

___ The background necessary for a particular career

___ How to appreciate my own and other cultures

Step 2. Now pick the learning goal of other students that you value most and write it below as your top learning goal. This goal may be one of the learning goals you checked off above or it could be different.

My top learning goal is

_____

Step 3. List some concrete steps you can take to reach it during the next year.

Three actions I can take to reach this goal:

1. Take courses in _____, _____, _____, and _____.

2. Join this extracurricular activity _____

   _____.

3. Do volunteer work at _____

   _____.

The Choice Exercise

Step 1. Think about two majors in which you are interested. Ask yourself the following questions and rate the likelihood of each. Are my chances of . . . poor, good, or very good?

1. Being accepted into the major _____

2. Making the grades necessary to graduate in the major _____

3. Making the grades required for graduate study in the major _____

If you are able to answer "very good" to the first two of these questions for any majors you are considering, go to Step 2 and evaluate and compare the majors by using the following rating scheme.

Step 2. For any major you are considering, rate the following factors in terms of their importance to you, using this scale: 1 = no importance, 2 = some importance, 3 = moderate importance, 4 = great importance.

Factors	Rate Importance to you
Good bachelor's-level job prospects	_____
Available career-oriented departmental advising	_____
Good contacts and relations between faculty and community	_____
Good general background for any career	_____
Good skills training for any career	_____
Good graduate-level job prospects	_____
Available independent study opportunities	_____
Available job-related fieldwork	_____
Major close to my career interests	_____
Good department reputation	_____
Highly interesting subject matter	_____

Step 3. You may want to use this exercise several times while you are choosing a major. Use it to evaluate psychology or any other major you are considering.

Write in the majors you are considering.

Psychology
_____
_____
_____
_____

Now, how do you believe each major rates at your college? Do one at a time. Using the same factors as in Step 2, rate each major, using the same point scale as before: 1 = none, 2 = some, 3 = moderate, 4 = great. Enter these points in column A. Then multiply the amount of each factor by the corresponding importance rating that you provided in Step 2 (column B). Complete the following table for each major being evaluated.

Column A Rating of major	Column B Your importance values from Step 2	Column C Multiply columns A and B
_____ Good bachelor's-level job prospects	_____	_____
_____ Available career-oriented departmental advising	_____	_____
_____ Good contacts and relations between faculty and community	_____	_____
_____ Good general background for any career	_____	_____
_____ Good skills training for any career	_____	_____
_____ Good graduate-level job prospects	_____	_____
_____ Available independent study opportunities	_____	_____
_____ Available job-related fieldwork	_____	_____
_____ Major close to my career interests	_____	_____
_____ Good department reputation	_____	_____
_____ Highly interesting subject matter	_____	_____
	_____ SUM	_____

What is the sum of these multiplied values? Add up column C to find out. Compare the various majors. The highest score wins!

What to do for students at the clarification stage

Once students have chosen a major, they must clarify that choice and their career direction. If they choose psychology as their major, they must ask themselves which of the following will be their primary goal? Which might be their alternate goal?

• A career requiring a bachelor's degree, related to psychology

• A career requiring a bachelor's degree, not related to psychology

• A career requiring graduate study in psychology

• A career requiring graduate study in another area

For both bachelor's-level plans, students will also have to clarify what supplementary area(s) of study to choose. The possibilities are numerous, including business administration, communications, economics, English, health, sociology, urban planning, wildlife science, and so forth. Minoring or taking a concentration of courses in a particular area of study can greatly strengthen the degree.

Chapter 3

Selecting psychology as a major: Some practical considerations

Bernardo J. Carducci, Indiana University Southeast

What is a psychologist?

Before considering whether or not to major in psychology, students need to ask themselves if this is really what they want. For example, when students are asked why they are majoring in psychology, they tend to give several general answers. Two of the most common answers given are "Because I want to be a psychologist" and "Because I want to help people." In response to the first answer, they need to be aware that the term *psychologist* implies that they have advanced training in psychology beyond the bachelor's degree. This training typically involves 2 to 5 additional years of postgraduate education, depending on whether one pursues a master's or a doctoral degree from a graduate program in psychology. So, if students really want to major in psychology because they want to "be a psychologist," or, more appropriately, be called a psychologist, they should plan on spending some additional time as an undergraduate thinking about how to get into graduate school, as well as preparing themselves to do well after they are admitted.

Becoming a psychologist requires that students receive training in psychology. There are many different types of educational programs that offer "psychology-related" training (Grosslight, 1984). Such training does not necessarily mean that they will be educated by psychologists. It could mean that they will be taught by individuals who have some training in psychology but do not have degrees in psychology and, therefore, are not psychologists. Such psychology-related training might be offered by schools of education, human services departments, counseling and guidance programs, schools of divinity, or sem-

inaries. If students are considering advanced training in psychology as preparation for becoming a psychologist, they should consult the American Psychological Association's (1988) *Graduate Study in Psychology and Associated Fields.* This book provides a brief description of many graduate programs in the United States and Canada that offer advanced training in psychology. Before applying to or entering any graduate program, students should inquire about the nature of the program and the academic background of the faculty.

Helping professions outside of psychology

As noted earlier, many students express a desire to major in psychology because they want to help people solve their problems. Such concern for others is extremely noble. However, there are a few things they should consider before using this reason as a basis for selecting psychology as a major. First of all, psychologists are not the only individuals who help others solve their problems. For example, when a loved one dies, a funeral director or member of the clergy may be of more emotional assistance than a psychologist. In helping individuals to cope with the trauma of rape, a sex therapist, who is not necessarily a psychologist, might be more helpful than a psychologist. In an effort to help minimize the stress related to adjusting to college and completing a college degree, many students seek emotional support by going to the student counseling center. In such settings, the people you talk to might be social workers or counselors whose training may not necessarily be from a psychology department. Individuals who work in a mental health center or mental hospital as psychiatric assistants, nursing aides, or orderlies may not have any formal academic training in psychology other than the in-house training sessions provided by the center or hospital. Yet, through their constant social support, such individuals can be of tremendous help to those suffering from emotional problems. The point of all this is that there are a variety of individuals helping people to solve their problems who are not necessarily psychologists. These individuals vary in the nature of problems they are qualified to treat and the nature of their professional training.

Before deciding to major in psychology because they want to help people, students probably should ask themselves what types of problems they want to help people solve. After they have made this decision, their next decision will be to determine what type of training will best prepare them to help these people. It could be that the best training might be in a discipline other than psychology. On the other hand, a major in psychology may be precisely the training they will need to meet their occupational goals.

An informational approach to career decision making

In an attempt to help students determine if psychology is the major for them, there are some suggestions you can make. Encourage students to read the bulletin of your college or university to see what courses are required for a psychology major. What they find out may cause them to change their minds. For example, to become a psychologist, undergraduates will have to take courses in statistics at the undergraduate and graduate levels. A non-mathematical person may not be able to meet some of the basic requirements for an undergraduate and graduate degree in psychology. Students may ask: What does being a mathematical person have to do with helping people solve their problems? The answer is that it has quite a bit to do with it if you take what you do seriously by maintaining a certain amount of continuous professional development. For example, as part of their continued professional development, many psychologists conduct research that is designed to assess the effectiveness of different approaches for dealing with certain problems. In order to accurately assess if one treatment is superior

to another, these psychologists have to statistically analyze their results.

Some students, however, have no intentions of ever doing such research. Why should they be required to take statistics? The answer is that even if one does not personally conduct research, solid knowledge of statistics is required to read, critically evaluate, and keep up to date on other's research. This is why psychology majors are required to take statistics. Thus, having some math skills is important to being a good psychologist, because students who want to be psychologists will have to take some statistics.

Another valuable source of information that students can use to decide if psychology is the major for them is to talk to individuals who are doing what they would like to be doing when they complete their educational training. When speaking with such people, students should ask them to indicate what they think is valuable training for the job. Such individuals will typically not only provide information about what courses students should take but also what type of experience they should have before deciding on their occupational choice. For example, those who want to work with alcoholics as a substance abuse counselor might find it useful to serve as a student volunteer in a substance abuse treatment center. It could be that after actually working with these individuals in a limited capacity, the student may decide that helping people solve their drinking problem is just not the right occupation. Finding out such things about oneself early in one's educational career is extremely important. Such a discovery can prevent students from wasting a lot of time and money on a college degree for an occupation that they will eventually discover is not right for them.

The career planning center on campus is another place for students to obtain valuable information concerning their occupational aspirations. For example, the career planning center can provide students with the names and phone numbers of individuals working in various areas of psychology, as well as make the initial arrangements for a visit. Because actually performing a job is probably the best way of determining whether or not one can and will enjoy doing it, career planning centers typically have arrangements with many local agencies and businesses for the utilization of students as volunteers or paid employees as a means of their gaining firsthand career experiences. Career counselors can be a valuable source of information for helping students discover what careers might be best suited for them. In this regard, occcupational interest tests and career counseling are two career-decision making services provided by these on-campus career centers. The earlier students visit the career planning center in their academic career, the more informed they will be about their occupational and professional career alternatives, and the sooner they will be able to start formulating a career-development strategy.

If, after discussing career objectives with a career counselor and other professionals working in the profession, the student decides to major in psychology, there are still a few more things to know about being a psychology major and about psychologists. This additional information has to do with how to utilize the knowledge about psychology he or she will obtain as a psychology major.

What do psychologists do?

One of the most frequently asked questions by students enrolled in psychology courses is "What can you do with a degree in psychology?" One way to respond to this question is to tell students some of the activities that psychologists are engaged in.

Teaching: The dispensing of knowledge

One principal activity engaged in by psychologists, particularly those working at a college or university, is teaching. Students probably think this is the only thing psychologists do. This is a natural assumption to make because interacting with instructors is probably the role students are most likely to associate with someone who is a psychologist. However, psychologists do a variety of other rather interesting things besides teach psychology.

The erroneous assumption that all psychologists do is teach may be one reason many students might shy away from psychology as a major. As most students are aware, teaching positions are becoming more and more difficult to obtain. As a result, if students thought that the only thing they could do with a psychology degree would be to enter a profession with shrinking opportunities, they would probably elect to major in something more promising, such as business, nursing, or computer science. However, as I hope to demonstrate, psychologists do many other things besides teach psychology.

Research: The quest for knowledge

Another principal activity of psychologists is conducting research. One type of research is basic research. Basic research is designed to test or develop theories about behavior. For example, psychologists doing basic research might be concerned with investigating how we see color, how information is organized in our memory system, or what causes depression. Applied research, on the other hand, has more to do with utilizing the information from basic research to deal with problems of a more practical nature. For example, psychologists might apply what they know about color vision to help design road signs or the packaging of breakfast cereal boxes. Information about human memory might be used in a school setting to help students with poor study habits improve their grades. Information about what factors cause depression can be used to help design rooms for the elderly living in nursing homes and college students living in dormitories so that individuals in both environments might function more effectively. Research conducted by psychologists can be performed within the confines of a university or privately owned company.

Clinical and counseling activities: Helping others to help themselves

Many psychologists are engaged in clinical or counseling activities. In this capacity, they might be working with severely depressed individuals in a mental hospital or with college students to help them overcome their test anxiety. Such activities can be done in both the public sector (e.g., university counseling center or state mental hospital) or the private sector (e.g., working with a company's alcoholic employees).

Business and industry activities: Psychology for profit

Psychologists are also engaged in a number of activities in the business sector. For example, industrial psychologists might be involved in the activities of a personnel office, performing such duties as screening and selecting potential employees, designing personnel training and development programs, and measuring employee proficiency. They might also be involved in the research and development aspect of the company. For example, a psychologist trained in personality psychology might be involved in the development of a test to help identify accident-prone individuals for the research and development department of an insurance company. Finally, a psychologist trained in physiological psychology might be employed by a pharmaceutical company that is testing the side effects of certain drugs being developed.

Where do psychologists work?

As you can see, psychologists are engaged in a variety of activities. However, the question students really want answered is not what psychologists actually do but: "Where can you find employment as a psychologist?" In response to this question, I have already shown that psychologists are engaged in a variety of activities, only some of which involve being an employee of a college or university. To illustrate this point, a recent survey indicated that the percentage of psychologists employed outside of academic settings is increasing, particularly in business, government, and human service settings (Stapp, Fulcher, Nelson, Pallak, & Wicherski, 1981). More specifically, in addition to working at a college or university, psychologists are employed by school systems and other educational settings; federal, state, and local government agencies; all branches of the military; both profit and nonprofit hospitals; human and social service agencies; a variety of businesses; and research and survey centers (cf. Boneau, 1968; Cates, 1970; Compton, 1966; Stapp & Fulcher, 1981, 1982).

As you can see, in response to the question concerning the employment opportunities with an advanced degree in psychology, it seems that one thing you can do is find employment. In fact, a survey (Stapp & Fulcher, 1983) of some 28,500 individuals with advanced psychology degrees indicated that 86.1% of those with doctoral degrees were employed full time, 7.8% were employed part time, .6% were unemployed but seeking employment, 1.3% were unemployed but not seeking employment, and 3.5% were retired. In the same survey of some 4,100 individuals with a master's-level degree, 73.3% were employed full time, 12.3% were employed part time, 1.3% were unemployed but seeking employment, 5.9% were unemployed but not seeking employment, and 6.9% were retired. Thus, the employment picture for those individuals with an advanced degree in psychology appears to be rather diverse and promising.

What can students do with a bachelor's degree in psychology?

While the employment prospects for those with an advanced degree in psychology appear very good, many psychology majors are proba-bly not interested in going on after graduation for the extra 2 to 3 years needed to obtain a master's degree or the additional 4 to 5 years needed to obtain a doctoral degree in psychology. If this is the case, the question students are probably asking themselves is: "What can I do with a bachelor's degree in psychology?" First of all, remind students that the field of psychology is essentially the study of people. And, as a result of this, in virtually any employment setting where the student works with people, a solid base of knowledge in psychology should make it possible for him or her to work more effectively with people. To be more specific, individuals having undergraduate degrees in psychology have found employment in a variety of different areas. For example, recent surveys of individuals holding bachelor's degrees in psychology report that psychology majors have found employment in such occupations as management trainee, fire fighter, salesclerk, library assistant, health services survey interviewer, flight attendant, college financial aid officer, computer analyst, advertising account executive, claims adjuster, and IRS examiner, to name just a few (Davis, 1979; Titley, 1979).

The important point for students to remember here is that the knowledge acquired in psychology can be put to work in a variety of employment settings. The key is being able to recognize where psychology can be applied, as well as supplementing coursework in psychology with courses related to the occupational career they wish to pursue (Carducci & Wheat, 1984). For example, as a psychology major interested in pursuing a career in management, they should take courses in principles of management, organizational behavior, economics, and accounting in the business department, as well as courses in psychology.

Should students select psychology as a major?

As you can see, the decision to select psychology as a major and to pursue a career utilizing one's knowledge of psychology involves some serious decisions. In this chapter, I have tried to make you aware of some of these relevant questions. In addition, I have attempted to provide you with some information and recommendations concerning some of the people students can talk to and places they can go for help to find some possible answers to these important questions

Should they become psychology majors? Returning to this initial question, the answer depends upon what they want to do, the kinds of people they like to work with, and the issues they wish to address. To help students make this decision, I would like to add that my own life is more interesting and exciting since I have become involved in the study of psychology as both a student and a psychologist.

References

American Psychological Association (1988). *Graduate study in psychology and associated fields*, 1988 ed. Washington, DC: Author.

Boneau, A. (1968). Psychology's manpower: Report on the 1966 national register of scientific and technical personnel. *American Psychologist, 23*, 325–334.

Carducci, B. J., & Wheat, J. E. (1984). Business: Open door for psych majors. *APA Monitor, 15*, 20.

Cates, J. (1970). Psychology's manpower: Report on the 1968 national register of scientific and technical personnel. *American Psychologist, 25*, 254–263.

Compton, B. E. (1966) Psychology's manpower: Characteristics, employment, and earnings. *American Psychologist, 21*, 224–229.

Davis, J. R. (1979). Where did they all go? A job survey of BA graduates. In P. J. Wood (Ed.). *The psychology major: Training and employment strategies* (pp. 110–114). Washington, DC: American Psychological Association.

Grosslight, J.H. (1984, March). *What the hell is going on—Will a real psychologist please stand up*. Paper presented at the meeting of the Southeastern Psychological Association, New Orleans.

Stapp, J., & Fulcher, R. (1981). The employment of APA members. *American Psychologist, 36*, 1263–1314.

Stapp, J., & Fulcher, R. (1982). The employment of 1979 and 1980 doctorate recipients in psychology. *American Psychologists, 37*, 1159–1185.

Stapp, J., & Fulcher, R. (1983). The employment of APA members: 1982. *American Psychologist, 38*, 1298–1320.

Stapp, J., Fulcher, R., Nelson, S. D., Pallack, M. S., & Wicherski, M. (1981). The employment of recent doctorate recipients in psychology: 1975 through 1978. *American Psychologist, 36*, 1211–1254.

Titley, R. W. (1979). Whatever happened to the class of '67? Psychology baccalaurate holders, one, five, and ten years after graduation. In P.J. Woods (Ed.), *The psychology major: Training and employment strategies* (pp. 103–109). Washington, DC: American Psychological Association.

PART 2

Surveys of the psychology major

Goals, curricula, employment

Chapter 4

Thirty years of psychology majors

Robert S. Harper, Knox College

ho are psychology undergraduate majors, and what do they do when they graduate? These are questions commonly asked by students considering a major in psychology. These are also questions that should be asked by faculty as they monitor their departmental curriculum. In reviewing the 30-year history of the psychology department of a small midwestern liberal arts college, some interesting answers emerge. Although the number of students involved and the absolute values of the percentages reported undoubtedly will vary from college to college, the trends probably will be very similar.

The study was carried out by grouping all of the graduates into 5-year units, beginning with psychology majors graduating in June 1954. As can be seen in Figure 4-1, the absolute number of psychology majors increased markedly through the 1969–1973 period and then dropped. This drop was associated with the economic changes of the early 1970s that adversely affected private colleges. Figure 4-2 shows that in the past 10 years approximately 60% of the psychology majors have been women, as contrasted with approximately 30% over the preceding 20 years. Figures 4-1 and 4-2 indicate that (a) the number of psychology majors has about doubled over the past 30 years, and (b) the majority of those majors now are women.

In Figure 4-3 the solid line represents the percentage of all psychology majors who continued on to graduate school. The dotted line represents those who entered a graduate program in psychology. When this figure is compared with Figure 4-1, it is apparent that the absolute number of psychology majors who have gone on to a graduate program has not changed markedly over the 30-year period; however, the percentage of psychology gradu-

ates going immediately into a graduate program in any field has declined noticeably since its peak in the 1959–1963 period. Since 1954 a steady 10% of psychology majors who had not gone directly into a graduate psychology program have entered graduate school in psychology later. The proportion of psychology majors who are going on to some graduate program has declined but is now stabilized at about 30%, and about 10% of the total graduates are going on to graduate school in psychology.

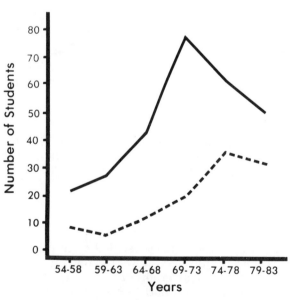

Figure 4-1. The number of students majoring in psychology at a small midwestern liberal arts college. The numbers are grouped in 5-year units from 1954-1983. The solid line represents the total number of students; the dotted line represents the number of female majors only.

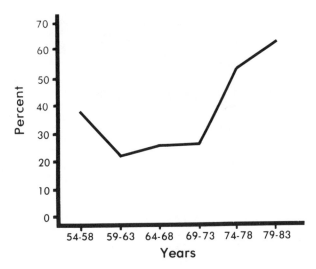

Figure 4-2. The solid line represents the percentage of all female psychology majors from the same midwestern college.

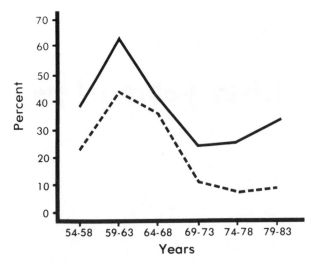

Figure 4-3. The percentage of all psychology majors who continued on to graduate school. The solid line represents those psychology majors who went on to any graduate program; the dotted line represents those who went on to a graduate psychology program.

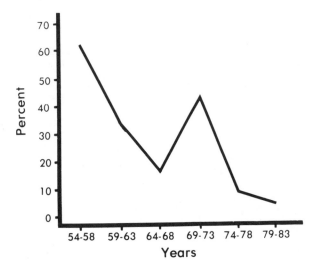

Figure 4-4. The solid line represents the percentage of all female psychology graduates of the small midwestern college who married soon after graduation.

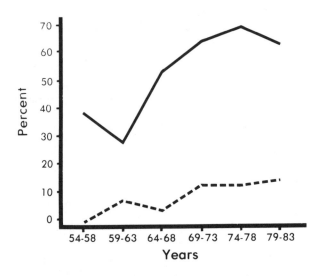

Figure 4-5. The percentage of psychology majors who took jobs after graduation. The solid line represents the percentage of those who took any job; the dotted line represents those who took psychology-related jobs.

Figures 4-4 and 4-5 present the strongest messages. Figure 4-4 shows the percentage of women psychology graduates who married immediately after graduation. Except for one upswing the figure shows an overall decline. I have no simple explanation for the 1969–1973 upswing, but the trend is obvious — almost two thirds of the women graduating in 1954–1958 reported that they married soon after graduation and were homemakers.

Women are now less likely to marry immediately after graduation.

What are the increasing number of women psychology graduates doing instead of becoming homemakers? Figure 4-5 shows that the majority of psychology graduates are entering the nonacademic work force, and most are entering the work force in positions that do not derive directly from their undergraduate psychology major.

In response to my initial questions, "What do undergraduate psychology majors do when they graduate?" and "What are the curricular implications of these postgraduate activities?" the figures show the following. About 10% of the psychology majors enter graduate programs in psychology, about 10% enter psychology-related jobs, about 20% enter other graduate programs, and about 60% enter the work force in positions not directly related to psychology. Approximately 10% of those not immediately entering a graduate program will do so later; 60% of the graduates are women, rather evenly distributed across the preceding four categories.

While a psychology department has an obligation to offer a sound curriculum to those entering graduate programs in psychology, departments cannot ignore the much larger group of graduates who are going into non-psychology-related careers. The greatest service an undergraduate psychology department can provide this group is to offer them training that increases their abilities to identify problems, to devise strategies for finding tenable solutions to those problems, and to be able to communicate their results and conclusions to others. This kind of training might be cloaked in some more attractive courses — industrial organizational psychology rather than experimental social, human engineering rather than sensation and perception. The undergraduate liberal arts college is not the proper site for technical applied courses in psychology. As Dr. Thomas E. Kurtz, one of the nation's most outstanding computer scientists, recently said, the liberal arts college is where students learn computer programming theory, not where they learn to become computer programmers. So it is with psychology — all undergraduate psychology majors must learn psychological theory and the theory of research, which they can use later to solve the problems they may confront.

Chapter 5

Occupations of psychology alumni: A comparison of three surveys

Frank E. Fulkerson, Paula S. Wise, and Gene F. Smith
Western Illinois University

This chapter presents the results of a survey of occupations of psychology alumni, which was conducted in the fall semester of 1984 and compares the 1984 survey data with data obtained from 1977 and 1979 alumni surveys. Results of the 1979 survey have been reported previously (Wise, Smith, & Fulkerson, 1983).

The Department of Psychology at Western Illinois University (WIU) was established in 1961; the first psychology majors were graduated in 1964. Therefore, the 1984 survey reflects 20 years of alumni. Master's level graduate programs began in 1968 with the first master's degree granted in 1969.

The surveys

The first edition of the WIU Psychology Department *Newsletter* contained the 1984 survey. Of the 1700 alumni who received bachelor's degrees and/or master's degrees from the Psychology Department addresses were available for only 1372 alumni.

Of the 1372 surveys mailed, a return rate of 17% represents the 231 completed and returned surveys: 149 from graduates with only a bachelor's degree in psychology from WIU; 57 from students with only a master's degree in psychology from WIU; and 25 from students with both bachelor's and master's degrees in psychology from WIU. Of the 600 questionnaires mailed in the 1979 survey, a return rate of 30.5% represents 183 completed and returned questionnaires. A total of 113 surveys were completed and returned in 1977; however, there are no records of the number sent. Although the percentage of response to the 1984 survey is small, comparisons with the other surveys are valuable.

The low return rate of the 1984 survey is somewhat difficult to understand or explain. Perhaps the fact that it was included as part of the *Newsletter* made it a less visible reminder than a separate survey would have been. In addition, elsewhere in the *Newsletter* there was a request for contributions for the Psychology Scholarship Fund. Alumni may have been reluctant to respond to the survey, for fear of being targeted for further fund-raising attempts. Also, some of the addresses may actually have been addresses of the parents of alumni instead of the alumni themselves. Thus, they may never have been received by the former student. Finally, some of the alumni may have suffered "survey burnout" since the 1984 survey was the third survey they were asked to complete in eight years.

All of these explanations are conjectures, and regardless of the reason for the low return rate, we believe that the responses of 224 alumni in 1984 are worthwhile to report and to compare with the 1977 and 1979 responses.

The 1977, 1979, and 1984 surveys varied somewhat in format. In all three surveys, former students were asked for general information, including name, address, year of graduation, employment history, and additional education since graduation. The 1977 survey also contained questions regarding the positive and negative aspects of graduates' psychology training and asked for suggestions for improving the psychology curriculum at WIU.

In the 1979 survey, alumni reported which courses or aspects of training had proved the most valuable since graduation, what improvements they would suggest for the undergraduate curriculum, when and why they decided to major in psychology, and why they would not mayor in psychology in the 1980s. Finally, alumni rated eight aspects of their training in psychology at WIU, for example, the quality of professors and the difficulty of coursework.

The authors categorized the 1977 and 1979 respondents' current occupations into nine categories, which were selected after examining the data and looking through other studies, (e.g., Davis, 1979; Titley, 1979). The social services category included, but was not limited to, respondents working as counselors, therapists, and social workers; education included teachers, professors, and school psychologists; management included nearly all business-related personnel not considered to be in sales or clerical positions; sales included stockbrokers and insurance agents as well as others directly involved in selling; professional trades included mail carriers, police officers, construction workers, and so on; clerical included secretaries, cashiers, and bank tellers; and miscellaneous included those whose occupations did not fit into any classification, as well as those individuals labeling themselves self-employed. Identifying categories was tedious and somewhat arbitrary as well. For example, if a person called himself a "nursing home administrator," we had difficulty deciding whether his job was social services or management. In the 1984 survey, we asked alumni to categorize themselves.

The 1984 survey condensed the aforementioned eight training-related queries into three more comprehensive questions: How satisfied were you with your coursework and experiences at WIU?, how satisfied are you with your choice of psychology as a major?, and how satisfied are you with your present employment?

Although we sent surveys to all of our former students, this study includes only replies from alumni who received bachelor's degrees from WIU's Psychology Department. In other words students who received bachelor's degrees elsewhere but master's degrees from WIU are not included, while students who received bachelor's and master's degrees from WIU are included.

Results and discussion

Table 5-1 presents the percentages of graduates in each of the nine occupational categories across the three surveys. An examination of the data reveals that the percentages in most categories remained fairly constant.

The occupational category most frequently mentioned in all three surveys was social services. In 1977 and 1979 we classified

30.0% and 30.6%, respectively, of the responses in this category; in 1984, 34.5% of the respondents classified themselves as employed in social services. Not only did the total percentage in social services remain consistent across surveys, there was little evidence of a change in the percentages by sex. While some of the other categories clearly were dominated by men or women, social services was not a sex-specific category for our alumni.

The next most frequently indicated occupation was education, although there has been an overall decline in the percentage of alumni employed in this area. Simply citing the overall percentages in education masks an important sex trend. There has been a dramatic decline in the percentage of women employed in education: 37.2% in 1977, 24.3% in 1979, to 18.3% in 1984. The percentage of men employed in education has always been lower than the percentage for women, but the percentage of men is constant.

In the remaining occupational categories, there was less consistency across the three surveys in relative frequency. The results of the three surveys are compared within each of the remaining categories.

The trends in full-time graduate school enrollment are markedly different from the trends within the education category. There has been a dramatic and continuing increase in the percentage of women who report current full-time graduate school enrollment: 4.7% in 1977, 11.4% in 1979, to 17.2% in 1984. On the other hand, 1984 reflects the lowest (6.2%) full-time graduate enrollment for men.

The trends in management are more difficult to summarize. There has been a steady increase in the percentage of men employed in management: 10.0% in 1977, 14.2% in 1979, to 18.5% in 1984. The percentages for 1977 and 1984 are about twice as high for men as compared to women. However, in 1979 the percentages for the two sexes were almost equal (14.2% and 15.7%, respectively).

Perhaps the most interesting trends occurred in sales. As indicated in Table 5-1, 27.1% of the men were involved in sales in 1977, 14% in 1979, and 11% in 1984. The percentage of women in sales, on the other hand, has never been greater than 3%.

In the remaining categories shown in Table 5-1 professional trades are dominated by men while clerical positions are dominated by women. Finally, very small numbers of respondents fell into the miscellaneous and unemployed categories.

In addition to occupation, we collected information on the number of students who had

TABLE 5-1. Occupational Trends of Western Illinois University Psychology Graduates

	1977			1979			1984		
	% men	% women	% total	% men	% women	% total	% men	% women	% total

Social services
  counselors
  therapists
  social workers
	30.0	30.2	30.0	31.0	30.0	30.6	34.6	34.4	34.5

Education
  teachers
  professors
  school psychologists
	11.4	37.2	21.2	15.1	24.3	18.6	12.3	18.3	15.5

Management	10.0	4.7	8.0	14.2	15.7	14.8	18.5	9.7	13.8

Sales
  stockbrokers
  insurance agents
  sales representatives
	27.1	2.3	17.7	14.2	2.9	9.8	11.1	2.2	6.3

Graduate school	8.6	4.7	7.1	10.6	11.4	10.9	6.2	17.2	12.1

Professional trades
  mail carriers
  police officers
  construction workers
	12.9	4.7	9.7	10.6	2.9	7.7	9.9	4.3	6.9

Clerical
  secretaries
  cashiers
  bank tellers
	0.0	7.0	2.7	0.9	11.4	4.9	4.9	8.6	6.9

Miscellaneous/ self-employed	0.0	2.3	0.9	3.5	0.0	2.2	2.5	2.2	2.3
Unemployed	0.0	7.0	2.7	0.0	1.4	0.5	0.0	3.2	1.7

Note: Respondents to 1977 survey include all psychology graduates from 1964 to 1977; respondents to 1979 survey include all from 1964 to 1979; respondents to 1984 survey from 1964 to 1984. Percentages represent totals of all respondents in the survey year.

completed graduate study. Of the 183 respondents in 1979, 69 had received graduate or professional degrees, and 20 were currently in graduate school. Approximately 34% completed graduate degrees in 1979, while an additional 10.9% currently attended graduate school. An additional 40 former students (21.9%) reported at least some graduate coursework. The 1984 survey yields comparable percentages: 36.8% of the respondents completed graduate degrees, 12.1% in graduate programs, and 15.5% with some graduate coursework.

In the 1979 and 1984 surveys alumni rated the quality of their education in the Psychology Department at WIU. In the 1979 survey respondents rated eight aspects of their education: the quality of professors, variety of courses, difficulty of coursework, quality of academic advice, preparation for graduate school, helpfulness of faculty, opportunities for students to engage in research, and quality of textbooks. Ratings were highest for quality of professors (73.4% assigned ratings of excellent

or very good); quality of textbooks (60.4% assigned ratings of excellent or very good); and helpfulness of faculty (59.4% assigned ratings of excellent or very good).

In 1979, alumni responded to the question, "If you were starting at WIU in 1980, would you still want to major in psychology?" as follows: 42.4% answered with an unqualified *yes;* 8.2% gave a qualified *yes;* 10.4% were *undecided;* 7.1% gave a qualified *no;* 30.6% gave an unqualified *no.* The reason given most frequently for not wanting to major in psychology again was a perceived lack of appropriate employment opportunities or low salaries in related jobs.

In the 1984 survey, respondents rated their satisfaction with their coursework, their psychology major, and their current job: 96.2% were either satisfied or very satisfied with their coursework; 88.1% were satisfied or very satisfied with their major; and 88.5% were satisfied or very satisfied with their job. Clearly, the respondents to our surveys gave their undergraduate education good ratings;

similar findings were reported by Lunneborg and Wilson (1985).

Perhaps the concern raised most frequently by students considering a psychology major is employment opportunities for the baccalaureate. The results of our surveys and those of others (e.g., Ware & Meyer, 1981) indicate that employment opportunities exist. Virtually none of the respondents reported unemployment. A second, frequently raised question was, "What types of jobs do people obtain with a bachelor's degree in psychology?" This question is more difficult to answer because of the broad range of jobs reported.

Information regarding alumni employment in positions *related* to their studies in psychology is more difficult to address, as it requires a more subjective judgment than a listing of occupations cited by respondents. It might be said that only working as a psychologist relates to the study of psychology. On the other hand it might be argued that there are few, if any, occupations unrelated to psychology. Examining the list of categories in Table 5-1, social services, education, management, sales, and graduate school relate, at least indirectly, to undergraduate training in psychology. These five categories represent the occupational categories of 84% of alumni responding to the survey in 1977, 84.7% of alumni in 1979, and 82.2% of alumni in 1984.

We believe that the results of our survey study provide valuable information about the employment and educational histories of psychology alumni. Responses to all three surveys have aided us in advising current and potential psychology majors and have led to curriculum modifications.

References

Davis, J. R. (1979). Where did they all go? A job survey of BA graduates. In P. J. Woods (Ed.), *The psychology major: Training and employment strategies* (pp. 110–114). Washington, DC: American Psychological Association.

Lunneborg, P. W., & Wilson, V. M. (1985). Would you major in psychology again? *Teaching of Psychology, 12,* 17–20.

Titley, R. W. (1979). Whatever happened to the class of '67? Psychology baccalaureate holders one, five, and ten years after graduation. In P. J. Woods (Ed.), *The psychology major: Training and employment strategies* (pp. 103–109). Washington, DC: American Psychological Association.

Ware, M. E., & Meyer, A. E. (1981). Career versatility of the psychology major: A survey of graduates. *Teaching of Psychology, 8,* 12–15.

Wise, P. S., Smith, G. F., & Fulkerson, F. E. (1983). Occupations of psychology majors receiving undergraduate degrees from Western Illinois University. *Teaching of Psychology, 10,* 53–54.

Chapter 6

"Would you major in psychology again?"

Patricia W. Lunneborg and Vicki M. Wilson, University of Washington

A pivotal criterion for evaluating the success of an undergraduate program is whether baccalaureates would repeat the program. This criterion was the focus of the following study, which succeeds previous attempts to determine what psychology graduates were doing with their education, and how they felt about it retrospectively (Lunneborg, 1974; Lunneborg & Wilson, 1982). Titley and Titley (1982) recommended that surveys investigating the potential of a degree in psychology can improve academic advising of current majors. The results of this study are dedicated to that end.

The Department of Psychology at the University of Washington offers two undergraduate degrees: the bachelor of science (BS), designed as preparation for doctoral (PhD) programs in psychology, and the bachelor of arts (BA), intended for everything else. In contrast to many requirements for the BS, a BA requires only a 2.0 grade-point average (GPA) and courses in the following: introductory psychology, methodology, statistics, and laboratory. The remaining hours of the 50 quarter-credits for a BA are elective. Students seeking BAs are urged to supplement psychology with another field and to adopt a career orientation, to take both basic-skills courses such as English composition and job-related courses such as computer programming.

Method

Of the 1,437 psychology majors who graduated from the University of Washington between 1978 and 1982, 1240 graduates with available addresses received the survey. The authors

sent postcard surveys in November 1983, and follow-ups in December 1983 and February 1984.

The sample is comprised of 797 psychology baccalaureates. The proportions in the total sample graduating in each of the 5 years ranged from 19% (1978 graduates) to 23% (1982 graduates). The sample consisted of 67% women and 33% men; 72% of the graduates held a BA and 28% held a BS. These percentages are essentially the same as for the population as a whole. Of the sample, 33% (N = 260) supplemented psychology with another major as undergraduates, 48% (N = 380) pursued further education; and 81% (N = 646) were currently employed. Jobs were coded by Lunneborg using Roe's (1956) occupational interest framework which includes eight groups: service, business contact, organization, technical, outdoor, science, general cultural, and arts and entertainment.

The postcard survey asked graduates to provide occupational and educational information and to rate their satisfaction with their undergraduate degrees in six aspects. Following these ratings, one of four career items appeared on the postcards. Thus, approximately one fourth of the sample responded to each of the four items. Only three items are of interest here: importance of college experiences to one's career, usefulness of psychology courses to one's current job, and satisfaction with aspects gained from the psychology major in one's work. The fourth item, a complex job satisfaction measure, is the subject of a separate article (Lunneborg, 1985).

All career items were rated: 0 = not, 1 = some, 2 = medium, and 3 = very. These ratings were of satisfaction, importance, or usefulness, depending on the item. We analyzed data using chi square and analysis of variance. All differences reported here were significant at the .05 level.

Results

The relationships between the statement that the respondent would major in psychology again, and various objective and subjective measures of satisfaction with the degree are of primary interest. Of the 754 graduates who responded to the question regarding a major in psychology, 69% (N = 522) said *yes*, although 48 of the 522 said they would supplement it with business administration, computer science, or other areas.

For the 11 objective variables possibly related to majoring in psychology again, there were no differences for these three: no differences between the men and women, no differences between those who had supplemented with another major or not, and no differences among the five areas of supplementation (humanities, social science, natural science and technical, business, and education courses).

The most recent graduates reported that they were more inclined to major in psychology again than earlier graduates, BS recipients were more apt to major again more than BA recipients, and those who had continued their education were more likely to major in psychology again than those with no further schooling. The level of additional degree made a significant difference as well; 92% of PhD recipients would elect to major again, while only 59% of those who continued study at the bachelor's level would major again. The area of further study was also important: Psychology, humanities, and medical and dental graduate students were most inclined to major in psychology again; and engineering and technical, and business administration students were least inclined. Only 11% of the respondents did graduate study in psychology.

In addition to the five significant differences just given, those who indicated that their employment was related to psychology and those whose employment was their career choice were more likely to indicate that they would major in psychology again. However, employment interest area (service, business contact, etc.) was not related to majoring in psychology again. This ends the consideration of the 11 objective variables.

Looking next at the six subjective ratings of the major, mean scores in Table 6-1 show that the degree was most satisfying as a means to personal growth and a liberal arts education, less satisfying as preparation for graduate study outside psychology, and least satisfying as career preparation. Chi-square analyses of proportions of those who would major again or not, at each of the four levels of satisfaction, were highly significant for all six ratings—the strongest values being for overall satisfaction and career preparation. Those most satisfied with the degree as career preparation were most likely (100%) to say they would major in psychology again. Those most satisfied with the degree overall were next most likely (91%) to say that they would major in psychology again.

Now for a summary of the significant relationships observed between the 11 objective postcard variables in relation to the 6 satisfaction with degree measures followed by the relation of the objective variables to the 3 career questions.

Summary findings

Personal growth and liberal arts education

For both of these measures, respondents who did not continue their education and those who continued their education in law or business reported higher satisfaction with their degrees. In addition, there was significantly greater satisfaction with the degree as a means for personal growth among more recent graduates, among those pursuing a second bachelor's degree or a law degree, and those employed in business, organization, and artistic fields.

Table 6-1. Satisfaction with Degree and Proportions Who Would Major in Psychology Again

Satisfaction measure	Mean	SD	N	Proportions rating satisfaction 0 and 3 who would major again	
Personal growth	2.38	.75	786	50%	79%
Liberal arts	2.23	.75	747	58	77
Overall	2.17	.66	776	20	91
Graduate preparation in psychology	1.78	1.08	523	55	80
Graduate preparation outside psychology	1.61	.90	610	51	89
Career preparation	1.49	.87	771	43	100

Preparation for graduate study in and outside psychology

Data showed only three significant relationships for the degree as preparation for graduate study outside psychology: BS recipients were more satisfied than BA recipients, those with further education were more satisfied than those without further education, and among those with further education, satisfaction was highest at the master's level.

We recorded a higher rate of satisfaction with the degree as preparation for graduate study in psychology among BS graduates than among BAs, among graduates pursuing PhDs than other degrees, among those who went on to study psychology or humanities, and among people employed in service and business contact occupations. Those respondents working in psychology-related jobs were more satisfied than others, as were those who had not supplemented the major with another field of study.

Career preparation and overall satisfaction

There was significantly greater satisfaction in both of these areas among BS recipients, people pursuing PhD degrees, individuals in psychology-related jobs, and those in their career choice areas. Greater satisfaction overall was also associated with further education in psychology, humanities, and social sciences, while greater satisfaction with the degree as career preparation existed in those studying psychology and medicine. Career preparation satisfaction was also higher among those employed in service and teaching, law, and social sciences, and among male than female baccalaureates.

This ends our consideration of the six satisfaction with degree items. In the following, we consider the three different career items.

Importance of college experiences to one's career

Two hundred eight (208) 1981–1982 graduates answered this item. Analyses of variance conducted for each experience determined if there were gender or degree (BA vs. BS) differences in responses. There were none. One importance rating stood out as most important—doing well enough for graduate school acceptance (mean of 2.28). The other six experiences varied only slightly from 1.83 to 1.60 (in descending order the other six college experiences are: liberal arts education, contacts made, jobs held, college GPA, the psychology major, and extracurricular activities). Performing well enough to continue one's education eclipsed the psychology major as a college experience important to one's career.

Usefulness of psychology courses to one's current job

We collected responses from 197 1980–1981 graduates. Analyses of variance were conducted for each type of course to see if there were gender or degree (BA vs. BS) differences in responses.

Responses can only be interpreted for the two required courses—laboratory and statistics. Men rated both of these courses significantly more useful than women did, and those who received a BS rated statistics more useful than those who received a BA. For the other five courses, a zero rating could have meant that the course was of no utility or that the person had not taken that course: mean scores proved uninterpretable. Nevertheless, graduates with a BA rated child, personality, and social courses as more useful than graduates with a BS, while those with a BS rated the research course as more useful than those with a BA. These results seem eminently reasonable, given the different goals of the two programs. The BS is intended as preparation for graduate school, the BA is not.

Satisfaction with aspects of psychology major in one's work

The 214 graduates of 1979–180 completed this item. The seven aspects with their mean ratings in parentheses were: knowledge of people (2.36), self-understanding (2.30), information-gathering skills (2.24), analytic and thinking skills (2.21), interpersonal skills (2.19), research skills (2.08), and writing skills (1.79). These general aspects received higher ratings than the specific psychology courses. Women indicated significantly more satisfaction than the men with the psychology major in terms of acquired self-understanding, analytic and thinking skills, and interpersonal skills. Also, BS holders were significantly more satisfied than BA holders with their analytic and thinking skills.

Aspects most related to the six satisfaction measures

We conducted analyses of variance for each of these seven aspects with the six degree satisfaction measures. Which aspects were most associated with satisfaction with the major? Referring to Table 6-1, the top three degree satisfaction measures—personal growth, liberal arts, and overall—were more strongly related to all aspects of the major than the bottom three measures. The aspects most responsible for this satisfaction were self-understanding, knowledge of people, and analytic and thinking skills. The aspects least related to all satisfaction measures were writing skills and interpersonal skills. Career preparation and graduate school preparation in and out of psychology, were most strongly related to research, information-gathering, and analytic and thinking skills.

What interest areas are the career choice areas of today's psychology graduates? Of the 601 employed persons who responded to the career choice item, the percentages of respondents who said their jobs were in their career area were: general cultural, 92%; science, 89%; service, 78%; arts and entertainment, 77%; outdoor, 67%; business contact, 66%; technical, 49%; and organization, 46%. A potential problem is the fact that more graduates were employed in organizational jobs than any other kind, and, as noted earlier, there was a significant relationship overall between saying you would major in psychology again and being in your career choice area. The percentages of employed graduates in Roe's different areas were: service, 22%; business contact, 6%; organization, 37%; technical, 8%; outdoor, 1%; science, 9%; general cultural, 15%; and arts and entertainment, 2%.

Discussion

What are the implications of these results for those involved in advising psychology majors? If we want to find them answering "yes" to "Would you major in psychology again?" what can we tell them now?

As in previous surveys (Davis, 1979; Lunneborg, 1974), approximately 70% of the respondents indicated that they would major in psychology again, for whatever reasons. Further, data show that students who complete a graduate school preparation program are more likely to be satisfied with the psychology major than those who did not. Those planning to continue their education, regardless of the area, are more satisfied with their psychology baccalaureates. Graduates continuing their education in psychology, the humanities, medicine and dentistry indicated the most satisfaction, and those continuing in technical fields and business administration the least satisfaction. Being academically eligible for graduate school was a top priority among students, more important than contacts made, jobs held, or extracurricular activities, although only a minority actually did that graduate study in psychology.

Psychology majors should be aware that graduates rated their degrees as most valued in later years for contributing to their personal growth and providing them with a liberal arts background. They valued the major least as career preparation, in spite of (or perhaps because of) the wide variety of jobs which they can enter (Ware & Meyer, 1981). These findings are not unlike those of Malin and Timmreck (1979) at the University of Houston where psychology majors felt their strongest need— career preparation—was not being met. However, it appears here that if psychology majors are able to construct a bachelor's degree on which to build a career, they become, in effect, 100% committed to the psychology major.

Psychology majors can be told that retrospectively they will consider the most valuable aspects of the major to be their increased self-understanding, knowledge of people, and analytic and thinking skills. However, they should also be aware that satisfaction with the major as career and graduate school preparation are most strongly related to having acquired skills for researching, information gathering, and analytical thinking. They may continue to lament over statistics and laboratories, but they will, at the same time, value greatly the variety of skills these courses teach.

While jobs in business are those most often secured by current psychology graduates, these jobs are least likely to be considered career choices. In contrast, salient career areas, for this group of graduates at least, were general cultural, science, and service.

The efficacy of supplementing psychology with another area was not demonstrated here. Nonetheless, rather than abandon the idea of supplementing the major, perhaps it would be more constructive to note the top two areas chosen by those who would *not* major in psychology again—business administration and computer science. If these two fields had more frequently been supplements perhaps more graduates would have said "yes" to majoring in psychology the second time around.

References

Davis, J. R. (1979). Where did they all go? A job survey of BA graduates. In P. J. Woods (Ed.), *The psychology major: Training and employment strategies* (pp. 110–114). Washington, DC: American Psychological Association.

Lunneborg, P. W. (1974). Can college graduates in psychology find employment in their field? *Vocational Guidance Quarterly, 23,* 159–166.

Lunneborg, P. W. (1985). Job satisfactions in different occupational areas among psychology baccalaureates. *Teaching of Psychology, 12,* 21–22.

Lunneborg, P. W., & Wilson, V. M. (1982). Job satisfaction correlates for college graduates in psychology. *Teaching of Psychology, 9,* 199–201.

Malin, J. T., & Timmreck, C. (1979). Student goals and the undergraduate curriculum. *Teaching of Psychology, 6,* 136–139.

Roe, A. (1956). *The psychology of occupations.* New York: John Wiley.

Titley, R. W., & Titley, B. S. (1982). Academic advising: The neglected dimension in designs for undergraduate education. *Teaching of Psychology, 9,* 45–49.

Ware, M. E., & Meyer, A. E. (1981). Career versatility of the psychology major: A survey of graduates. *Teaching of Psychology, 8,* 12–15.

Chapter 7

The undergraduate psychology major: A 10-year follow-up study

Harry J. Parker, John J. Hedl, Jr., and Fong Chan, The University of Texas, *Southwestern Medical Center at Dallas*

Interest in undergraduate psychology education has increased over the past 15 years. In the 1950s and 1960s, the primary interest of educators concerned graduate-level instruction and the scientific-practitioner model. In the early to mid-1970s, a number of studies appeared that examined various aspects of undergraduate education. Kulik (1973) conducted a study of undergraduate psychology looking at several aspects, for example, field experiences and employment potential. Parker (1973) and Pinkus and Korn (1973) examined graduate employment options in public, private, and government sectors. Studies in Texas (Parker, 1975) and the Southwest (Parker & Hedl, 1976) examined the purposes of the psychology department vis-a-vis the undergraduate major, practicum experience, employment of graduates, and curricular variety. Davis (1979), Erdwins and Mendelsohn (1979), Fretz (1979), Fryrear (1979), Lunneborg (1979), Titley (1979), and Woods (1979) studied employment entry and surveyed graduates as well.

In 1985, the American Psychological Association (APA) completed their second national study examining selected characteristics of faculty members and students, introductory psychology courses, the psychology major, courses for nonmajors, independent study, and other aspects of the undergraduate curriculum (Scheirer & Rogers, 1985). This study was designed to be the first in a series of surveys performed every 3 years by APA on the subject of undergraduate education in psychology. The study focused on an in-depth examination of courses offered throughout the U.S. and did not present the data on a state or regional basis.

In contrast to this national focus, the purpose of the study described next was to examine undergraduate psychology education in the Southwest in 1985 and to compare the findings with available information from Parker (1975) and Parker and Hedl (1976). The project was undertaken in the fall of 1984 after securing support from the Texas Psychological Association.

Specifically, the present study was a replication and extension of early work by Parker (1975) and Parker and Hedl (1976) which focused on seven Southwestern states (Arkansas, Arizona, Kansas, Louisiana, New Mexico, Oklahoma, and Texas). The major questions from the original surveys were included to determine any significant changes in the mission or purpose(s) of the undergraduate psychology major curriculum in the 1975–1985 period, perceived employment opportunities (job titles, occupational settings), or requirements for fieldwork practica.

We sought additional information to examine changes, and reasons for the changes, in undergraduate enrollment or departmental resources (faculty, space, funding, etc.). We were also interested in the nature and sources of information that psychology departments find useful for formulating decisions about the undergraduate curriculum or evaluating programs. Finally, we were interested in the self-generated perceptions of chairpersons as they reflected on the major problem confronting undergraduate psychology at the time of the study and in the next decade. Consistent with our original studies we examined similarities and differences between public and private colleges and universities in the seven states under consideration. Comparisons to the recent APA study were developed where appropriate.

Method and procedure

Lists of public and private institutions of higher learning offering an undergraduate major in psychology came from multiple sources: state education governing bodies, federal government directories of higher education, directories related to college entrance and recruiting, and state psychological associations. From these lists 156 institutions of higher learning offering a bachelor's degree in psychology were identified. These public and private schools in Arkansas (20), Arizona (5), Kansas (23), Louisiana (22), New Mexico (9), Oklahoma (20), and Texas (57) were sent the survey. The two-page survey was sent to the chairperson of the psychology department in each school in early November, 1984, with a requested return date of 30 days later. We described the purpose of the study in a cover letter, which included the endorsement of the Texas Psychological Association (the original sponsor of the survey in 1975), and a statement that the 1985 findings would be compared with those of 1975. The unique geographic focus was also specified since no other studies related to this geographic area. We sent a second mailing to nonrespondents in early January, 1985. No other means of communication was used.

By March 1, 1985, returns totaled 113 (72% of the population). Of six private schools that responded, five indicated that they did not offer a major in psychology. One of the six schools had ceased operation. This, then, provided a usable data base of 57 public and 50 private schools, or 69% of the population surveyed. This return rate compares favorably to the 72% obtained by Scheirer and Rogers (1985) in the national APA study.

The survey form contained 12 questions, the first 6 from the 1975 study (Parker, 1975) and 6 additional questions which will be addressed in the Results and Discussion section.

Results and discussion

An initial set of nonparametric analyses compared the responses of the public and private schools to the survey questions. Chi-square and Kruskal-Wallis Tests for Ordered Contingency Tables (Marascuilo & McSweeney, 1977) were the major techniques employed. These data are generally presented combined for all schools in the sample since, in most cases, nonsignificant differences were the rule. Significant differences are discussed where appropriate. These data are presented combined across the seven southwestern states as well. The 1985 responses were also compared to previous data from the Parker (1975) and Parker and Hedl (1976) studies for this region to determine the presence of significant trends related to undergraduate psychology education over the previous decade.

Reasons and purposes for the psychology major

Question 1 read, "Listed below are statements representing prominent reasons or purposes for the curriculum design of a psychology major. Please *rank* in order of importance only those statements characterizing your major. Put a '1' before the most important, a '2' before the next, etc." Five purposes were listed with one category for "other," making six possible ranks. Data from Question 1 are contained in Table 7-1 and are expressed in percentages for both 1975 and 1985.

Forty percent of 118 schools indicated that graduate school admission was their primary curricular purpose in 1975. Thirty-four percent of the schools indicated that this was their secondary purpose.

In 1985, Purpose E, provide a base in behavioral science as part of a liberal arts and science education, dominated, with 81% of the schools using the first and second ranks, followed closely by Purpose A, graduate school admission (77%). Purpose C, prepare for employment in psychologically oriented occupations, was third in rank (47%). In 1975 the same top three purposes (E, A, C) prevailed with similar ranks, 78%, 75%, and 34% respectively.

Differences in rank for Purposes E and A in 1975 and 1985 were not statistically significant, but differences in C were ($p < .05$). Purpose B, prepare teachers of high school behavioral science, did not achieve high ranks (the top two ranks for 1985 = 5%, 1975 = 8%), 1985 differed statistically from 1975 in assigning more in the middle ranks (3rd and 4th) than in lower ranks, suggesting more interest or commitment in the last decade. Purpose D, fulfill an academic offering as established by faculties and governing officials, revealed no statistical differences between ranks of the 1975 and 1985 responses in the top two ranks (1975 = 23%, 1985 = 21%).

These data suggest that the primary purposes of the psychology major in the Southwest have changed little in the past 10 years and few differences were noted between the public and private schools. A nearly equal emphasis in 1975 for rank and sequence was found between public and private schools

(Spearman rank-order correlation (rho) = .93). For 1985, the correlation was .88.

The basic curricular concerns were preparing for graduate school admission and providing a broad base in behavioral science as part of a liberal arts education. However, a growing development and interest was noted in 1985 regarding employment preparation. Little change was noted related to the purpose of fulfilling an academic offering.

Employment in psychologically oriented occupations

Question 2 stated "If your major has for one of its purposes C, prepare for employment in psychologically oriented occupations, please print three (3) specific occupations your graduates enter." As shown in Table 7-1, Purpose C in Question 1 was ranked third in priority for all schools in 1985 and 1975. For 1985, 72% of the public schools ranked Purpose C and provided 98 work settings while 82% of the private schools listed 102 work settings. Although private schools were more disposed to choose C than were public schools, the number of entries of work settings were comparable. Table 7-2 shows the incidence of 22 specific occupations by type of school for the two time periods.

In 1985, for both public and private schools, there was considerable similarity in frequency of occupational titles cited. The most obvious were counselor and psychology aide, along with personnel clerk and probation-parole-correction officer. In 1975, a similar profile of responses was found. The 1975 data revealed that public schools were less concerned with job information and job relevance than were

Table 7-2. Specific Occupations Graduates Enter Upon Completion of a Major in Psychology

Specific occupation	1975		1985	
	Public N = 36	Private N = 40	Public N = 50	Private N = 38
Psychology aide—technician	7	7	10	4
Personnel clerk	1	1	5	3
Child-care worker	0	4	2	1
Caseworker	3	7	4	2
Probation/Parole officer	4	3	6	3
Teacher (elem. & secondary)	2	2	2	0
Counselor (voc. rehab., probation, alcohol & drug)	5	4	5	5
Test construction specialist	0	1	0	0
Counselor, unspecified	4	14	3	3
Psychological—rehab. tester	5	2	1	0
Social worker	1	2	2	2
Community planner	1	1	0	0
House-cottage parent	0	2	1	0
Clinical psychologist	2	1	1	3
School psychologist	2	0	0	0
Behavior modification/ management	4	0	0	2
University teacher	1	0	0	2
Special education worker	1	0	0	2
Research assistant	1	0	1	1
Computer programmer	0	0	1	0
Youth worker	0	0	1	2
Supervisor—sheltered workshop	0	0	3	4

Note: Schools were asked to supply three specific occupations; numbers indicate frequency of their responses, but not all schools provided three occupations.

Table 7-1. Ranking in Percent for Reasons/Purposes of Curriculum Design of Undergraduate Major

Reason/purposes of curriculum design		1975 schools rank							1985 schools rank						Significance
	N	1 %	2 %	3 %	4 %	5 %	6 %	N	1 %	2 %	3 %	4 %	5 %	6 %	
A. For graduate school admission	118	40	34	20	4	1	0	104	32	45	16	5	2	0	N.S.
B. Prepare teachers of high school behavioral science	89	3	5	18	22	48	3	58	0	5	29	35	31	0	p < .05
C. Prepare for employment in psychologically oriented occupations	105	12	22	31	30	5	0	81	16	31	35	16	2	0	p < .05
D. Fulfill an academic offering as established by faculties and governing officials	97	5	18	17	32	27	2	67	5	16	24	25	30	0	N.S.
E. Provide a broad base in behavioral science as part of a liberal arts and science education	115	57	21	13	4	3	2	99	61	20	14	3	2	0	N.S.
F. Other	17	29	12	12	12	12	23	4	50	25	0	25	0	0	N.S.

Note: Kruskal-Wallis Test for Ordered Contingency Table revealed no statistical significance in ranks of public and private schools and were combined. Total public schools for 1975 = 64; 1985 = 57. Total private schools for 1975 = 58; 1985 = 50.

private schools. In 1975 and 1985, schools did not always provide specific occupational titles, but gave work settings or generic areas instead. These responses (Table 7-3) clarify the chairpersons' perception of employment entry patterns of graduates.

Some new areas were cited in 1985, but in general they were similar to 1975. Mental health/MR, industry/business, social/community agencies, and social work were frequently identified settings for both types of schools. More diversification was found among private schools than public schools.

While 35% of the schools in 1985 chose preparation for employment (C) in Question 1 as a purpose of the major in undergraduate psychology, departmental chairs continued to prefer a work setting rather than a specific work title to characterize the entry-level employment of graduates. A lack of consistent

and accurate feedback mechanisms may contribute to this inability to identify the specific job titles of graduates entering the work force. Less than one half of the public and private schools cited graduates as a major or minor source of information, and only 23% used employers as a major source to identify work (see Table 7-8). However, Table 7-9 shows that 65% of the schools sought graduates' type of employment as specific information.

Emphasis of the psychology major

In Question 3 departmental chairs were asked to rank their curriculum emphases, and in Question 4 they were asked for percentage of emphasis. Multiple ranks could be used. Table 7-4 presents the distribution of ranks for the various curriculum emphases in 1975 and 1985, expressed in percentages of schools selecting a given emphasis.

There were no statistical differences between the mean ranks reported by public and by private schools on general psychology or experimental. Private schools identified more emphasis on applied than did the public schools ($p < .05$ for both 1975 and 1985). Private schools reported greater emphasis on Category D, educational/social, used only in 1985, than did the public schools ($p < .05$). Degree of emphasis on other areas was not computed because few schools reported other options.

In terms of mean percentage emphasis, *general* was the primary label for the curriculum in public and private schools for both 1975 and 1985. The secondary emphasis differed; public schools cited experimental, while private schools cited applied in both 1975 and 1985. In 1985 Category D, educational/social, appeared to better characterize emphasis than the 1975 data. Category E, other, had a larger mean percentage of emphasis in 1975 than it did in 1985, suggesting that the educational/social category was an accurate designation. Thus, schools have not changed their emphases in the past decade, maintaining general psychology as the major portion of the curriculum, with experimental being second most important in public schools and applied in private schools. In 1985 the educational/social emphasis could be identified as basically applied rather than as general or experimental. Hence, private schools were clearly more disposed to adopt a broad interpretation of applied preparation.

Requirements for fieldwork practica

Question 5 asked, "As part of your major in psychology do you *require* the student to spend time in fieldwork or practica within a

Table 7-3. Occupational Settings of Graduates After Completing Major in Psychology

Job setting	1975		1985	
	Public N = 36	Private N = 40	Public N = 51	Private N = 50
Mental health, mental retardation	9	11	7	7
Hospitals/mental hospitals	3	1	0	2
Social and community agencies	6	1	6	6
Welfare/child care	3	7	2	3
Probation—correction	1	6	5	4
Social work	2	9	5	7
Church-related work	1	3	0	6
Personnel	5	6	4	2
Clinics	2	2	2	1
Indust. mgmt./business research/advertising	10	4	7	6
Institution/agency research	1	2	1	0
Teaching—preschool programs	3	2	2	1
Criminal justice—law enforcement	1	3	0	0
Rest/nursing homes	0	1	0	0
Government programs and agencies	2	2	0	0
Graduate training (all types)	1	0	0	1
Laboratories, medicine	1	1	0	3
Sales (assorted products)	2	0	3	1
Human services	0	0	3	3
Law	0	0	0	3
Health aide	0	0	0	1
Children homes	0	0	0	3
Counseling	0	0	3	3

Note: These data are derived from question asking for three specific occupations.

mental hospital, clinic, health agency, business/industry, school, etc.?" The response requested was either a *yes* or *no*. In 1985, 5% of the public schools had such a requirement, compared with 64% of the private schools. In 1975, 8% of the public schools and 24% of the private schools responded *yes*. Private schools showed more disposition for the requirement as part of the major in psychology than did public schools, and this is somewhat consistent with private schools citing more occupations than did public schools. These two periods for comparison over time suggests that public schools' requirements have remained the same while private schools have made more commitment to providing a required experience. By comparison, the APA survey indicated 2.6% of the 4-year schools

had courses that involved a significant fieldwork component (Scheirer & Rogers, 1985).

Part 2 of Question 5 stated, "If Yes, indicate the total hours for any time in the field that is required in your major." In 1985, three public schools reported a range of 30 to 190 clock hours, with a mean of 98 clock hours required for a 16-week semester. Fourteen private schools reported a range of 30 to 400 clock hours, with a mean of 134 clock hours required for a 16-week semester. Thus, private schools were more committed to this requirement than were public schools. In 1975, five public schools reported a range of 6 to 320 clock hours and a mean of 114. Thirteen private schools in 1975 reported a range of 8 to 1040 clock hours and a mean of 207 clock hours. Thus, the 1975 average for private

Table 7-4. Distribution of Rank by Percent in Curriculum Emphasis for Schools in 1975 and 1985

Curriculum emphasis	1975				1985[a]			
	Public school		Private school		Public school		Private school	
	N	Mean %	N	Mean %	N	Mean %	N	Mean %
A. General	41	47	27	53	55	42	42	39
B. Experimental	38	30	25	25	52	31	36	23
C. Applied	37	18	23	28	47	23	41	28
D. Educational/social	not included in 1975 survey				32	13	35	18
E. Other	9	23	6	16	7	7	8	9

Note: In 1975 respondents were not asked to rank, only to indicate emphasis. Number of public schools surveyed in 1975 and 1985 was 42 and 57 respectively; 31 and 50 private schools were surveyed in 1975 and 1985 respectively.
[a] No statistical significance between public and private schools in A and B, C and D were significant (p < .05), and E was not computed.

Table 7-5. Percent Changes in Emphases for Undergraduate Curriculum in Past Decade for Combined Public and Private Schools

Curriculum Emphasis (es)	N	Increased in importance Public and private schools	Remained the same Public and private schools	Decreased in importance Public and private schools	Eliminated as a mission Public and private schools
A. Preparation for graduate school admission	103	37	56	7	0
B. Preparation of high school behavioral science teacher	89	7	61	22	9
C. Preparation for employment in psychologically oriented professions	95	37	55	7	1
D. Fulfillment of an academic offering as established by faculty and governing officials	87	9	79	12	0
E. Provision of a broad base in behavioral science as part of the liberal arts and science education	103	37	63	0	0
F. Other	103	5	0	0	0

Note: Total N for public schools = 57, private schools = 50. No statistical differences were found between public and private schools; designation of changes hence was combined.

schools was almost twice that of public schools. In the past decade, then, the number of schools remained nearly the same, with private schools reducing required hours on site and showing less variability in hours. Of course, the small number of schools responding to this question for 1975 and 1985 prohibit any extensive analysis of these data.

Question 6 read "If you have a requirement for field work practicum, please rank the manner in which the setting is chosen." In 1985, the public schools reported that choice of setting related most strongly to physical proximity of the school and to the opportunity for approved supervision. Having students, faculty and setting jointly share in the decision of setting was also important. Private schools emphasized the latter. Data from 1975 for 3 public and 7 private schools, though limited, showed that all persons shared equally in the decision of selecting a setting.

Limited responses in 1975 and 1985 prevent any meaningful statistical comparison. Further, selection of a practicum is not a critical issue. The department heads, in public and private schools, seem to express little variance in the decision-making process.

Major changes in undergraduate psychology programs

Question 7 concerned changes in the past decade in the undergraduate program. The intent was to determine if changes in mission(s) or purpose(s) had: "increased in importance," "remained the same," "decreased in importance," or were "eliminated as a mission." Table 7-5 shows the distribution of responses, which generally reinforce those from Question 1. No statistically significant differences were found between responses of the public and private schools, hence these data were combined for discussion.

Under "increased in importance," Categories A, preparation for graduate school admission; C, preparation for employment in psychologically oriented professions; and E, provision of a broad base in behavioral science as part of a liberal arts and science education, are all 37%. "Remained the same" was the status prominently chosen by all schools for D, fulfillment of an academic offering as established by faculty was E (63%), followed by B, preparation of high school behavioral science teacher (61%), A (56%), and C (55%).

Schools used "decreased in importance" in a limited status with only B showing 22% followed by D at 12%. These two categories likewise showed limited use of "increased in importance" (B = 7%, D = 9%).

These data convey that graduate school admission, preparation for employment, and a

Table 7-6. Changes in Enrollment for Undergraduate Psychology Course in the Past Decade for all Schools

Statement best describing enrollment change	Public school N = 56 %	Private school N = 50 %
A. Essentially stable each year, no real growth or fluctuations	30	34
B. Varies from year to year; no trends apparent	4	14
C. Enrollments have declined due to:		
1. Less service courses	2	0
2. Less psychology majors	9	6
3. Both	2	4
4. Other (Explain)	7	6
D. Enrollments have increased due to:	7	0
1. More service courses		
2. More psychology majors	13	16
3. Both	27	18
4. Other (Explain)	0	2

Note: One public school did not respond to this question.

broad base in behavioral science as part of liberal arts and science represent the major emphases of public and private schools in the past decade. Preparing high school teachers in behavioral sciences has diminished in importance.

Changes in undergraduate enrollment

The intent of Question 8 was to determine the growth, stability, or decline of enrollments in undergraduate psychology in the Southwest during the decade 1975–1985 and the underlying reason(s) for any change. Table 7-6 presents a summary of the responses to this question for public and private schools. In general, 42% of the schools (combined) indicated an increase in enrollment, 32% indicated stable enrollment, 18% reported a decrease, and 8% indicated some variation.

In public schools, 47% of the respondents felt that the source of their increased enrollment resulted from a combination of the increase in psychology majors and an increase of nonpsychology majors. Private schools reported a 34% enrollment increase of psychology majors.

Twenty percent of the public schools and 16% of the private schools noted an enrollment decline. In both cases, a decline in psychology majors, rather than less service courses, appears to be the cause. Other causes for the decline were unexplained.

Overall, the responses to Question 8 are optimistic and indicate increased enrollment in the past decade, especially in public schools.

Changes in departmental resources

The purpose of Question 9 was to identify various types of resources related to the undergraduate psychology program (e.g., faculty, students, space, library funds) and to determine the direction of any change(s) in the past decade. Department chairs were asked to rate eight sources on a 4-point scale: increase, same, decrease, not applicable. Table 7-7 shows these data in percentages for the entire sample of schools; 86% of the public schools and 98% of the private schools provided answers for analysis. Consistent with the increased enrollment reported by 42% of the schools, overall growth in 75% (6 of 8) of the resources for the undergraduate program (range of 40%–55% schools) is cited. However, resources in significant number of schools remained the same (range of 27% –46%), while declines were considerably smaller (range of 10%–22%).

By far, institutional library allocation increased the most. Significant increases in faculty (both full-time and part-time), space, equipment, and quality of majors in psychology also occurred. Public schools indicated a significant increase in full-time faculty whereas private schools' faculty remained the same. A similar pattern occurred in equipment allocation.

The largest decline reported by schools (22%) is in full-time faculty, suggesting that if decline occurs the full-time faculty is the resource most affected. The range of schools reporting declines by category was somewhat narrow (10%–16%).

Interestingly, schools reported the lowest percentage of increase in research grant funds and gifts and other private contributions. One quarter of the schools did not feel that these two resources were applicable to their mission at the undergraduate level.

Feedback for curriculum decision-making

Question 10 concerned the nature and importance of feedback that was perceived by the departmental chair as useful in formulating decisions about the undergraduate curriculum in psychology. Chairs were asked to rate ten potential sources of feedback on a 3-point scale: major source, minor source, and not a source. Combined data for all schools are presented in Table 7-8 because no statistically significant differences were noted except for the importance of the psychology department chairperson. The pattern of results suggests that curriculum decision-making is influenced by various internal and external groups.

Clearly, the major source of curriculum decision-making for all schools is the psychology faculty, as reported by 94% of the schools. Other institutional faculty were viewed as a minor source by 64% of the schools or not a source by 20% of the schools.

The second ranking source of influence in curriculum decision-making is the department chair, rated as a major source by 64% of the schools. For private schools, they were a minor source in 36% of the schools. In contrast, the chairs were a minor source of influence for 21% of the public schools and not a source of influence for 14% of them. Overall, data indicates that chairs have less influence in the private institutions.

Recent graduates were a major source of influence for 44% of the schools and a minor source for 48%. In contrast, alumni were viewed as a minor source of feedback by the majority (58%) of schools or not a source by 32%. Only 10% of the schools considered alumni as a major source of feedback.

Consistent with the previously noted importance of graduate school admissions, graduate

Table 7-7. Percent Changes in Departmental Resources for the Past Decade (1975–1985), All Schools Combined

Type of resource	N	Not applicable	Increased	Same	Decreased
A. Number of full-time faculty	107	0	45	33	22
B. Number of part-time faculty	104	9	40	38	13
C. Space allocation for department	107	2	42	46	10
D. Institutional library allocation	106	2	55	27	16
E. Equipment allocation	105	3	47	34	16
F. Academic quality of psychology majors	107	1	49	38	12
G. Grant funds for research	106	22	26	37	15
H. Gifts, private contributions to department	103	25	20	45	10

Note: No statistical differences were found between public and private schools except in A and E, p < .05. In A, public schools were greater in "increased" while private schools greater in "same." The same pattern applied to E.

Table 7-8. Percentage of Importance of Feedback Sources in Making Decisions about Curriculum, All Schools Combined

Potential sources of feedback	N	Major source	Minor source	Not a source
A. Graduates	105	44	48	8
B. Employers	101	23	51	26
C. Graduate schools attended by our students	102	41	44	15
D. Psychology faculty	105	94	6	0
E. Other institutional faculty	103	16	64	20
F. Alumni	98	10	58	32
G. Institutional administrations	100	14	56	30
H. Psychology department chairperson	101	64	28	8
I. Accrediting body recommendations	98	29	40	31
J. Public/legislative bodies	97	6	40	54

Note: Total number of public schools = 57, private schools = 50.
No statistical differences were found between public and private schools except in H (p < .05), category D was not compared.

Table 7-9. Percentages for Methods of Obtaining Information on Graduates for All Schools Combined

Types or methods of information on graduates	Public and private schools		
	N	Yes	No
A. Current employment status (Employed or not)	98	70%	30%
B. Type of employment	106	65	35
C. Salary range	93	26	74
D. Evaluation of undergraduate curriculum/specific courses	94	50	50
E. Graduate school enrollment status	99	81	19
F. Evaluation of department faculty teaching effectiveness	97	66	34

Note: Total number of public schools = 57, private schools = 50.
No statistically significant differences were found between public and private schools, hence were combined.

schools were considered a major source of feedback for 41% of the schools and a minor source by 44%. Interestingly, employers were viewed as a major source by 23% of the schools or a minor source by 51%. This is consistent with the previous findings of an increasing importance ascribed to job-related concerns on the part of the departmental chair. Other institutional faculty, institutional administration, and public and legislative bodies are not reported to have substantial influence.

Information obtained from graduates

Question 11 was designed to determine the types of graduate information a psychology department chair collects on employment status (type of employment, salary, yes/no), graduate school status, and whether alumni are used to evaluate curriculum and/or faculty teaching effectiveness (see Table 7-9). No statistically significant differences were found between public and private schools.

Both public and private schools stated that primary information on psychology graduates included graduate school status (81%), current employment status (70%), and type of employment (65%). Only 26% of the department chairs sought information on graduates.

Both types of schools consider graduates an important source of information in evaluating faculty's teaching (66%). One half of the schools find graduates useful in evaluating curriculum and specific courses.

Overall, the two important variables for evaluating the undergraduate major in psychology are graduate school admission, which was a primary stated purpose of the major (see Question 1), and employment status. Graduates were seen either as a major or minor source of information by 92% of the schools for the evaluation of teaching effectiveness, but not necessarily for curriculum evaluation. These data combined with those from Question 10 strongly indicate the prominent role of psychology faculty and chair in determining curriculum. In light of the departments' stated concern regarding employment for graduates, former student feedback on curriculum and courses might enhance departments' ability to place a larger percentage of graduates in the work force.

Single problem confronting undergraduate psychology today and in the next decade

In Question 12, chairs were asked to identify "What single problem do you see confronting undergraduate psychology today and then in the next decade?" We tabulated and grouped according to common themes and the frequencies of designation the open-ended responses to this question. The four most common themes are presented separately in Table 7-10 for *today* and the *next decade*. Selected problems with only single nominations have been deleted from consideration here.

Today. We analyzed responses from 43 public schools (75%) and 43 private schools (86%). Four major themes emerged: employment, curriculum, student quality, and program funding. The most salient concerns of the chairs related to employment, particularly for the private schools. Fifty-eight percent of the private schools (43) and 40% of the public schools (43) responding to this question expressed concerns about job opportunities for

Table 7-10. Issues Confronting Undergraduate Psychology Today and in the Next Decade

Today

Employment concerns	Public	Private
Job opportunities for the bachelor's	6	15
Curriculum shaped for better employment	5	3
Whether psychology taught as science or an applied subject	3	1
Maintaining psychology as liberal arts rather than para-professional training for job-oriented students	3	6
Sub Total	17 (40%)	25 (58%)
Curriculum—Maintenance and quality of subject matter	3	3
Students—Recruitment of capable students	6	2
Resources—Program funding	5	5
43 of 57 public schools responded [75%] 34 of 50 private schools responded [80%]	31	35

Next Decade

Employment Concerns		
Job opportunities, lack of career shifts	6	11
Psychology as liberal arts rather than paraprofessional training for job-oriented students	7	6
Broadening background and skill to make bachelor's more marketable	8	7
Curriculum—How to integrate advances in technology, information, computers, and neuroscience into the curriculum	6	3
Resources—Program funding	3	1
Encroachment—Psychology taught by departments other than psychology	2	1
41 of 47 public schools responded [72%] 34 of 50 private schools responded [68%]	41	34

the undergraduate major and job-related curriculum issues. Student recruitment was a public school concern, whereas program funding was of similar concern to public and private schools. Curriculum, the maintenance and quality of subject matter, was mentioned by 7% of the schools overall.

Next decade. We analyzed responses from 41 public schools (72%) and 34 private schools (68%). Again, four themes emerged: employment, curriculum, program funding, and encroachment. *Next decade* responses accounted for 78% of the public school responses and 85% of the private schools'.

Similar to the *today* issues, job opportunities for the undergraduate was foremost. Again, the private schools (71%) indicated higher concern than did the public schools (51%). Integration of recent advances in computers, technology, information, and neurosciences into the curriculum was the second most frequent category of concern, slightly more frequent for public schools (15%) than for private schools (9%). Program funding was again cited, but with a lower frequency of concern than in the *today* section. Finally, a new theme, encroachment, emerged. A small percentage of schools (4% overall) expressed concern about psychology being taught by other departments in the college or university.

These free-response data reinforce previously noted findings in the survey related to psychology's concern over job opportunities and curricular relevance for the undergraduate major. The increased interest of private schools in these two areas was again noted both for today's problems and for those anticipated in the next decade.

Summary and conclusions

The present survey of undergraduate psychology in the Southwest provides confirmation of previous findings in curriculum and presents new information on changes in this region of the country. In both 1975 and 1985, graduate school admission and the provision of a broad base in behavioral science as part of a liberal arts tradition were the two primary purposes cited for the undergraduate major at both public and private schools in the Southwest. Not only were the ranks of these purposes similar for the two time periods, but an additional question added in the 1985 study indicated that both purposes had increased in perceived importance for approximately 50% of the schools responding to the survey.

Preparation for employment ranked third in importance for all schools; 37% of the respondents stated that this purpose had increased in importance in the past decade. The importance of employment preparation also changed significantly, whereas the other two purposes did not. Employment focus was also the most frequently self-generated response to the major problem facing undergraduate psychology today and in the next decade. In terms of curricular emphasis, public schools ranked general psychology, experimental, and applied in that order of importance. In comparison, private schools ranked in order general psychology, applied, and experimental following closely. Private schools were also more knowledgeable about occupations and job titles and had more required practicum experiences than the public schools.

Other trends worthy of mention were also found. The chairpersons at approximately 50% of the schools indicated that enrollments at the undergraduate level were increasing while only 20% stated a decrease. This increase in enrollment was matched with an increase in a number of critical resources (faculty, space, equipment, etc.). While some colleges and universities in the Southwest are experiencing a decline in psychology, the undergraduate major appears to be thriving at the majority of educational institutions surveyed.

Overall, the picture for undergraduate education in psychology is promising. Enrollments are on the increase, and departments are increasingly recognizing the importance of employment possibilities for the bachelor's degree. While a significant emphasis is directed toward graduate school preparation, the employment potential of the undergraduate major appears to have increased in importance as an issue in the states surveyed. This finding fits nicely with the observation that 47% of the undergraduates nationally are concerned with employment entry upon graduation and not concerned about graduate school (Scheirer & Rogers, 1985).

References

Davis, J. R. (1979). Where did they all go?: A job survey of B.A. graduates. In P. J. Woods (Ed.), *The psychology major: Training and employment strategies.* (pp. 110–114). Washington, DC: American Psychological Association.

Erdwins, C. J., & Mendelsohn, M. B. (1979). A survey of paraprofessional positions in human service settings. In P. J. Woods (Ed.), *The psychology major: Training and employment strat-*

egies. (pp. 81–86). Washington, DC: American Psychological Association.

Fretz, B. R. (1979). Where to look for positions. In P. J. Woods (Ed.), *The psychology major: Training and employment strategies* (pp. 27–29). Washington, DC: American Psychological Association.

Fryrear, J. L. (1979). Community agency employment opportunities and requirements. In P. J. Woods (Ed.), *The psychology major: Training and employment strategies* (pp. 75–80). Washington, DC: American Psychological Association.

Kulik, J. A., in collaboration with Brown, D. R., Vestewig, R. E., & Wright, J. (1973). *Undergraduate education in psychology.* Washington, DC: American Psychological Association.

Lunneborg, P. W. (1979). Jobs in research for those with bachelor's degrees in psychology. In P. J. Woods (Ed.), *The psychology major: Training and employment strategies* (pp. 94–102). Washington, DC: American Psychological Association.

Marascuilo, L. A., & McSweeney, M. (1977). *Nonparametric and distribution-free methods for the social sciences.* Monterey, CA: Brooks/Cole.

Parker, H. J. (1973, December). Employment opportunities for a baccalaureate degree in psychology. Paper presented at the meeting of the Texas Psychological Association, Dallas.

Parker, H. J. (1975). The baccalaureate degree in psychology: Purpose, curricula, training, and employability in Texas. *Texas Psychologist, 27,* 25–30.

Parker, H. J., & Hedl, J. J., Jr. (1976). The bachelor's degree in psychology: Its status in the Southwest. *Texas Psychologist, 28,* 41–46.

Pinkus, R. B., & Korn, J. H. (1973). The professional option: An alternative to graduate work in psychology. *American Psychologist, 28,* 363–372.

Scheirer, C. J., & Rogers, A. M. (1985). *The undergraduate psychology curriculum: 1984.* Washington, DC: American Psychological Association.

Titley, R. W. (1979). Whatever happened to the Class of '67? Psychology baccalaureate holders one, five, and ten years after graduation. In P. J. Woods (Ed.), *The psychology major: Training and employment strategies* (pp. 103–109). Washington, DC: American Psychological Association.

Woods, P. J. (1979). Employment following two different undergraduate programs in psychology. In P. J. Woods (Ed.), *The psychology major: Training and employment strategies.* Washington, DC: American Psychological Association.

Authors' Notes

The authors wish to thank the Texas Psychological Association for support to conduct this follow-up study. The authors wish to thank Patsy Moore for typing assistance in the development of the survey instrument. Ora Lee Parker was extremely helpful in preparing preliminary drafts of the paper and the tables. Jackie L. Hedl was very helpful with technical editing of the final manuscript.

PART 3

Advising the psychology major

Reports on career preparation, counseling, and development options

Chapter 8

A liberal education

John K. Bare, Carleton College

In *Beyond the Present and the Particular: A Theory of Liberal Education*, Bailey (1984) recognized that the proposals for a liberal education that he makes must be justified, and thus be considered the topic of justification immediately at the end of the first chapter. "Justification is the production of reasons for beliefs and actions, not the [number] of supporters [for a particular position]; it is a matter of reason rather than rhetoric, of conviction rather than persuasion. Justification is required as a feature of the attempt to make human life rational, to make our activities and beliefs parts of an intelligible and coherent whole, to understand what we are about" (p. 12). *This* essay is an attempt to justify a liberal education in Bailey's sense.

What is to be justified? What is the nature of a liberal education? According to Bailey (1984), a liberal education is society's attempt to involve the student in the most fundamental and the most general knowledge that the society possesses. As a consequence, liberal arts students are liberated from the tyranny of the immediate present, for that fundamental and general knowledge, together with their imaginative conjectures and hypotheses, permits them to determine how things *might* be. Everyone is "born into specific and limited circumstances of geography, economy, social class, and personal encounter and relationships. . . . Education can . . . be of a kind that will entrap or confirm . . . young persons in the limiting circumstances of [their] birth or it can be of a kind that will widen [their] horizons, increase [their] awareness of choice, reveal [their] prejudices and superstitions as such, and multiply [their] points of reference and comparison" (p. 21). It follows that the more fundamental and general the knowledge, the greater the liberation. The educated person is liberated "to become . . . a free chooser of beliefs and actions—in a word, a free moral agent" (p. 21).

Psychology, as part of the liberal arts, provides reasons for the justification of a liberal education from its data and conclusions. Cognitive development, the nature of psychotherapy, and data from a study of a liberal arts institution are sources of some of those reasons.

The findings of Jean Piaget (e.g., 1970) are responsible in part for the remarkable growth in the understanding of human cognitive processes, which has occurred in the last three decades. If we are concerned with the cognitive changes that a liberal arts education provides, we can review his conclusions.

Assimilation and accommodation are familiar Piagetian concepts; they are the simultaneous and complementary aspects of the cognitive system. At any moment we have available to us ways of thinking about things called schemas, and we use those ways to interpret and understand external objects and events. We assimilate objects and events in terms of what we already know. At the same time, our schemas are now changing by the very process of incorporating these new objects and events into our experience; we accommodate our ways of thinking to take account of the new objects and events. These cognitive processes, or the "human knowledge acquisition device that has been designed by evolution's architect," as Flavell (1977) puts it, is spontaneously active, requires no external rewards, and is "biased to attend to those situations that present it with the most information. . . . Novel, surprising, puzzling, discrepant, uncertainty- and curiosity-provoking, or put more generally not readily assimilable happenings—these are precisely the ones a learning, developing organism *ought* to be designed to notice, explore, and seek to understand, for they constitute the essential nutriments for its cognitive progress" (p. 24). The richer our schemas, the greater the number of objects and events that will be incorporated into our schemas, and, as a consequence, the nearer we ought to come to understanding the world about us and our role in it.

Education of any kind, but particularly a liberal education, is carefully designed to provide the opportunity for contact with a wide array of provocative, insightful, and important happenings that are grist for our cognitive mill. They activate our cognitive processes and modify the ways in which we think and understand. No one can read Freud and not have a modified view of human motivation; no one can read Bandura and imagine that operant conditioning in humans exactly parallels that in animals; no one can read Piaget and continue to think about human learning simply in terms of assocations; and no one can read about attribution theory and think that the perceptions of others is veridical.

Hobbs (1962) provided a second context in which to think about the importance of a liberal education.

> All approaches to psychotherapy seem to have a more or less elaborated conception of the nature of man, which they, in essence, teach to the client. In doing so, they tie in with an ongoing process which is a unique and most exciting and engaging characteristic of man. Man constantly engages in building and repairing and extending and modifying cognitive structures that help him make personal sense of the world. The individual has got to have a cognitive house to live in to protect himself from the incomprehensibilities of existence as well as to provide some architecture for daily experiencing. He has to build defenses against the absurd in the human condition and at the same time find a scheme that will make possible reasonably accurate predictions of his own behavior and of the behavior of his wife, his boss, his professor, his physician, his neighbor, and of the policeman on the corner. He must adopt or invent a personal cosmology. When he invests this cosmology with passion, we may call it his personal mystique. (p. 746).[1]

As we build our cognitive houses, it is imperative that they be built with the soundest materials available—the best that the best minds known to us can provide. The strength, flexibility, and the quality of our cognitive houses will be improved by coming into contact with the thoughts of the intellectual giants of the human race.

As their first task, Winter, McClelland, and Stewart (1981, pp. 12-13) catalogued the following proposed outcomes of a liberal education.

1. Thinking critically or possessing broad analytical skill
   - differentiating and discriminating within a broad range of particular phenomena
   - formulating abstract concepts
   - integrating abstract concepts with particular phenomema or concrete instances
   - evaluating evidence and revising abstract concepts and hypotheses as appropriate
   - articulating and communicating abstract concepts
   - identifying abstract concepts and differentiating and discriminating between abstractions
   - comprehending the logic governing the relationships among abstract concepts

2. Learning how to learn

3. Thinking independently

4. Empathizing, recognizing one's own assumptions, and seeing all sides of an issue

5. Exercising self-control for the sake of broader loyalties

6. Showing self-assurance in leadership ability

7. Demonstrating mature social and emotional judgment

8. Holding equalitarian, liberal, proscience, and antiauthoritarian values and beliefs

9. Participating in and enjoying cultural experience[2]

These investigators tested for the outcomes of a liberal education at "Ivy College" with a variety of instruments: a newly developed Test of Thematic Analysis; a newly developed Analysis of Argument test; a modification of Heidbreder's Concept Attainment test; Hudson's Divergence of Thinking test; Rosenthal's Profile of Non-verbal Sensitivity (PONS); a test for learning of new material; five measures based on the Thematic Apperception test (achievement motivation, leadership motive pattern, fear of success self-definition, and maturity of adaptation); and self-ratings.

The data led them to conclude that a liberal arts education:

1. Increases the students' capacity for mature adaptation to the environment when students encounter new experiences;

2. Increases the students' critical thinking and conceptual skills by demanding that they integrate broad ranges of novel experiences;

3. Increases the students' independence of thought, their instrumentality, and their self-definition by setting them free from elaborate restraints on behavior and thought; and

4. Increases the students' motivation for leadership by endowing them with a sense of being special. (177–178)[3]

The parallel among these findings, the development of our cognitions, and the construction of our cognitive houses is apparent.

Those who feel passionately about the importance of a liberal education or who have, in Hobb's words a "personal mystique," often reveal that passion in their prose. Philosopher Brand Blanshard (1949) provides a description of the process of a liberal education.

To educate a human mind is not merely to add something to it, but to do something to it. It is to transform it at a vital point, the point where its secret ends reside. Change what a man prizes and you change him as a whole, for the essential thing about him is what he wants to be. . . . What is significant about a person or a people is the invisible things about them, the place where they keep their treasures stored, the unseen sun behind the clouds that determines the orbit of their lives. And curiously enough, it is these unseen things that are most nearly eternal. The educators of the West were those restlessly active people, the Greeks. But not one ship or bridge, not one palace or fortress or temple that their impatient activity erected has come down to us except as a ruin; and the state they built so proudly was already a ruin two thousand years ago. Does anything of them remain? Yes, the Greek spirit remains. The thought of Plato remains, the art of Sophocles, the logic and ethics of Aristotle. No doubt there were hard-headed practical men in Athens who stopped before the door of Plato's Academy and asked what was the use of it all. They and their names have vanished; the little Academy became a thousand academies like [the one from which you have graduated]. (pp. 20–21)

References

Bailey, C. (1984). *Beyond the present and the particular: A theory of liberal education.* London Routlege & Kagan Paul.

Blanshard, B. (1949). *The uses of a liberal education* (Pamphlet 26). New Haven: Hazen Foundation.

Flavell, J. H. (1977). *Cognitive development.* Englewood Cliffs, NJ: Prentice-Hall.

Hobbs, N. (1962). Sources of gain in psychotherapy. *American Psychologist, 17,* 741–747.

Piaget, J. (1970). *Genetic epistemology.* New York: Columbia University.

Winter, D. G., McClelland, D. C., & Stewart, A. J. (1981). *A new case for the liberal arts: Assessing institutional goals and student development.* San Francisco: Jossey-Bass.

Footnotes

1. Reprinted from Hobbs (1962) by permission of APA. Copyright 1962 by APA.
2. Adapted from Winter, McClelland, and Stewart (1981) by permission of author. Copyright 1981 by Jossey-Bass.
3. Adapted from Winter, McClelland, and Stewart (1981) by permission of author. Copyright 1981 by Jossey-Bass.

Chapter 9

Teaching critical thinking at the undergraduate level: A golden opportunity worth its weight in gold

John J. Furedy, *University of Toronto*

The emphasis on the importance of critical thinking, which has elsewhere been called the "Socratic strain" (Furedy & Furedy, 1982; see also Kimble, 1984) is generally considered to be among the hallmarks of higher education. However, I suggest that the fostering of the Socratic strain—a questioning, critical attitude—has not been particularly effective. It is one of those "motherhood" issues, in which emotional feelings predominate over cognitive analysis. Few teachers can readily explain precisely how they attempt to encourage critical thinking in their students or how they incorporate it into their own research and their interactions with their colleagues. A common, though seldom explicitly stated, view is that the time to teach critical thinking is only after the student has mastered the subject being studied; such mastery is correctly not considered to have been achieved by the completion of an undergraduate major. Finally, perhaps because the critical attitude is considered to be a luxury for use only by impractical academics, there is a view that it is of no value in the practical world of business into which the psychology major is most likely to enter.

As suggested by its title, this chapter is intended to argue against such views. The first section provides groundwork for this argument by elaborating the essential elements in the Western tradition of critical thinking which derive from Socrates. It is through the influence of this tradition that higher education is not just quantitatively, but qualitatively, different from indoctrinal or merely informational education. I shall then argue that the undergraduate level is actually better suited for the teaching of critical thinking than the graduate levels of psychology; in fact, the undergraduate level constitutes the golden oppor-

tunity. Finally, I shall suggest that even in practical terms, psychology majors who have acquired the critical attitude have gained a valuable tool, even though they must still learn to judge what the appropriate circumstances are for its use. In this sense, then, critical thinking is "worth its weight in gold" for psychology majors and any prospective employers.

Critical thinking: Education, higher education, and Socrates

Among the essential elements in the Western tradition of critical thinking are a disposition for disciplined inquiry based on a readiness to question all assumptions and an ability to recognize when it is necessary so to question. Critical thinking also entails the capacity to evaluate and analyze in a rational manner and an understanding of disinterested scholarship. These elements are most clearly seen in the life of Socrates and the move from indoctrinational-informational to higher education.

Many civilizations that preceded that of the ancient Greeks (and many that followed) had educational systems concerned only with the passing on of culture, ritual, or the skills of living. The cognitive complexity of this sort of education can be enormous even in so-called primitive societies. The "dos" and "don'ts" of traditional medicine, genealogical history, or court astrology in the Middle Ages probably demanded more memorization of information than does research in nuclear physics. Nevertheless, despite its complexity, this sort of education does not qualify as higher education in my terms, because it is largely doctrinal in nature. In other words, the central assumptions of what is passed on from generation to generation are not questioned, but rather accepted by both student and teacher. This is the sense in which Socrates maintained that he was not a teacher. Only his intellectual opponents, the Sophists, were teachers, inasmuch as they sought to elevate tradtion by rhetoric instead of examining its assumptions by logic.

In marked opposition to the Sophist tradition, the concept of critical thinking first emerged with clear emphasis in the Western world with Socrates. This is not to deny that Sophists, such as the philosopher Protagoras, made significant contributions to thought. However, with the Socratic education, a new and higher form had emerged. In this form, education was not indoctrinational, but rather required that both the student and the teacher come together to examine and question the premises underlying certain positions that had been hallowed by tradition.

This questioning attitude allowed the Sophist opponents of Socrates to convince the Athenian citizens that he was "corrupting the youth." In this regard, it is important to remember that it was not Socrates' behavior that was held against him. He was no profligate hedonist, who by his behavior led youth into corrupt practices; nor did he preach any particular doctrine that was contrary to the religion of the citizenry. Nevertheless, he did pose a serious threat to the establishment, because he was prepared to question all assumptions and believed that the uninquiring life was not a truly human one.[1]

The threat that the Socratic education posed for traditional education is also indicated by the assertion that, for Socrates, the "uncritical acceptance of tradition . . . is no education at all," because any tradition "requires the most careful scrutiny, and until this process of examination has begun, education has not begun" (Anderson, 1962a, p. 207). Moreover, Socratic scrutiny is indifferent to the fact that an overwhelming majority of one's peers may hold the view under examination with complete conviction. Although this conviction may be dangerous for those who question the majority view, nevertheless, "as Socrates says in the *Crito*, though 'the many can kill us', that is no reason for setting their opinions on a level with the opinions of the wise, for believing, though they have a certain power over life and death, that they have any power over truth" (Anderson, 1962b, p. 199).

The questioning, critical attitude that Socrates so clearly embraced established a new

sort of education. At this higher educational level, both teacher and student are prepared to study issues in a passionately *disinterested* way.[2] Socrates' life dramatically exemplified a passion for disinterested inquiry, an attitude that has been called the "Greek way" of thinking about the world (Burnet, 1930). The Greeks (including the pre-Socratic philosophers who flourished in Ionia) were the first to introduce the notion of considering problems for their own sakes, rather than considering them primarily in relation to current human needs.

Socrates' way of thinking about the world led him to emphasize considerations that seemed unimportant to most of his contemporaries, but which are relevant for higher education and critical thinking. The *Euthyphro* stresses the need to define terms in a dialogue. Although most of us have little interest today in the concept of piety, which is the subject of the *Euthyphro*, this dialogue still provides a useful analysis of the nature of adequate definitions and serves to illustrate the importance of definitional discussions during the process of higher education. On the way to his trial for treason, Socrates meets Euthypro, a self-styled expert on piety, who is also on his way to the Athenian court. Socrates pretends to seek Euthyphro's help in defining piety so that, armed with the expert's definition, he can prove to the court that his actions were pious. The dialogue that ensues soon shows that Euthyphro's expertise is rhetorical rather than logical. If Socrates had wanted to use Euthyphro's rhetorical skills, he would not have wasted time on "logic chopping," but would instead have consulted Euthyphro on how best to persuade the court by various rhetorical tricks.

An even more dramatic illustration of the Socratic emphasis on critical discussion is provided by the dialogue telling of Socrates' death—the *Phaedo*. At the outset of this dialogue, Socrates, having been condemned to die by a reluctant Athenian court, is urged to escape by his friends. Escape would have been relatively easy, because the Athenians felt embarassed at having to execute a 70-year-old former soldier whose crimes did not seem heinous. However, Socrates refuses offers of help and insists on spending his last few hours doing what he loved most—critically discussing issues. The topic he picks is apropos: whether or not the soul is immortal. What is unusual, however, is that two of his best-loved students, Simmias and Cebes, take the opposite position; they argue for mortality. Surely at a time like this and on a topic of this sort, one would exect his students to humor the condemned man and leave him his little bit of hope. But the followers of Socrates are his students, not his disciples.[3] It is the discussion of issues that matters, rather than what particular doctrinal conclusion is reached. Even at this 11th hour, his students are ready to subject to critical examination Socrates' view that the soul is immortal.

To understand the conception of critical thinking as embodied in Socrates' teaching one must develop a general disposition for evaluative inquiry, an understanding of what it is to be disinterested, and the ability to carry out evaluation and analysis according to the canons of rationality. Evaluative inquiry or reflection has been called one's "pondered sense of things" (Hart, 1978, p. 210) and leads naturally to a consideration of a corpus of values and attitudes associated with the critical thinker. The attitudinal aspect of critical thinking has been elaborated by Seigel (1980):

> In order to be a critical thinker, a student must have certain attitudes, dispositions, habits, and character traits, which together may be labelled the *critical spirit* or *critical attitude*. It is not enough for a student to be able to evaluate claims on the basis of evidence, for example; a student, in order to be a critical thinker, must be disposed to do so. A critical thinker must have a willingness to conform to judgment, to principle, not simply an ability to so conform. One who possesses the critical spirit has a certain character as well as certain skills: a character that is inclined to seek reasons; that rejects partiality and arbitrariness; and that is committed to the objective evaluation of relevant evidence. A critical attitude demands not simply an ability to seek reasons, but a commitment to seek reasons; not simply an ability to judge impartially, but a willingness to so judge; even when impartial judgment is not in one's self-interest. A possessor of the critical spirit is inclined to seek reasons and evidence; to demand justifications; to query and investigate unsubstantiated claims. Moreover a critical spirit possesses habits of enquiry and assessment consonant with [these considerations]: a critical spirit habitually seeks evidence and reasons and is predisposed so to seek. (p. 10)[4]

To insist that an attitudinal component is part of the definition of a critical thinker is not necessarily to adopt the student-oriented, subjective approach exemplified by, for instance, McKeachie's characterization of the Socratic method as the establishment of a deep human relationship in which, "in Langston Hughes' words, 'I become part of you and you become part of me'" (1982, pp. 62–63). The Socratic approach is subject-oriented rather than subjective. The critical thinker, as an individual

and in relations with others, is concerned with exploring issues rather than with the subjective merging of identities. For instance, in the *Phaedo*, Simmias and Cebes refused to "become part of" Socrates on the question of whether the soul is immortal.

It is also important to recognize that the critical thinkers are not necessarily emotionless, if only because, like Socrates, they can possess a passionate commitment to inquiry. Furthermore, to emphasize only the questioning of assumptions and the analysis of argument by logic in defining critical thinking is to take too narrow a view of the concept. Critical thinking does not consist merely of raising questions or of indiscriminate skepticism: "it is the appropriate use of *reflective scepticism* within the problem area under consideration" (McPeck, 1981, p. 7). One must allow that critical thinking can be displayed in reflection, in musing and puzzling over a problem, and in venturing into new areas of inquiry. However, I do not concur with the next step in McPeck's argument, that to reflect effectively one must know a good deal about the field of inquiry and, thus, that the ability to be a critical thinker in one field may not transfer to other areas (pp. 7–8). On the contrary, critical thinkers could effectively question and assess ideas, even when discussing issues outside of their particular areas of expertise. However, one will not be as proficient in specialized evaluation in an unfamiliar field.

The questioning, critical attitude is one of the hallmarks of higher or university education. It is not accidental that it was Socrates' most famous pupil, Plato, who founded the first Western university, the Academy. What differentiated Plato's Academy from the other professional schools (e.g., the Egyptians had, for a long time, maintained excellent medical schools) was that tradition was not merely passed on but was examined. Of course, this is not to say that critical examination is the only function of a university either then or now; an academic institution cannot be run on Socratic educational principles alone. However, I would contend that teaching critical thinking is an essential part of a university education, because, as I have argued, it is this Socratic aspect that differentiates higher education from one that is solely indoctrinational or bound to tradition.

It is, of course, a more complicated question whether such higher education is better, because the answer depends on one's values. For those who prize inquiry for its own sake, it is obvious that the Socratic strain has merit. However, even from a more practical viewpoint, there are grounds (e.g., technological progress) for suggesting that society benefits from having at least some people engage in higher education. To the extent that scientific advances are socially beneficial, the emphasis on criticism is socially helpful, because the critical attitude is necessary for scientific advancement. Moreover, I suggest that even those who emphasize the detrimental effects of the applications of scientific principles stand to benefit from a critical attitude which questions widely held opinions. This is because these detrimental effects are often glossed over by the experts and are exposed only through the nonexpert generalists who are ready to question the pronouncements of experts. The Socratic strain, therefore, appears to be not only important for higher education but also beneficial for the social fabric.

The application of critical thinking

When considering the approaches likely to promote the Socratic strain in teaching and learning, it is important to recognize that critical thinking cannot be reduced to a bag of tricks that students can be taught in a mechanical way. Critical thinking consists both of an attitude towards inquiry and a set of proficiencies necessary for the effective expression of that attitude in scholarship and discussion. There is no pat way to guide a teacher in how to call forth these qualities and attributes in students. We often recognize when a teacher possesses this ability, but it is not possible to present ready formulas for its creation.

Nevertheless, as detailed elsewhere (Furedy & Furedy, 1983), critical thinking can be encouraged by certain styles of assignments and course structures. Beyond the limited contexts of critical analysis exercises, position papers, and simulation courses, I suggest that the Socratic strain should be reinforced in all the important contexts of university life for students and faculty. It is relatively easy to devise written assignments that require critical thinking; faculty also must consider how students can be encouraged to develop this ability in other contexts: while listening to lectures, while participating in seminar discussions, while working with a group in solving a problem, while reflecting on something they have read or heard, and while writing examinations. Furthermore, faculty must allow room in their courses for general discussions of the values that uphold scholarship and inquiry.

For each context, current teaching practices must be closely scrutinized. If critical thinking is to be truly promoted in an essay examination, the exam questions must be formulated in such a manner that they require genuine discussion of the relevant issues (Furedy & Furedy, 1983). Furthermore, the students must understand what is meant by genuine discussion, and they must be confident that they will not be penalized for a sound, but independent, approach to the issues. There is a widespread belief among students that the way to do well in examinations (or in course work in general) is to discover what the professor thinks and to echo or elaborate upon these views. Even when students are mistaken about "psyching out" a particular teacher, the influence of such reasoning is often very strong. Thus, faculty cannot assume that students feel ready to question the assumptions of their professors. Students may need reassurance that faculty encourage criticism. Indeed, they may need more than reassurance; they may need to be goaded into independent thinking! Faculty must be prepared to reward independence by the way in which they grade students' work.

Another reason why students may fear to criticize is their belief that criticism yields only unproductive negativism. A related false belief is that the instruction to analyze an idea critically means merely to find fault with it. It may be necessary to discuss the notion of academic criticism, to explain objective criticism, and to distinguish it from ad hominem arguments in order to overcome considerable resistance to criticizing authorities (whether in the form of course materials or the instructor).

Encouraging students to question prevailing views, and even those we hold ourselves, is not the equivalent of saying: "There are no right or wrong answers." In the Socratic approach, entitlement to opinion is won by defense of the opinion according to canons of rational argument. We all know how dispiriting it is to see students swept along in a free flow of unsubstantiated opinions. Critical thinking implies a process in which right is sifted from wrong by an unceasing process of dialogue. This process must be initiated by encouraging students to express their opinion openly, which does not entail an assumption that all opinions are valid. The chief worth of openness is to begin the process of rational argument by which opinion is put to the test.

It is not just the students' opinions that will be subject to critical scrutiny. The faculty must be prepared to encounter students' challenges to their own views. The fear that such challenges will undermine convictions or imply inadequate understanding on the faculty's part may be a strong inhibition to explicit teaching of critical thinking. The inherent conflict has been characterized by Flew (1982): "Your desire to get the right, or at least the reasonable, answer [must be] stronger than any possibly conflicting desire to hold fast to particular cherished positions" (p. 352).

The notion that the clash of ideas is an important part of higher education can be put into practice at all levels of undergraduate learning. However, the concept of critical thinking is perhaps most clearly exemplified in the way in which undergraduate thesis research is conducted. A common mode is the arrangement where the faculty supervisor is more or less the sole arbiter both in the design and in the evaluation of the study. A more critically oriented model is the "adversarial" one (see Furedy & Furedy, 1977), in which evaluation is partly by other faculty who have had nothing to do with the thesis, and critical input into the design of the study is provided by other students in the course as well as by other faculty members.

Just as the Sophists were opposed to the educational methods of Socrates, there are forces even within universities that tend to promote an uncritical approach. Some of the forces that may inhibit or even work against the teaching of critical thinking are a negative societal attitude toward criticism; vocational preoccupations and aspirations of students and teachers; misperceptions of the Socratic method; faculty perceptions (versus the reality) of the extent to which critical thinking is induced in students in university courses; the implicit acceptance that teaching basic skills is sufficient to produce critical thinkers; and the content-coverage compulsion of many teachers.

Many sins are laid at the door of vocational preoccupations, especially within liberal arts programs. There is a long standing tension within institutions of higher education between the desire to shape students for particular jobs or professions in society and the fostering of an independent critical spirit. These tensions have recently been discussed with respect to legal education and research in Canada in the report, "Law and Learning," presented to the Social Sciences and Humanities Research Council by the Consultative Group on Research and Education in Law (1983). The report pointed to prior traditions of legal training as expository and doctrinal rather than critical and reflective and remarked on the continuing tension between the intellectual goals of law faculties and their professional-training duties. Although the tension perhaps does not manifest itself in the

same way in nonprofessional programs, it may be present in American psychology (McKeachie, 1982, p. 63). In particular, the teaching of popular topics such as biofeedback at the undergraduate level may be particularly vulnerable to an uncritical, use-oriented approach (Furedy, 1982).[5] More emphasis is placed on how to use biofeedback than on whether it is, in fact, useful and what, indeed, the phenomenon is. Despite this vulnerability, the undergraduate level of education is, nevertheless, a stage where the Socratic strain can be brought to full fruition, and the psychology major is, in particular, a golden opportunity for teaching critical thinking.

Why the undergraduate level of education is a golden opportunity

At the undergraduate level both students and faculty have the luxury of being able to reflect on their subject. At the postgraduate level, the opportunity for reflection is severely curtailed. This is the case not only for those students who are going into business, but also for those going into further academic work in professions such as medicine and law. The nature of the academic work in any profession is such that certain assumptions are no longer open to question, and the focus must be on the more information-transmitting aspect of education. Moreover, even if the student continues with graduate work in a basic research area such as physiological psychology, I suggest that the luxury of reflection is no longer available. Both the graduate student and his or her supervisor have to focus on specific research topics and cannot really afford to question assumptions in the Socratic way. Furthermore, the financial connections between supervisor and student at American graduate schools, as well as the power of the supervisor over the employment prospects of the graduate student, tend to detract from the purely academic relationship between graduate student and supervisor and, hence, from the possibility of adopting a more Socratic approach to inquiry.

I do not want to suggest that the potential for reflection is always actualized in most undergraduate courses. To the extent students consider that critical thinking is not rewarded and that grades are given on the basis of following the professor's "line," most students will not opt for a critical attitude. The pressure to conform to professorial prejudices in order to obtain high grades is especially strong nowadays, when entry into professional schools is so difficult. Critical thinking can only be taught if the professor emphasizes that critical thinking, rather than conformity, will be rewarded and if professorial behavior is clearly seen to reflect this emphasis. In other words, provided that professors stress the Socratic emphasis, the opportunity for a genuinely liberal education is maximal at the undergraduate level. Moreover, psychology is particularly well suited for developing critical thinking, because, as one of the softer sciences, it is a field whose scientific status is under constant debate and one in which many important methodological issues remain unresolved.

Why liberal education is worth its weight in gold

Is this sort of liberal education of any practical use? The benefits of a liberal, critical education for a research career are reasonably obvious. Although there are other requisites, one cannot be a successful researcher unless one has acquired the habit of independent thought. This is not to deny that research is also a joint enterprise and that the concepts of one researcher are heavily dependent on those of others. Nor is it to ignore the many instances in which the researcher has to forego exercising her or his critical skills to survive. It also appears that professional schools for law and medicine consider liberal education to be useful, as evidenced by these schools' requirement of a bachelor's degree. Although professional education involves considerable memory work, it is the mark of any professional that she or he can exercise independent judgment. In contrast, the development of critical thinking is not generally considered useful for students entering business and may even be regarded as detrimental.

There is a grain of truth in this view. Any student who enters the business world and adopts a consistently Socratic stance is unlikely to win many friends or influence people. It is no accident that Socrates himself was a business failure, as well as a failure in the applied art of politics in the narrow sense of that term.

However, business employers themselves indicate in media interviews that they value the ability to think critically in their employees, because there are many situations that call for this skill. For example, although anyone in sales must be able to sell the product, managers must also be able to evaluate the product

beyond the sales "pitch." When a new plan is proposed with all the enthusiasm and customary color charts, it is important to have the ability to evaluate the plan in terms of the assumptions that lie behind it, assumptions which are not necessarily spelled out by the plan's enthusiastic presenter. When conflicts inevitably arise, it is essential to be able to analyze the competing arguments, assess what the conflicts really are (which are often not clearly identified by the opposing parties), and achieve the appropriate resolution.

Possessing a skill does not require its use under all circumstances. Employers expect their employees to have enough common sense not to use their critical skills in circumstances which are likely to be offensive. Determining these inappropriate circumstances is part of on-the-job training, which is gleaned through experience as the new employee matures in the organization. What is probably impossible for the new employee to pick up is the ability to evaluate a case and to consider what the assumptions are behind a particular position.

The ability to think critically and, when appropriate, to communicate one's criticism clearly is a valuable skill in business. When the circumstances call for rhetoric rather than logic, the successful rhetorician is likely to be the one who can distinguish betweeen those aspects of her on his position that are rhetorical and those that are logical. This skill is not something that can be learned in the hurly-burly world to which the new employee is introduced. Rather, it is a skill that is best taught through a critical, liberal education at the undergraduate level.

References

Adler, M. (1983, February), *How to speak, how to listen.* [Transcript of Firing Line, Public Television Service.]

Anderson, J. (1962a). Socrates as an educator. In J. Anderson, *Studies in empirical philosophy* (p. 207). Sydney: Angus & Robertson.

Anderson, J. (1962b). Classicism. In J. Anderson, *Studies in empirical philosophy* (p. 199). Sydney: Angus & Robertson.

Burnet, J. (1930). *Early Greek philosophy.* London: A & C Black.

Consultative Group on Research and Education in Law. (1983). *Law and learning. Report to the Social Sciences and Humanities Research Council of Canada.* Ottawa: Social Sciences and Humanities Research Council.

Flew, A. (1982). [Review of *Critical thinking and education*]. *British Journal of Educational Studies, 30,* 352–353.

Furedy, C., & Furedy, J. J. (1983). Ways to promote critical thinking in higher education. [*Higher Education Research and Development Society of Australasia News*, 5, 3–4.

Furedy, J. J. (1982). Comments on "Biofeedback in the Undergraduate Curriculum" from a more critical pedagogical perspective. *Teaching of Psychology, 9*, 224–226.

Furedy, J. J., & Furedy, C. (1982). Socratic versus Sophistic strains in the teaching of undergraduate psychology: Implicit conflicts made explicit. *Teaching of Psychology, 9*, 14–20.

Furedy, J. J. & Furedy, C. (1977). Modeling the realities of research experience: Collaboration against common and merciless foes. *Teaching of Psychology, 4*, 107–110.

Hart, W. A. (1978). Against skills. *Oxford Review of Education, 4* (2), 205–216.

Kimble, G. A. (1984). Psychology's two cultures. *American Psychologist, 8*, 833–839.

McKeachie, W. (1982). Undergraduate education in the next decade: Discussion. *Teaching of Psychology, 9*, 62–63.

McPeck, J. E. (1981). *Critical thinking and education*. Oxford: Martin Robinson.

Palladino, J. J., Tryon, W. W., Johnson, R., Motiff, J. P., Rich, M. L., & Zweig, J. T. (1982). Sophism revisited: Response to Furedy. *Teaching of Psychology, 9*, 226–227.

Plato, (1952) "The Euthyphron," "Apology," "Crito," and "Phaedo" in F. J. Church [translator], *The Trial and Death of Socrates*. London: MacMillan.

Seigel, H. (1980). Critical thinking as an educational ideal. *The Educational Forum, 45*, 7–23.

Author's Notes

The preparation of this chapter was partially supported by a grant from the National Science and Engineering Council of Canada. As suggested by the references, the views expressed in this paper draw heavily on previous papers with Dr. Christine Furedy, whose expertise on nonpsychological subjects and in instructional development continues to exert considerable influence on my thinking. I am also indebted to Dr. Amanda Walley for critical comments on earlier drafts of this chapter.

Footnotes

1. The usual translation of the Greek is: "The unexamined life is not worth living." I am indebted to Professor H. Ferguson of St. Andrews University for pointing out (personal communication, 1979) that this is a poor translation, and that a better one is "the uninquiring life is not the life for man." The usual translation is misleading as it suggests the self is the central concern. In contrast with such a subjective view, Socrates' life of inquiry was concerned with all matters of general interest, and the inquiry was conducted along objective, rational lines.

2. It has never been easy to foster contexts in which sustained dialogue of fundamental matters can take place. It was his sense of the lack of such contexts, even the decline of genuine conversation in Western society, that inspired Mortimer Adler to sponsor seminars that discuss issues such as "What is truth?" at the Aspen Institute. Adler even goes so far as to suggest that most marriages "dry up" because of the failure of conversation (Firing Line, 1983, p. 11). Without entering into matters of marriage counseling, we can at least agree that many teachers find that tutorials and seminars "dry up" because of the failure of genuine discussion to continue to occur.

3. A modern version of this distinction is that between graduate students who work with, rather than under, a faculty supervisor. The fact that this distinction is not one to which many are sensitive suggests that there has been an implicit acceptance of the disciple model of academic supervision in American universities.

4. Reprinted from Seigel (1980) by permission of Kappa Delta Pi Honor Society in Education. Copyright 1980 by Kappa Delta Pi Honor Society in Education.

5. Comments (Palladino, Tryon, Johnson, Motiff, Rich & Zweig, 1982) and my unpublished reply are available from me on request.

Chapter 10

Integrating conflicting needs in curriculum planning: Advice to faculty

Judith Waters and Benjamin Drew, Fairleigh Dickinson University

Justina Ayers, AT&T, Morristown, NJ

There is no doubt that curriculum planning has become an increasingly difficult task in recent years because of the educational and economic factors that must be taken into consideration. Certainly, there have been many changes in the career goals of psychology majors. There was a time, not so very long ago, when large numbers of psychology majors dreamed about going to graduate school. Even if that dream was essentially unrealistic, faculty could feel secure in designing a curriculum geared toward preparing students for doctoral-level programs with rigorous research requirements. The undergraduate curriculum in most schools was based on the need to offer students the type of course work necessary to succeed in traditional graduate schools. In order to be admitted to research-oriented master's and doctoral programs, students had to achieve high scores on the critical qualifying examinations. The Graduate Record Examinations (GREs) evaluated and still evaluate knowledge in several experimental areas and expertise in statistics and research methodology. There are few applied questions in the applied subjects. Because admission committees still emphasize grades and high scores on the GREs (Undergraduate Advising Office, 1987), it is particularly important for students from relatively unknown undergraduate institutions to perform well on both general and subject parts of the test. There is always the problem of grade inflation, which committees consider when reviewing the credentials of applicants.

Planning for today's psychology majors presents a more complex situation than many faculty have previously had to face. Contemporary undergraduates come from a variety of backgrounds and interests and have some career goals that my prove difficult to achieve utilizing the traditional, although by no means obsolete, curriculum designed to prepare them for most doctoral-level programs. In the authors' experience, students interested in psychology have the following educational or occupational goals and related issues that must be addressed:

1. A graduate education in one of the traditional research-oriented areas such as sensation and perception, cognitive psychology, or human development.

2. Admission to graduate school in one of the applied areas. The applied degree programs also have a research component.

3. Temporary employment, either before or during graduate school, in order to get practical experience and make a relatively permanent career decision or to earn enough money to pay for tuition and living expenses. Some students hope to have their companies pay their educational expenses. In that case, they can go to school only part-time, a problem for the graduate school faculty planners.

4. Employment immediately after graduation that would utilize the skills acquired in an undergraduate course of study. Students with immediate career plans often state that they have no interest in going to graduate school at any time in the future. It is only later, perhaps years later, that some of them change their minds and recognize the short sightedness of their earlier academic decisions. Without guidance in their undergraduate years, they may cut off some of their options or add unnecessary barriers to achieving their new goals.

The essential responsibility of each faculty member is to engage in a curriculum-planning process that will meet the needs of as many psychology majors as possible, as well as meeting the needs of students who minor in psychology and students from other majors who are either required to take some psychology courses or who do so out of interest in a particular topic. The curriculum plan also should give the faculty—who, unlike the students, are not just "passing through"—an opportunity to develop courses beyond those basic areas tested on the GREs.

In sum, the planning process must take into account the academic needs of students aspiring to careers that (a) depend upon a traditional doctoral-level education, which students may defer for several years, (b) require some undergraduate experience in the workplace, and (c) require undergraduate training that is appropriate to those careers, but not necessarily relevant to getting into graduate school. The first category needs no clarification. An example of the second category would be a career in drug and alcohol counseling, and an example of the third would be a job in a personnel department. Thus, psychology departments have to offer courses in the traditional areas tapped by the GREs and applied courses such as Crisis Intervention or Personnel Psychology and Interviewing Techniques. The selection for each student of courses both in and out of the major requires good advising and an understanding of the choices facing all students. Students need to be convinced that they should avoid reducing their options too soon. This objective can be achieved by the use of advising manuals including *Is Psychology The Major For You?* (Woods & Wilkinson, 1987) and individually produced materials, as well as through workshops and counseling sessions.

Graduate school orientation

Purdy, Reinehr, and Swartz (1987) reviewed the undergraduate curricula of 50 "elite" psychology departments that they identified as "those that provided the most undergraduates who subsequently received their doctorates in psychology from 1920 to 1980" (p. 757). They concluded that although each program had some unique characteristics, there were more similarities in course requirements than differences. The average number of hours required to complete the major and the hours required for introductory psychology and for statistics and experimental design were almost identical. They also noted that in some pro-

grams students appeared to be given considerable freedom of choice in selecting courses beyond the core courses. However, they felt that implicit departmental policy probably limited that flexibility. If, for example, the faculty of a particular institution were aware of the proportionate area coverage of the Psychology Test of the GREs, which is an important factor in the admission decisions of many graduate schools, they would utilize that information in advising students about which courses to take.

The Psychology Tests of the GRE are composed of two subscores, an experimental or natural science orientation and a social or social science orientation (Educational Testing Service, 1986). The Experimental subscore is divided into two sections, with an equal number of questions in each of these sections for the specified topics. The first subsection of the Experimental subscore covers questions in learning, cognition, and perception. The second subsection covers ethology, comparative psychology, sensation, and physiology. The Social subscore includes an equal number of questions in personality, clinical, abnormal, developmental, and social psychology. The questions assess knowledge of theory and the ability to identify the psychologists associated with those theories, the ability to draw conclusions from experimental data, and the ability to evaluate experiments.

Palmer (1984), while noting that percentages of questions devoted to a subject area may vary somewhat from one test administration to another, listed the percentages that he found as follows:

Physiological and comparative psychology	13.6%
Developmental psychology	12.2%
Learning and motivation	12.2%
Sensation and perception	12.2%
Clinical psychology and psychopathology	10.8%
Personality and social psychology	10.8%
Cognition and complex human learning	10.0%
Applied psychology	9.1%
Methodology	9.1%

Students can score very well on the General Test, have excellent grades in all their courses, and still not perform adequately on the Psychology Test if they have not taken the critical courses. Those students who wish to pursue careers in industry either immediately or after graduate school may focus on such courses as industrial/organizational, personnel, or consumer psychology while avoiding most of the courses in the experimental area. Even if there are a few questions that assess knowledge in the applied areas, most of the questions are based on knowledge in the traditional research areas. Although some graduate institutions no longer utilize the GRE Subject Test in Psychology as a factor in their decision-making process, others still use it because they need a standard for comparison for students from a variety of programs. If responsible faculty members do not feel that the Educational Testing Service is developing tests that are useful in selecting students for graduate school, then they must make their dissatisfactions known. If, however, faculty believe that the tests do, in fact, assess the appropriate subjects, then they must inform students about the classes that students will need to take in order to get high scores on the examination.

The GRE Board in conjunction with the Educational Testing Service is in the process of developing Major Field Achievement Tests. The stated purpose of these tests is to establish "appropriate, economical measures to assist departments and institutions in the assessment of the outcomes of undergraduate education in specific disciplines" (C.N. Mills, personal communication, October, 1987). In 1988, the pilot year, the test in psychology will have 140 questions to be distributed in the following manner:

Learning, cognition, and perception	23%
Developmental	14%
Clinical and abnormal	13%
Social	11%
Ethology and comparative psychology	10%
Measurement and methodology	9%
Sensory and physiological	8%
Personality	8%
General/historical	4%

The rationale for utilizing these tests involves applying the rules of management by objectives. Under such a system, one must have a means of measuring the outcomes. At the present time, both public and private academic institutions are designing tests to measure the proficiency of their students in the basic skills and substantive areas that are important in higher education. Many of these tests will be administered in the sophomore year. The implication is that only students who meet minimum standards would be allowed to continue their education without remedial work. Senior-level examinations given in the major fields of study could be used to disqualify candidates from graduation.

A serious aspect of the use of these tests involves perceptions of the quality of education delivered in a particular department. If, for example, the students at one school do not perform as well as the students from another institution, the former, especially those who have achieved high scores on other tests, may think that their training has been inadequate. The problem is similar to the situation previously discussed concerning the utilization of the GREs to evaluate applicants for graduate school. It is quite possible for a student to have a high grade-point-average and still not score well on the advanced subject test because of the discrepancy between the subject areas tapped by the test and the courses emphasized by the particular department. College and university administrators, unaware of the difference, may also blame the faculty for poor teaching. To remedy the situation, each department could simply construct its own test. The consequence would be a more representative test than the one produced by ETS with, however, a loss in terms of ability to compare the results with those of other schools. Since the development of the ETS test is in the pilot stage, concerned faculty might suggest to ETS that distinct subtests covering a broader range of topics, including industrial psychology, should be designed. Students could then be given the opportunity to choose 6 areas out of 10 alternatives (or whatever number seems appropriate). This pattern is similar to the way in which comprehensive examinations are given to doctoral students in many schools. Psychology majors might be required to take methodology and history and systems and then select four other areas such as human development, industrial and educational psychology. In that way, schools would have a realistic view of the skills of their students.

The study

Since many faculty committees work in relative isolation, the authors of this chapter thought it would be helpful to review the curriculum designs of a random sample of colleges and universities across the country, not just those geared toward sending students to graduate school. In the fall of 1987, we telephoned 96 departments in six geographic regions and explained the nature of the project. We asked not only for their course lists and departmental requirements for majors and minors, but also for any guidance materials that they provided for undergraduate students. Forty-six academic institutions submitted the requested information.

We received curriculum plans from small independent campuses of a few thousand mostly residential students and from large public universities with a population of over 30,000 residential and commuter students. The faculty of the schools that responded ranged in size from a low of 7 to a high of 91. Larger institutions can provide a greater variety in course offerings each semester than smaller schools. However, even if a school lists a large number of courses in its bulletin, some of these courses may be given very infrequently.

In analyzing the data, we encountered a few problems. For example, we discovered that many schools were not specific about the minimum and maximum number of credits required for the major. Although some schools did specify the minimum number of credits for the major, we found discrepancies with the stated minimum when we added up the total credits for required courses. In addition, it was difficult to discover which courses beyond introductory psychology, statistics, and experimental design were actually required. In some cases, there was so much flexibility that it appeared as though a student could easily graduate without studying theories of personality or social psychology.

Major results

1. The minimum number of credits required for the psychology major ranged from 18 to 53, the average being 33 with modes at 30 and 36 credits.

2. Every department required at least one introductory course for majors. Sixty-five percent of the respondents allotted 3 credits for a single course while 17% listed a 4-credit course, 4% required 6 credits (two courses), and 4% required 8 credits (also two courses). When there were two introductory courses, they were divided between the natural science areas and the social areas. Nonmajors were not always required to take both introductory courses.

3. All schools required at least one course in statistics. The breakdown of credits ranged from 3 credits required by 60% of the schools, 4 credits required by 30% of the schools to 8 credits (two courses) required by only 5% of the schools.

4. The distribution for experimental design courses was similar to that of statistics courses with 51% requiring 3 credits and 29% requiring 4 credits to 9% requiring 8 credits. We had some difficulty in interpreting the distinctions between courses with similar descriptions but with different titles. The same material seems to be presented in experimental design courses and psychology laboratory courses. However, sometimes courses called "Experimental Psychology" were essentially "chalk and talk," and sometimes they included a laboratory component.

5. Thirty-six percent of the schools required a course in the history and systems of psychology, while the rest made it optional. Most of the schools offered it as a 3-credit class.

6. Only 14% of the schools required some type of independent study or research.

7. About 20–30% of the schools required such courses as sensation and perception, cognitive psychology, and physiological psychology. Most, however, offered these classes as options to be selected from a limited list of basic courses.

8. In the applied areas, 83% of the schools listed industrial psychology, 48% offered personnel psychology, and 41% offered community psychology.

9. Forty-two percent of the schools offered some form of practical experience as part of the program.

10. Some psychology departments were also very specific about courses outside of the department and mandated requirements in philosophy (28%), for example. Others simply followed their institutions' general requirements for liberal arts major.

The results indicated very little difference in the required courses or in the options listed by our respondents. Purdy et al. (1987) also had found a similar pattern in their data utilizing only "elite" institutions. The real distinctions between schools that have a high record of success in sending students to graduate programs and those who do not probably are based either on the quality of the courses or on the type of courses chosen by the students (e.g., applied topics) rather than on the published list of required courses. As previously noted, students who are allowed to focus on the applied areas do not have the background to score well on the Subject Test of the GREs as it is presently designed.

The curriculum in psychology cannot rely on merely covering the content of the discipline. The opportunity to conduct a literature search, to review previous studies, and, perhaps, to collect and analyze new data should be integrated into almost every course. The ability to think critically; write clear, concise, and cogent arguments; and to present one's work before an audience of experts are all skills that our profession values. Moreover, they are also the skills that many corporation managers feel that recent college graduates lack (Waters, Ayers, & Drew, 1987; Weinman, 1988).

Based on the results of the study and on our own experience as curriculum planners, we decided to design what we considered, in all modesty, to be an ideal program. At least, we will provide the reader with a structure to attack. Our basic assumption was that we, as faculty, do know what courses an educated psychology major should take in order to keep all his or her options open.

1. Two semesters of introductory psychology to expose students to all the major topic areas, including the ones that they would like to avoid. One course would focus on natural science subjects, the other on social science subjects.

2. A 3-course sequence of statistics, introduction to experimental psychology, and research design (including survey techniques) and, finally, a laboratory and a field research experience.

3. A history and systems of psychology course to be taken in the junior year to prepare students for the Graduate Record Examination Subject Test.

4. A research project also to be conducted in the junior year so that the student will have a credible research paper to submit to a conference or for publication before applying to graduate school.

5. Several courses from the basic areas that are covered by the GREs.

6. Electives that prepare the student to earn a living directly after graduation, if necessary.

7. A practical experience in the senior year, if not earlier.

We have included a sample list of the major courses offered by the institutions in our study (see Table 10-1).

Career-oriented curriculum innovations

There have already been career-oriented programs developed that have met some of the students' occupational needs. Unfortunately, the "professional option" as outlined by

Table 10-1. A Sample of Courses

Introductory Psychology (Natural and Social Science Orientations)
Statistics (Basic and Advanced including Multivariate Analysis)
Experimental Design
Laboratory Research
Field Research
Tests and Measurements
History and Systems
Sensation and Perception
Cognitive Psychology
Comparative Psychology
Physiology
Learning Theory
Social Psychology (Theoretical and Applied)
Personality Theory
Abnormal Psychology
Human Development (Child, Adolescent, and Aging)
Motivation and Emotions
Clinical Psychology
Community Psychology
Educational Psychology
Behavioral Medicine
Forensic Psychology
Health Psychology
Human Sexuality
Psychology of Women
Environmental Psychology
Political Psychology
Industrial/Organizational Psychology
Human Resources
Personnel Psychology
Consumer Psychology
Advertising Psychology
Engineering Psychology
Human-machine Interactions
Psychology of Prejudice
Cross-Cultural Psychology

Electives

Afro-American Psychology
The Psychology of Sleep and Dreaming
Children and Television
The Psychological Foundations of Musical Behavior
Psychology and the Supernatural
Psychology and the Actor

Pinkus and Korn (1973) was discontinued at Carnegie Mellon University due to lack of funds and faculty support. The experiment, a 4-year curriculum specifically planned to assist students in getting employment after graduation, was implemented during an era when there was little or no recognition on the part of the academic world of its responsibility for providing students with career preparation. Resistance to the design and implementation of career-oriented university programs stems from a number of sources. Mink (1979) pointed out that the traditional model of education in liberal arts colleges has "emphasized intellectual values and minimized vocationalism, a function considered best left to other educational institutions" (p. 243). Furthermore, even when they acknowledged that career education was important, many faculty members were relatively unfamiliar with job opportunities for new graduates or sites for fieldwork placements for students. However, with the increasing number of faculty involved in consulting, especially in psychology departments, and with the growing interest on the part of some corporations and other types of organizations in providing realistic work experiences for students, the problem of modifying the curriculum to meet the vocational needs of students should all but disappear. In addition, many academic institutions have business people and corporate executives on their boards of advisors who can help with placements. Advisory boards can provide the link to the "real world" that is so necessary for the successful implementation of any fieldwork program.

There are several issues that must be considered in designing career-oriented curricula. The decision as to whether course credit should be given for the time spent in the workplace should be each school's option. The extent of the program and selection of sites are also choices that each planning committee will have to make for itself. However, a word of caution is necessary. From time to time, placements that we used at Fairleigh Dickinson University that appeared at the outset to be valuable experiences did not live up to their potential. Sometimes, it was merely a matter of the job supervisors not being as enthusiastic about training students as the personnel department staff were when the arrangements were made. Occasionally, the workload and the type of task assigned were beyond the level of skill that any undergraduate student could or should reasonably be expected to handle. At other times, students were given low-level clerical work to do when a more varied and enriching experience had been promised. In each situation, the student felt that he or she had been treated unfairly and that the placement was a waste of time. Despite these problems, the placement effort has proved to be very successful. Some students have even been hired by the organizations where they did their fieldwork.

Possible Types of Placement

1. Cooperative education programs consisting of 4- or 5-year plans in which the student may eventually spend as long as 1 year outside of academia working full time for a selected organization. In the first or second year, short work placements and preprofessional courses would be offered.

2. A 1-year fieldwork sequence with one semester devoted to preparation in terms of lectures, reports on chosen fields, and visits to worksites. The second semester should involve a regular full-time job placement.

3. Summer internships arranged by the school.

4. Volunteer work once a week or during vacation breaks. There are certainly other possible variations in fieldwork placements. The respondents in a study of corporate executives (Waters, Ayers, & Drew, 1987) stated that any experience that was less than a full-time commitment was relatively useless in preparing the student to make the final transition to the workplace. According to the respondents, students must learn to adjust to a normal business work schedule and they must also be involved continuously in the same project for as long as the project lasts. Having days of schooling interspersed between work days makes continuity difficult to achieve. Part-time employment does not provide the same experience that a regular full-time job placement does.

Several universities are considering strategies to provide a business education for liberal arts students. Fairleigh Dickinson University has planned a 5-year program leading to a baccalaureate degree in liberal arts and a master's degree in business administration. The major selected for the initial implementation of the combined degree is psychology because there is a greater overlap among the courses in both areas (e.g., human resources, industrial psychology, and consumer behavior). A second strategy would involve developing an undergraduate degree with a major in liberal arts, preferably psychology, and a 24- to 27-hour minor in business. Students would take introduction to business; 1 year of accounting, business administration, or management; and 1 year of economics to fulfill the requirements in business.

The tasks of projecting business needs in the coming years and planning for the curriculum changes necessary to be responsive to the job market and the changing composition of the student body require a closer working relationship between business leaders and the academic community. In these times of financial crisis, an increasing number of educational institutions are seeking support for their capital projects, and even for operating expenses, from corporations and foundations. Corporate philanthropy to education in the past few years has already exceeded donations to health agencies and hospitals. Business contributions to employees in the form of tuition benefits and the funding of academic chairs at universities are further indicators of corporate interest in the education of the workforce. However, many executives in charge of grants and other university relations are applying the rule of efficacy to their donations. In some cases, there are "strings attached" to educational support. The heyday of the generous unrestricted grant no longer exists. Managers now want to now how their organizations will benefit directly from grants to educational institutions. In order to develop programs that will meet the academic goals of higher education and deal with the needs of the workplace at the same time, there must be constant, open, and honest communication among the decision makers in government, business, and academia.

A cross-fertilization between the business world and universities has been in progress for a number of years. Business leaders have already been called upon for their expertise in designing internships and cooperative education programs. Some corporations have also paid the salary of executives who spend a semester or even a year or more in residence on a college campus. Lectures by industry representatives continue to provide the entire academic community with valuable insights into the functioning of the business world. The corporate community also utilizes the skills of academics. An increasing number of university faculty serve as consultants to industry and conduct research and workshops in problems such as conflict resolution and occupational stress. Moreover, some faculty are making the transition into the business world as the positions available in academia continue to decrease. Closer contact should result in a better understanding of the basic issues and the common goals of both communities.

A different perspective

In order to give the reader a different perspective on the issues, we asked our graduate students what they felt needed improvement in their undergraduate programs. They all emphasized advising, which they thought was often rushed or simply amounted to signing off on courses of study for registration. They suggested that students be given a more realistic view of the field of psychology ranging from standards in graduate school to job opportunities. As a group, the graduate students offered the opinion that many undergraduates are attracted to psychology because they think they will be able to answer cosmic questions such as "Who am I?" or because they think that their personal experiences will help them to understand the material (unlike chemistry where you actually have to know something). There are also the casual majors, students who are uncommitted elsewhere or who think that psychology is an easier or more interesting discipline than other disciplines such as biology. Therefore, it is critical that faculty emphasize the scientific basis of psychology, the pursuit of academic excellence, and the focus on research in the academic areas and problem solving in the applied areas.

When advising undergraduates about courses to take outside of psychology, advisers must focus on some of the demands of our discipline: research, writing, oral presentations, and utilizing material from other fields. For example, courses in public speaking and acting will assist students in improving their oral presentations.

The University of Minnesota (Undergraduate Advising Office, 1987) sent us an excellent advising manual that delineates the general requirements of the College of Liberal Arts, the departmental requirements, the career potential including jobs for students with a bachelor's degree, and the standards for admission to graduate school. The appropriate advising offices are also listed, as are important additional publications, so that students can find answers to many questions themselves. This excellent manual could easily serve as a model for other institutions.

Parting words

While reviewing our own suggestions, we came to the realization that a few of them may prove uneconomical in the short run. In some institutions, all academic departments are being treated as cost centers that must remain competitive with other cost centers in attracting students. If the number of credits required for an introductory experience in one department exceeds or even doubles the number in another department, the disparity is sure to effect enrollment. This is a very practical issue that will have to be resolved in each institution. Psychology, as a discipline, is still popular enough to be able to make curriculum decisions based less on "the numbers game" than other fields. However, we should not become overconfident. Our objective in writing this chapter was to inform the reader of what other institutions are presently offering and to share some reflections on fieldwork placements and advising needs.

References

Educational Testing Service. *Graduate Record Examinations.* (1986). *Practicing to take the GRE psychology test.* Princeton: Author.

Mink, W. (1979). The undergraduate major: Preparation for career or graduate school. In P. J. Woods (ed.), *The psychology major: Training and employment strategies* (pp. 240–248). Washington, DC: American Psychological Association.

Palmer, E. L. (1984). *How to prepare for the graduate record examination GRE psychology test,* (2nd Edition). Woodbury, NY: Barron's Educational Series.

Pinkus, R. B., & Korn, J. H. (1973). The preprofessional option: An alternative to graduate work in psychology. *American Psychologist, 28,* 710–718.

Purdy, J. E., Reinehr, R. C., & Swartz, J. D. (1987). Undergraduate curricula of leading psychology departments. *American Psychologist, 42,* 757–758.

Undergraduate Advising Office. (1987). *Psychology handbook 1987–1988.* Minneapolis: University of Minnesota, Department of Psychology, Undergraduate Advising Office.

Waters, J., Ayers, J., & Drew, B. (1987). [Survival manual for "new hires"]. Adapted in P. J. Woods (Ed.) with C. S. Wilkinson, *Is psychology the major for you?* (pp. 97–104). Washington, DC: American Psychological Association.

Weinman, G., & Waters, J. (April, 1988). *Corporate perceptions of communications skills: A needs analysis.* Paper presented at the Eastern Psychological Association, Buffalo, NY.

Woods, P. J. (Ed.) with Wilkinson, C. S. (1987). *Is psychology the major for you?* Washington, DC: American Psychological Association.

Authors' Notes

The authors wishes to thank Arthur Hirota and Jeffrey Brain for collecting and processing the data and Joan Barry-Gertz for producing the manuscript.

Chapter 11

Assessing psychology majors' career advising needs

Patricia W. Lunneborg, University of Washington

The results of an American Psychological Association survey (APA, 1983) of undergraduate department chairs underscored the need for improved career advising for psychology majors. APA found that (a) 65% of the chairs were concerned with balancing the curriculum between traditional psychology and courses to make students more employable, (b) 47% were worried about career prospects for baccalaureates, and (c) 26% were faced with losing students to other fields such as business.

I agree with Titley and Titley's (1982) claim that providing quality academic advising is a faculty responsibility and a professional obligation owed our paying consumers—undergraduate students. In keeping with this belief, I decided that an appropriate source of recommendations for improving departmental advising were psychology majors themselves. Ware's (1982) needs assessment of Creighton University students concluded that departments such as his needed a variety of sources of career information. His needs assessment survey was adopted and adapted for this study.

The University of Washington (UW) is a state-supported university with an enrollment of approximately 35,000 students on a single campus. UW places the value of research and graduate education above undergraduate instruction. The Psychology Department has 750 majors to 50 regular faculty. We award 300 baccalaureates annually. Eighty percent of our majors receive BAs (vocational and professional orientation) versus 20% BSs (graduate psychology orientation). Our majors are 80–90% upper-division students, and 70% of them are women. They tend to be commuters, employed part- or full-time, primarily interested in clinical/counseling and contain a significantly older segment of returning students.

Until 1967 there was only a highly restrictive BS program at UW. An administrative secretary handled the inevitable paperwork for these majors and the faculty informally advised them. After 1967, the department assigned one faculty member to the faculty advising function and, as enrollment quickly grew with the inception of a BA program, established a centralized office to advise all undergraduates.

Since 1967, the primary strategies for meeting our majors' needs emphasize efficiency, simplicity, and cost-effectiveness. They include: (a) a central departmental advising office with one professional and one faculty on the staff, who handle *all* advising; (b) (paid) employment of trained peer advisers, (c) a heavy reliance on easily available written materials; (d) a fieldwork course to provide work experience at literally hundreds of agencies for up to 18 credits (of the 50 required for the degree); (e) interdepartmental programs—organized sequences of supplementary courses utilizing other departmental courses and advisers; and (f) minority graduate students giving specialized advice to minority majors. These strategies are similar to those at the University of Massachusetts, which has the same numbers of faculty and students and whose strategies have met with enthusiastic approval from faculty, administration, and students (Halgin, 1983).

Our secondary strategies (reaching fewer students or addressing what have been regarded as ancillary needs) include: (a) 3–credit career development course, (b) 4 meetings per quarter on careers and graduate school, (c) quarterly newsletter mailed to all majors, and (d) library of career materials and graduate program information, student-authored career handouts, vocational interest testing and interpretation, and résumé writing workshops.

The following report summarizes the results of the needs assessment survey and offers recommendations for improving services to meet our majors' career planning needs.

Method

Participants

A random sample was drawn from the population of psychology majors enrolled in the spring quarter of 1983 (N = 640). By the quarter's end, 145 of 200 students had responded (73% return-rate). Seventy percent of the 145 respondents were women and had the following class status: 3% freshman, 7% sophomores, 35% juniors, 48% seniors, and 7% fifth-year students. The proportions of the sexes represented in each class were uniform, and the proportions of the various classes in the sample did not differ significantly from those observed in the total population of psychology majors.

The same two-sided, one-page survey distributed to Creighton University psychology majors the previous summer (Ware, 1982) was used with only minor modifications for comparison purposes. A cover letter explained the purpose of the survey and a stamped return envelope was enclosed. I sent follow-up letters and surveys to nonrespondents after 3 weeks and again after another 2 weeks.

Materials and procedures

The most important items on the survey had students rate the value of nine sources of career information and of 14 types of career-related information. The same sources of career information as at Creighton (minus two career courses not given at UW) were presented with instructions to rate items using a Likert-type scale ranging from 1 (not at all valuable) to 5 (very valuable) only if the student had used that source. The same procedure was used to rate the value of different types of information.

Postgraduation plans and frequency of advice were solicited as was the degree of assistance already received in preparing for postgraduation and degree of additional assistance desired. An open-ended question asked for the kinds of additional assistance students wanted from the psychology advising office to prepare for careers.

Results

The percentages of students' postgraduation plans are as follows: 44% full-time employment (including military), 28% graduate school in psychology, 24% graduate or professional program other than psychology, 4% "other" (additional undergraduate study, travel, part-time employment). The sexes did not differ in post-graduation plans.

The degree of assistance received in making career plans was rated 2.6 (below medium) with no difference between the sexes. The degree of additional assistance desired was rated overall 3.4, with a significant difference between the sexes (women = 3.6, men 3.0). Students indicated that they saw an adviser on the average of 2.4 times a year.

Table 11-1 presents the percentage of respondents who used various sources of information and their value. The most used and highly valued sources were department printed material and the two professional advisers. Although used by only 23% of respondents, the fieldwork course was also highly rated, significantly more so by women. Women rated both departmental presentations on careers and graduate school and the counseling center staff higher than men. The University placement office was the least used and most poorly rated source of career information.

Table 11-2 presents 14 types of career information, their use and value. Information about appropriate courses was most used, followed by career opportunities within and outside human services, and career activities of different kinds of psychologists. Women used information about career opportunities

Table 11-1. Students' Use and Evaluation of Career Information Sources

Source	% Use	Value#
1. Department printed material	74	3.7
2. Psychology advisors (faculty/staff)*	72	4.0
3. Classroom instructor in psychology	64	3.3
4. Psychology peer advisors*	41	3.4
5. Departmental presentations	30	3.1[1]
6. Other departments' advisors	29	3.1
7. Counseling center staff	25	3.0[2]
8. Fieldwork course (Psychology 497)	23	3.8[3]
9. Placement office	20	2.8

\# All footnote values significant at or beyond the .05 level.
1. Females = 3.3   Males = 2.6; 2. Females = 3.3   Males = 2.4; 3. Females = 4.2   Males = 3.0.
* On a separate question regarding the frequency of meeting with an advisor, the average number of contacts was 2.4 per year.

Table 11-2. Students' Use and Evaluation of Career Information Types

Source	% Use	Value#
1. Information about courses	50	3.7
2. Career opportunities within human services	48[1]	3.5
3. Career activities of different psychologists	46	3.6
4. Career opportunities outside human services	39[2]	3.2
5. How to identify your career interests	27	3.3
6. How to identify your career goals	23	3.1[3]
7. Career activities of health and law professionals	22	3.4
8. How select/apply to graduate school in psychology	20	3.2
9. How to select your career aptitudes	19	3.0
10. How select/apply nonpsychology professional program	16	3.0
11. Résumé writing	14	3.1
12. What kinds of people enter different careers	14	3.1
13. Interview skills	12	2.8
14. Job search skills	12	3.3

All footnote values were significant at or beyond the .05 level.
1. Females = 53%   Males = 34%; 2. Females = 45%   Males = 27%; 3. Females = 2.9   Males = 3.8.

more often but were less satisfied with information on identifying one's goals than men.

Fifty-eight suggestions for additional assistance were made by students. A desire for more career information followed by information on graduate school in psychology, general advising improvement, and information on professional training other than psychology were listed.

Discussion

There is an alarming gap between the career assistance psychology majors say they are going to need and the assistance obtained thus far. This point is illustrated vividly in Tables 11-1 and 11-2. While our results paralleled those at Creighton, UW students used career information sources and types much less. The ratings of the value of these items, on the other hand, does not appear to differ as much between the two departments, although there was a distinct trend for the least used types of information to be rated lower at UW than at Creighton. Thus, future advising strat-

egies will be aimed first at increasing the use made of available sources of information. As we have little control over the quality of types of information provided by the Placement and Counseling Centers, the low values placed on these types of information could remain a problem.

The findings in Table 11-1 indicate a need to increase the use made of all sources of career information. Use of peer advisers and departmental presentations, particularly, should receive attention. Judging from the 80% use of the top sources at Creighton University, 80% would be a goal to strive for for our five most popular sources, while doubling the current number (23%) who take fieldwork.

Looking at Table 11-2, a goal might be to have over 50% of respondents say they had used the top five types of information. For the rest of the list, our aim should be to get at least a third of our majors exposed. Most students apparently lack basic knowledge of résumé writing, interview skills, and job search skills, at the same time that only 20% of them have found their way to the placement office which specializes in free classes in all of these skills.

Below are some student suggestions our advising staff hopes to implement.

1. *Career resources on campus handout.* This comprehensive handout has already been prepared and is free, as are all our printed materials, to anyone who visits the advising office.

2. *Faculty conversation hours.* Typically when we have meetings devoted to preparation for graduate school we have graduate students describe the process they went through applying and "what graduate school is really like." Certainly faculty members could do this informally without extensive preparation and help narrow the void between undergraduates and our research-oriented faculty.

3. *Directory of advising publications.* A handout lists all the other handouts available.

4. *Psychology as preparation for other professions.* We need a handout and conversation hours devoted to careers based on postbaccalaureate study areas other than an MA in counseling or a Master's of Social Work (MSW). What do medical, dental, business, law, computer science programs require of psychology majors? As 24% of the respondents intended to do graduate work outside of psychology, this represents a real information need.

5. *Women and career goals.* We need a departmental presentation devoted to this topic to which we send special invitations to women age 28 and over. We should schedule it at the day's end from 4:30 until 6:00 and supply light refreshments.

6. *Where are they now?* Mail surveys should continue to be conducted which identify employers of psychology baccalaureates so that these firms can be researched by prospective graduates.

7. *Push the placement center.* Many of the types of information least used by students are provided free by the Placement Center, which also keeps files of letters of recommendation for all graduates and mails letters when requested. We need to advertise the Placement Center more among our majors and avoid duplication of services. We could also invite Placement and Counseling Center staff to give conversation hours in which they role play interviews, review job search strategies, clarify values and interests, and improve résumés.

8. *Updated career library.* We need new and relevant books including federal and state labor market statistics. We need files of relevant articles for students to copy and a careers corner in our waiting area with a bulletin board highlighting local newspaper articles on college graduates and magazine features on careers.

9. *Undergraduate organization.* Despite repeated past failures to organize a Psi Chi chapter or other undergraduate club, we must attempt this again and enlist the help of our majors in better meeting their career advising needs.

10. *Fieldwork expansion.* The fieldwork instructor has now added a fieldwork component to the community psychology class and could assist other instructors in adding fieldwork experiences to their courses, for example, tutoring at an in-

stitution for the mentally retarded as part of the developmental course, socializing with the elderly at senior citizen centers as part of the personality course, and helping student refugees in the public schools as part of social psychology.

11. *More frequent departmental presentations.* Perhaps the only way to meet the needs of students for more career and graduate school information is to have more presentations. Only 30% indicated they used this source in spite of quarterly newsletter and daily newspaper advertisements, special invitational mailings, and class announcements.

We have concluded that we are not reaching enough of our majors with our career development program. We need to increase the use of our departmental sources of career information and to concern ourselves with improving the values of the departmental information we offer students. Our chief sources of information should be used by 80% of majors and the chief types of information should be used by at least 50% of respondents to surveys such as this. These goals will guide our planning in the year to come.

References

American Psychological Association, Educational Affairs Office. (1983). *Results: Phase 1 survey of undergraduate department chairs* (Tech. Rep.). Washington, DC: Author.

Halgin, L. F. (1983, August). *An advising system for a large psychology department.* Paper presented at American Psychological Association, Anaheim, CA.

Titley, R. W., & Titley, B. S. (1982). Academic advising: the neglected dimension in designs for undergraduate education. *Teaching of Psychology, 9,* 45–49.

Ware, M. E. (1982). *Assessing psychology majors' career planning needs* (Tech. Rep.). Omaha, NE: Creighton University, Department of Psychology.

Chapter 12

The professional seminar:
A new method for student advisement

Henry J. Oles and Robert G. Cooper, Jr., Southwest Texas State University

The failure of student advisement

One of the most important jobs to be handled by the faculty is the proper advisement of their students in terms of both their academic and career plans. Unfortunately, the general lack of meaningful advisement, and even incorrect advisement, are frequent sources of numerous problems and recurring complaints from undergraduates. Obviously, student advisement is a responsibility that should be of serious concern. It is surprising, however, that very little has been written about the academic advising process, especially as it applies to psychology students. While the current state of advisement seems to please few, little is being done to bring about a significant change.

Most psychology departments offer a wide variety of courses from which to choose with relatively few required courses. This places a great deal of responsibility on the students. For example, courses such as statistics and experimental methods are considered fundamental and therefore should be taken early in one's academic career, but a particular sequence is not required. For a variety of reasons, students often do not get the advisement they need, and consequently they often enroll in the wrong courses. They frequently delay taking core courses and instead enroll in courses that may have no application to their overall career goals.

Unfortunately, many psychology majors have no career goals beyond completing their current semester. They have little awareness of the scope of the field of psychology and the employment possibilities that may be available

to them with a bachelor's, master's or doctoral degree. Many students drop out of psychology who might have not done so had they had better information about the field. On the other hand, a number of students complete the bachelor's degree in psychology only to find that they have no interest in continuing in the field. If students had more accurate information about the field of psychology, they could have made more intelligent decisions about their programs and not wasted so much of their time.

The fault lies with both the faculty and the students. In large psychology departments with a student-teacher ratio of 50–1 or more, it is difficult for individual faculty to become involved in a meaningful long-term relationship with individual students. On the other hand, students often avoid advisement, either because they simply do not want to take the time or because they fear an adviser will force them to take courses they do not want, even if there is good reason to take them. Many students have virtually no personal contact with faculty during their undergraduate years. Their first contact with advisement may be forced upon them when they file for a degree, only to learn that they have so many deficiencies that their graduation will be delayed.

Some departments try to combat the problem by using student advisers. The results of this plan are mixed. Student advisers provide little continuity and often give incorrect advice. Some institutions have resorted to the automatic "rubber stamp" approach which essentially is the advice that students get on their own from the university catalog, friends, or helpful faculty.

A review of the research on advising indicates that very little work has been done on the topic. Apparently, advisement is a process that the faculty assumes is taking place properly and therefore does not need to be researched or changed in any way.

The study

Advisement for psychology majors and minors at Southwest Texas State University has always been a problem. Both the University and the Department of Psychology have grown dramatically over the past 10 years. There have been a number of new faculty added to the staff who are not thoroughly familiar with departmental or university requirements. In addition, the entire staff shoulders a very heavy teaching load. As a result, advisement was at best haphazard. Students often took courses or avoided courses primarily because of lunchroom gossip. A variety of formal and informal advisement procedures were instituted, but none of them worked. Even compulsory advisement before registration was attempted, but it failed as students sought means to avoid it. As a result, advisement was reduced to a process that was available if and when a student asked for it. Most advisement took place at the registration table as students struggled to assemble a schedule.

A psychology faculty group at Southwest Texas State University was assigned the task of studying the advisement process and possibly developing a workable alternative. After many intensive meetings, the result of these group meetings was the formulation of an entirely new approach to advisement which was titled the Professional Seminar. This new 1-hour required course was designed to be taken by any student interested in a psychology major or minor after they had successfully completed their first course in psychology.

Professional Seminar was structured to introduce students to the psychology faculty, their areas of expertise and research, the courses they offered, requirements for those courses, degree requirements and to provide students with factual information about job possibilities in psychology or related fields. The seminar also presented information on graduate study including the problems of being a graduate student.

The professional seminar

Professional Seminar is structured to include 14 weekly class meetings. Currently, Southwest Texas State University's Department of Psychology offers three sections per semester, each meeting at noon on Monday, Wednesday, and Friday. This hour was designated as a time when full-time faculty would be free to make presentations in the Professional Seminar, as well as a time when students would not have many conflicting classes. Students are scheduled for a particular section but may, with permission, attend another section meeting the same week. One faculty member is designated as the Professional Seminar coordinator.

Weekly meetings are built around a particular specialty area within psychology, with the primary instructors in that area responsible for the presentation. During the course of the semester, students usually have an opportunity to hear presentations by the entire staff. Presenting faculty are encouraged to talk about their area of specialty, the courses they teach, their requirements for those courses, and their research interests and projects in which students may become involved. Presentations are semiformal; students are encouraged to ask questions at any time.

Professional Seminar also includes several special presentations. Near the beginning of the semester, a university librarian discusses how to use the library, especially in terms of psychology reference material and the use of the new computer search facilities. Another presentation near the end of the semester concentrates on the importance of research, even as an undergraduate, and how a student can find a suitable research topic and faculty research adviser. The final presentation includes a roundtable discussion by several faculty on the job market for students with the bachelor's, master's or doctoral degrees. Admission requirements for graduate school are also discussed.

Students are required to write a one-page typewritten paper each week, describing the previous week's presentation, and how it relates to their career goals and personal needs. They are also required to prepare two special papers, a short library report demonstrating their mastery of the use of *Psychological Abstracts* and a detailed analysis of why they are studying psychology, a list of the courses they have taken, a list of courses they will take to graduate, and their plans for graduate school or a career in a psychology-related field. For many students, this paper is the first time they are forced to seriously contemplate their long- and short-term goals.

Evaluation is based on a combination of factors. Attendance is of foremost importance and accounts for 50% of the student's grade. Weekly papers account for another 30%. Each paper is graded as a *3*, *2*, or *1*. Generally, any paper that demonstrates reasonable effort is graded a *3*. Graders are strict about the paper's format, grammar, spelling, and appearance. A secondary goal of the course is to promote professionalism. All papers must be neatly typewritten and turned in on the assigned date. Students who consistently demonstrate poor grammar, sentence structure, and spelling are identified and referred to the university remedial English program. The majority of students earn a final grade of *A* or *B*.

Professional Seminar is now completing its fourth year. Enrollment is held at less than 50 students per section or 150 students per semester. Student response to the seminar has been excellent. Most of the current students have just begun their course work in psychology. The Professional Seminar program has been evaluated by a number of different techniques. Evaluations by the students themselves are generally excellent and at least as good as those given to some of the most popular courses in the Psychology Department. A 96-item questionnaire assessing student attitudes toward 24 different psychology courses was administered at the beginning and again at the end of the Professional Seminar. Attitude changes were generally in the direction that the psychology faculty predicted. We counted the enrollment in several important, but not required and previously unpopular courses, such as Theory of Measurement, to determine if recommendations made in Professional Seminar are being followed. The results of that count demonstrate that enrollments in nonrequired courses can be manipulated by providing students with essential information about those courses.

Our results show that students often avoid enrolling in courses simply because they do not have sufficient information about their value.

Conclusions

In summary, we can conclude that the Professional Seminar program developed at Southwest Texas State University is a highly successful alternative method for providing large numbers of students with a vast array of reliable and valid information about specific course offerings, professors, rules and regulations, research activity, graduate school, and careers in psychology. The seminar program offers numerous advantages over traditional counseling methods, including giving students first-hand contact with a large number of faculty in a very cost- and time-effective format. One faculty member, together with volunteer help, can provide 150 students with 13–14 hours of academic advising each semester for a total of 1400 contact hours. Not only would it be impossible for the Psychology Department to provide this much advisement to each student on an individual basis, but the Department feels that it is advantageous for the student to learn about particular courses, and psychology in general, from a wide array of faculty members. Several other academic departments at Southwest Texas State University have begun seminar advisement programs of their own, based upon the model developed in the Psychology Department.

Chapter 13

Teaching and evaluating a career development course for psychology majors

Mark E. Ware, Creighton University

Career development programs at the collegiate level have grown in popularity over the last decade (Goodson, 1982; Haney & Howland, 1978). Goodson's survey revealed that less than one third of the reporting institutions evaluated various career development programs and that most evaluation instruments were constructed for local conditions. Both Goodson (1982) and Holland, Magoon, and Spokane (1981) emphasized the need for comprehensive evaluation of career development programs.

The research literature reflects the current status of evaluating career development programs. Several studies failed to employ a comparison or control group, pre- and posttesting, or both (Buckalew & Lewis, 1982; Evans & Rector, 1978; Gillingham & Lounsbury, 1979; Heppner & Krause, 1979; Reardon & Regan, 1981; Scrimgeour & Gilgannon, 1978). Several other studies, however, have included those requisites (Babcock & Kaufman, 1976; Barker, 1981; Bartsch & Hackett, 1979; Cochran, Hetherington, & Strand, 1980; Smith, 1981). Most studies (e.g., Barker, 1981) have evaluated career programs for freshmen and sophomores. Little is known about the problems of or the effectiveness of career programs for upper-level college students, in general, and psychology majors, in particular.

The objectives of this article are: (a) to describe one way of teaching a career development course, (b) to examine and interpret the results of a 5-year program of research to evaluate the effectiveness of a career course, and (c) to provide experientially based suggestions for developing and teaching a career course.

Career development course

The course consists of three components corresponding to the three objectives of the course. The objectives are to increase knowledge about one's self, about occupational and postgraduate educational opportunities, and about job-search skills.

The course employs traditional lecture format, small group discussion, written assignments and exercises, locally produced videotape programs and booklets, commercially produced audiovisual materials, career inventories, and out-of-class skill development tasks. This multidimensional approach to the course highlights the instructor's effort to engage the students at as many levels as possible and the belief that significant learning occurs in association with relevant materials and practical problems (Rogers, 1969).

The course requires at least two short-answer essay examinations. The results of the tests constitute about 40% of the final grade. The bases for the remainder of the grade are class attendance and participation and the quality and timely completion of assignments.

The class meets for 50 minutes, three times a week, for 14 weeks. Structured paper-and-pencil exercises guide students in exploring and clarifying their values, interests, and abilities. Figler (1975) provides excellent illustrations of the types of exercises an instructor can use. Students complete exercises outside of class. Small group, in-class discussion of the results of the exercises aim to foster student disclosure and peer support.

The administration and interpretation of

two career inventories stimulate exploration of personal characteristics and of occupational alternatives. Students complete the Self-Directed Search (Holland, 1974) and the System for Career Decision-Making (Harrington & O'Shea, 1980) during the first and second half of the semester, respectively. Moreover, students use paper-and-pencil assignments to evaluate the degree of match between their interests and abilities and their prospective careers. From the evaluations, students select two careers from each inventory that have a high degree of consistency with their personal characteristics. The students use the *Dictionary of Occupational Titles* (U.S. Dept. of Labor, 1977) and the *Occupational Outlook Handbook* (U.S. Dept. of Labor, 1982) to conduct an in-depth investigation of and to write reports about four careers. Finally, students conduct a structured interview of persons who work in any two of the four occupations reported on. The interview includes questions about the specific duties performed, the degree of stress associated with the position, effects of the work on one's health, and major satisfactions and dissatisfactions associated with the work. Students write a summary report about each interview.

Ware and Sroufe (1984a) produced a videotape, "Career Development and Opportunities for Psychology Majors." The tape provides a summary of the first two components of the course. The narrator points out that psychology majors come from a variety of backgrounds and that they select psychology as a major because it serves one or more personal interests and values. Interviews of four students document those conclusions. The narrator describes the similarities between deciding about a college major and deciding about an occupation. In addition, he states that assessing and developing one's skills are an integral part of career development. Excerpts from interviews of six former students, include some who went immediately into the job market in business, human services, and collegiate settings, and others who went to graduate school in psychology or professional school in medicine and law. The contents of the interviews illustrate the general and specific skills required for various occupational pursuits and the variety of career paths available to psychology majors. The program concludes with a summary of the major issues in the program and with an invitation to students to make use of their academic advisers and other available resources. A 20-page booklet, "Career Development and Opportunities for Psychology Majors," (Ware, 1987) elaborates on the issues that the videotape presents.

Exploration of graduate and professional school opportunities focuses on postgraduate work in psychology and related disciplines and the professions of medicine, dentistry, and law. During the semester, four to six invited speakers come to class to describe their work activities, graduate preparation, and career satisfaction and dissatisfaction. Visitors include doctoral-level psychologists, a social worker, and a lawyer. The topics of searching for, preparing for, and applying to graduate school in psychology require four 50-minute periods. The instructor also points out how the principles associated with each process are transferable to professional school. Finally, discussion of issues associated with gaining admission to medical, dental, and law school constitute one class period. This latter feature may be peculiar to Creighton because of the large number of preprofessional students.

Ware and Sroufe (1984b) also produced a videotape, "Pursuing Graduate Study in Psychology," highlighting the factors associated with preparing one's self for graduate school. This tape contains excerpts from interviews of faculty, students, and a graduate school dean. Ware and Sroufe describe the role of personal motivation, research experience, coursework, and field experience for gaining admission to graduate school. An 18-page booklet, "Pursuing Graduate Study in Psychology," (Ware, 1984b) describes factors associated with searching for, preparing for, and applying to graduate school.

The last component of the course develops job-search skills and requires about one third of the semester. Lectures and activities focus on developing skills in assertive communication, decision making, job hunting, résumé writing, and interviewing. Moreover, all students submit a formal résumé, and they may participate in a videotaped, simulated job interview. Formal, written feedback provides each student with an evaluation of his or her interview performance. Each student also has an opportunity to view his or her taped interview.

Texts for the course include Figler (1979) and Super and Super (1982). Requirements also include readings from portions of Figler (1975), Powell (1978), Woods (1979), and other selected articles.

A 5-year program of research evaluated the effectiveness of the career course. The Method and Results section describes the participants, materials, and results of that research program.

Method and results

Study 1 (Ware & Beischel, 1979)

Participants. The 12 junior and senior psychology majors enrolled in the course constituted the treatment group, and the 13 junior and senior psychology majors not enrolled in the course constituted the comparison group.

Materials. Materials consisted of two questionnaires. The What Should They Do (WSTD) competency scale from the Career Maturity Inventory (Crites, 1973) was the first questionnaire. The WSTD scale measures skill in solving career-related problems. The Identify scale (Holland, Gottfredson, & Nafziger, 1975) was the second questionnaire. High scores on the scale reflect a clear and stable self-picture of personality, interest, and talent. Finally, students rated their degree of decisiveness about the choice of a career. Students in both groups completed the three measures at the beginning and at the end of the semester.

Results. Table 13-1 contains the pre- and postcourse results for treatment and comparison groups on measures of cognitive skill (WSTD), identity, and decisiveness about a career. A 2 × 2 analysis of variance with repeated measures on the second factor was used. The results of analysis of the cognitive skill measure revealed a significant difference between treatment and comparison groups, $F(1,21) = 13.80$, $p < .01$. Analysis of identity scores revealed a significant increase for both groups from the beginning to the end of the semester, $F(1,23) = 8.34$, $p < .01$. Analysis of decisiveness ratings indicated a significant increase in scores from the beginning to the end of the course, $F(1,21) = 4.39$, $p < .05.$, and a significant interaction between groups and trials, $F(1,21) = 8.38$, $p < .01$. Inspection of Table 13-1 indicates that the treatment group experienced an increase in decisiveness but the control group remained unchanged.

Study 2 (Ware, 1981)

Participants. The 31 psychology majors who enrolled in the course constituted the treatment (T) group. The 59 psychology majors enrolled in other upper-level psychology courses made up the comparison, major (CM) group. The 29 nonpsychology majors who were not in the course made up the comparison, nonmajor (CNM) group. Inclusion of the CNM group permitted an evaluation of the similarities and differences between students majoring in psychology and a heterogeneous group of students from other disciplines.

Table 13-1. Means and Standard Deviations for Treatment and Comparison Groups at Pre- and Posttest for 3 Dependent Variables

Groups	Measures					
	Cognitive Skill		Identity		Decisiveness	
	Pre	Post	Pre	Post	Pre	Post
Treatment						
Mean	13.9	13.9	12.7	13.7	4.6	5.3
SD	1.4	2.0	2.4	1.6	.7	.7
Comparison						
Mean	11.4	12.2	11.7	12.9	4.3	4.3
SD	2.2	1.1	2.5	1.6	1.1	1.4

There was a slightly greater number of men than women in each of the groups.

Materials. The materials used in this study consisted of several forms. The first form instructed students to rate their degree of knowledge about themselves, job opportunities, résumé writing and interview skills. The rating scale was a 6-point Likert-type scale that varied from low (*1*) to high (*6*).

The second form was the vocational checklist (Aiken & Johnston, 1973). The checklist consisted of 50 sentence stems that asked students to indicate the approximate number of times they emitted a specific information-seeking response during the preceding 3 weeks. The checklist provided two scores, including a cognitive or thought response and a behavioral or action response.

The Career Maturity Inventory-Attitude Scale (CMI-AS) constituted the third form (Crites, 1973). The CMI-AS consists of 50 true-false items. The resultant score provides a measure of career maturity in which higher scores indicate higher levels of maturity. The Results section includes items from a course evaluation.

Analyses. A 3 × 2 analysis of variance was used to evaluate the results. The unequal number of participants in the cells of the factorial design required the use of harmonic-mean analysis. In the first set of analyses, students' post- minus pre-course difference scores were the data. These analyses evaluated whether significant differences in the difference scores existed between the groups. In the second set of analyses, students' pre-course scores were the data. The analyses provided one way to identify the similarities and differences between those who elected to take or not to take the course, as well as to compare psychology and nonpsychology majors.

Results. Table 13-2 contains the mean post-minus pre-course difference scores between the groups. Analysis of the self knowledge ratings revealed a significant difference for the treatment variable, $F(2,113) = 3.31$, $p < .05$. Results of protected t-tests (Welkowitz, Ewen, & Cohen, 1976) revealed that students in the T group reported significantly greater increases in self-knowledge than those in the CM group.

Analysis of the job knowledge ratings revealed a significant difference for the treatment variable, $F(2,113) = 24.59$, $p < .01$. Protected t-tests revealed that students in the T group reported significantly greater increases in job knowledge than students in the CM and the CNM groups.

Analysis of the skills' knowledge ratings revealed a significant difference for the treatment variable, $F(2,113) = 34.88$, $p < .01$. Protected t-tests revealed that students in the T group reported significantly greater increases in skills' knowledge than students in the CM and the CNM groups.

Analysis of the cognitive vocational information-seeking revealed a significant difference for the treatment variable, $F(2,113) = 6.17$, $p < .01$. Protected t-tests revealed that students in the T group exhibited significantly greater increases in cognitive information seeking than students in either the CM or in the CNM groups.

Analysis of behavioral vocational information seeking revealed a significant difference for the treatment variable, $F(2,113) = 12.53$, $p < .01$. Protected t-tests revealed that students in the T group exhibited significantly greater increases in behavioral information seeking than student in either the CM or the CNM groups.

Analysis of the career maturity scores revealed a significant difference for the treatment variable, $F(2,113) = 4.41$, $p < .05$. Protected t-tests revealed that students in the T group exhibited significantly greater increases in career maturity than students in the CM groups.

Table 13-2 also contains the mean pre-course scores for the treatment and comparison groups. Analysis of variance revealed significant differences between groups only for the skills' knowledge and career maturity scores.

Analysis of the skills' knowledge ratings revealed significant differences for the treatment variable, $F(2,113) = 6.67$, $p < .01$. Protected t-tests revealed that students in the T group reported significantly less skills' knowledge than students in either the CM or the CNM groups.

Analysis of pre-course maturity scores revealed a significant difference for the treat-

Table 13-2. Means and Standard Deviations for Treatment Groups

Groups	Knowledge			Vocational information seeking		
	Self	Job	Skills	Cognitive	Behavioral	Career maturity
Post- minus pre-course difference scores						
Treatment						
Mean	.45	1.52	2.52	13.90	30.35	2.45
SD	.89	1.15	1.91	16.38	36.83	4.03
Comparison, major						
Mean	−.03	.12	.22	−.64	5.24	.00
SD	.76	1.10	1.00	18.81	17.69	3.55
Comparison, nonmajor						
Mean	.17	.14	.31	2.21	1.14	.79
SD	.66	1.27	.97	18.60	25.68	3.94
Pre-course scores						
Treatment						
Mean	4.77	3.45	2.42	53.97	40.58	36.03
SD	.92	.89	1.36	20.16	27.15	5.37
Comparison, major						
Mean	4.95	3.69	3.33	54.37	35.20	38.54
SD	1.02	1.28	1.33	24.84	20.85	5.04
Comparison, nonmajor						
Mean	4.76	4.03	3.52	51.79	44.52	39.45
SD	.69	1.32	1.40	19.23	25.04	3.98

ment variable, $F(2,113) = 4.89$, $p < .01$. Protected t-tests revealed that students in the T group exhibited significantly lower career maturity scores than students in either the CM or the CNM groups.

Listed below are items from the students' course evaluation, including the percent of students who agreed or strongly agreed with each item. Inspection reveals that students discriminated among the several course components and that more than 75% of the students responded favorably to all class activities.

Self-Knowledge

1. The self-exploration exercises in the beginning of the course helped me to know myself better. (81%)

Job Knowledge

2. It was very important for me to have the areas or jobs in psychology differentiated. (90%)

3. Realizing job opportunity and salary level in areas of psychology was very important to me. (90%)

4. The videotapes and professionals who came to class helped me very much in my own decision making. (84%)

5. The lectures on graduate school application and acceptance were very important for me. (77%)

Skills Knowledge

6. The lectures on résumé writing and letter of application were very important to me. (100%)

7. The résumé and letter of application writing exercises were very important to me. (97%)

8. The lectures on the interviewing process were very important to me. (97%)

9. The opportunity to practice interviewing in class was very important to me. (84%)

Study 3 (Ware, 1982b)

Participants and materials. The 31 psychology majors who enrolled in the career class reported previously (Ware, 1981) also participated in this study. Students completed a course evaluation by providing narrative responses to the following questions:

1. At the start of the semester, you had certain aspirations that you hoped the course would help you to realize. Identify the components of the course that you think helped you the most and explain how they helped. Indicate something important you know or can do that you did not know or could not do before taking the course.

2. Describe how your attitudes about postgraduate education and employment are different as a consequence of taking this course.

3. Imagine that a psychology major asked you about taking this course. Describe your reactions indicating what kinds of person can benefit most from this course and how.

Students' responses about the course were assigned to one of four categories: (a) self-discovery, (b) information about the world of work and postgraduate education, (c) development of job-search skills, or (d) other. The results reported below do not include responses in category (d).

Results. The following direct quotations illustrate students' responses to the course. Remarks are organized into three areas corresponding to the course goals: increasing knowledge about one's self, the world of work and postgraduate education, and job-search skills. After each set of quotations, students' statements are summarized.

Self-Discovery

Student A: The first section of the course, the knowledge of self part, was beneficial for me since it provided an opportunity to evaluate myself and my perception of myself. I think a large number of people are reluctant to elaborate on their good points, and I am no exception. The exercises provided me with a chance to learn how to talk about myself without feeling guilty or embarrassed about it. The discussions of the results in the small group setting also enhanced these aspects of my own personal evaluation and development.

Student B: These (self-exploration) exercises gave me a broader perspective on what I can and cannot do. I found out that I have interests in science, art, and music, but was more skilled in teaching and managerial skills.

Student C: The first day of class, we were all asked what we hoped to get out of this course. My response was that when I asked the question, "What are you going to do with a psychology degree?", I could give an intellectually sound answer. At the time I knew I wanted a psychology degree because I saw much of my life centering around psychology. Yet, I had other interests which I wanted to try. For example, I have always had an interest in the arts and fashion. At the time, I did not see the correlation between psychology and my secret interests. After taking the first self inventory test, these secret interests proved to be a domineering part of my life. But, I did not know how to fit it all together. I learned that by taking some courses in journalism/communications my degree could be highly marketable in the field of fashion and business.

Student D: I learned about transferable skills. There are things I do every day that I can apply to the world of work. It was important to me to find this out because now I think that I have a lot more to offer a prospective employer than I was aware of before.

Student E: My attitudes toward employment for women, especially the conflict between the practice of medicine and family life, have been altered through the semester. I have come to the realization that one can limit the amount of time that he or she spends on the job without limiting the amounts of what he or she can contribute to that job. The resolution of these conflicting ideas has led to my commitment to attempt to enter medical school.

The students indicated that the course helped to clarify and verify self-impressions, allowed them to acknowledge "hidden" impressions, provided an opportunity to resolve conflicts, and enhanced their self-confidence.

The World of Work and Postgraduate Education

In the following quotations students express views regarding a first full-time job following graduation.

I think the most important thing I learned in this section is that I have been thinking in a very narrow-minded manner. I no longer think of myself as having one occupational option the rest of my life.

In this course I have learned that you can try out different jobs until you have found one that meets your own personal needs.

The following quotations are some views about employment options.

It opened up to me a wide range of alternatives to graduate school. I have never had experience in the business world, but I learned that I possess many qualifications that could give me a rewarding career in business if I so choose.

The thing I didn't know before the course was that you could do so much with an undergraduate degree in psychology. I found out that the avenues were endless. Another thing that could be used as a subheading to this is, "What can you do with a law degree?" So often you hear lawyers are starving. Well the ones that are must have no initiative, or be dead.

By gaining knowledge of various careers, I realized that there are many careers in this world that I would be happy to pursue and that not getting into dental school is not the end of the world. This knowledge served to relieve my many pressures and anxieties and gave me reassurance about my future.

The students indicated that the course provided career alternatives that were unknown to them previously, pointed out that one's first career choice need not be for a lifetime, and reduced the anxiety level associated with career plans.

My attitude towards postgraduate education on the whole has only been more firmly established. My desire for a postgraduate degree has altered from a shaky possibility of attending medical school to a firm commitment to this goal.

When I went into this course I was still tentatively thinking about medicine. During the semester I pretty much decided against medicine. However, I began to think more seriously about graduate school. I was able to identify several areas that may interest me, both within and outside of psychology. I thought about counseling psychology, and perhaps organizational/industrial psychology. I never really considered graduate school, only professional school. I'm taking it much more seriously.

I still want to do postgraduate work after college, but I no longer feel it is absolutely necessary to plunge into graduate school the instant I obtain my BA. The notion of waiting a year and getting a variety of things in my life straightened out (marriage?) seems much more plausible and was, in fact, reinforced by the statistics that I read. I don't really know if I will wait before entering graduate school but I do know that if I decide to wait, I won't be struck down by unconquerable guilt.

I feel more assured about the path I was and am going to follow. I am graduating in December and have a job lined up for January 1982. I was apprehensive about doing this because most people I know are continuing their education immediately, without a break. After taking the course I saw that taking time out to work can actually be beneficial in making it into a graduate school because of first hand experience.

During the course I went through a change and am now comfortable with my new plans. That is, being a full-time mother and working part-time to keep in touch with the working world until my child (or children) are in school.

The students indicated that the course clarified feelings about going to professional school, changed opinions regarding postgraduate education, reduced pressure to pursue postgraduate education immediately, reduced reactions such as guilt and anxiety to post-graduate plans, and discovered that being a mother is acceptable and is part of a career.

Job-Search Skills

Students reported the following about the exercises of writing a résumé and participating in a simulated job interview.

I have found that reviewing my values and abilities sheets just prior to an interview makes it easier for me to talk about myself during an interview, and to come across with greater confidence in myself. That is one thing I definitely could not do before this course. And although it is still difficult to speak highly of myself, I now realize that it is possible to maintain your positive assets without feeling as though you are bragging about yourself.

The stimulated interviews and the skills we learned in preparing for them were probably the best parts of this course. They were the most practical for the fu-

ture and I feel that I am now a step ahead of future applicants—that the confidence and skills I have now could be an important deciding factor in helping me stand apart from the rest.

Another important thing I learned is how to write a résumé. I was scared to death at this prospect and never thought I could do it. Well, I did. The important thing is that I now possess the skills and if I have to revise it or write a whole new one, I can do it alone.

The idea of doing an interview terrified me; even a simulated one. But I decided to try it thinking the experience would do me good. I was amazed with myself. I was not half as terrified or nervous when I was doing it as I thought I would be. Now, when I am asked, "What are you going to do with a psychology degree?", I can say exactly what and how I intend to use it. Besides having an answer to this question, I feel that I have more confidence in what I am doing and where I want to go.

The students indicated that the course densensitized the prospect of undertaking a job interview and increased confidence in one's self and toward résumé writing and interviewing.

Summary. The results of these descriptive statements provide increased evidence for asserting that the career course can provide students with perspectives about themselves, the world of work, and job-search skills. Moreover, students indicated that the course helped them reduce anxiety, guilt, and fear associated with this stage of career development.

Study 4 (Ware, 1985)

Participants. Seventy junior and senior psychology majors completed the study. During the two semesters, the 44 students enrolled in the course constituted the treatment group, and the 26 students enrolled in another upper-level psychology course constituted the comparison group. The investigator taught both classes. There were about an equal number of men and women in each group.

Materials. One set of measures consisted of three scales from *My Vocational Situation* (Holland, Daiger, & Power, 1980): vocational identity (VI), occupational information (OI), and barriers (B). VI measures how clear and stable a picture a person has of his or her goals, interests, personality, and talents. OI provides an indication of the amount and kind of vocational information the person needs. B describes the number and type of perceived obstacles to achieving one's career choice.

The VI scale was most consistent with the course objective of increasing knowledge about one's self. The OI assesses skills associated with increasing knowledge about the world of work and job-search skills. The B scale was most consistent with the course objective of increasing knowledge about one's self. A second set of measures consisted of two of the competence tests from the Career Maturity Inventory (Crites, 1973): Knowing Yourself (KY) and choosing a job (CJ). KY and CJ are two of five scales designed to assess different components in the career decision-making process. These two scales were chosen because previous research (Ware & Beischel, 1979) revealed that they were the least likely of the five to have ceiling effects with college students and because they were consistent with those parts of the course emphasizing information about one's self and job-search skills.

Analyses. Analysis of covariance of the post-course scores with pre-course scores as the covariate was used to evaluate the course's effectiveness. Analysis of covariance is not a substitute for random assignment of participants to groups, but the analysis is designed to adjust for pre-course scores in evaluating post-course performance.

One-way analysis of variance of pre-course scores was used to identify the characteristics of those enrolled in the course. Analysis of pre-course scores also provides a reference point to evaluate the direction of change in performance as a consequence of taking the class.

Results The results of the covariance analysis of post-course scores revealed significant differences between treatment groups for each of the three Holland measures but for none of Crites' measures. Specifically, significant dif-

ferences were found for Vocational Identity ($F(1,67) = 7.16$, $p<.01$), Occupational Information ($F(1,67) = 18.31$, $p<.01$), and Barriers ($F(1,67) = 5.37$, $p<.05$). Table 13-3 contains the mean, standard deviation and sample size for each post-course measure. The mean post-course scores for treatment and comparison groups were 13.6 and 13.4 for Vocational Identity, 1.0 and 2.2 for Occupational Information, and 0.4 and 0.6 for Barriers, respectively.

The results of the analysis of variance of pre-course scores revealed significant differences between groups for Vocational Identity ($F(1,68) = 10.73$, $p<.01$) and Occupational Information ($F(1,68) = 17.54$, $p<.01$). Table 13-3 also contains the mean, standard deviation and sample size for each pre-course measure. The mean pre-course scores for treatment and comparison groups was 9.4 and 12.8 for Vocational Identity, and 3.3 and 2.0 for Occupational Information, respectively.

Discussion

Interpretations

The results of all four studies provide a comprehensive perspective about the course's effectiveness in increasing students' knowledge about themselves, the world of work, and job-search skills. Each of those issues will be examined individually. Several sources provide evidence for an increase in information about one's self. Study 2 demonstrated that students enrolled in the career course gave higher ratings of self-knowledge, obtained higher career maturity scores, and reported greater information seeking thoughts and behaviors. Study 4 found that by the end of the course students obtained higher scores in Vocational Identity

Table 13-3. Post- and Pretest Means, Standard Deviations, and Sample Sizes

					Variable					
	Vocational identity		Occupational information		Barriers		Know self		Choose job	
Group	T	C	T	C	T	C	T	C	T	C
					Posttest					
M	13.55	13.42	1.02	2.15	0.36	0.58	16.05	16.39	17.11	16.19
SD	3.00	3.85	1.29	1.52	0.65	0.81	1.75	1.77	2.23	2.74
					Pretest					
M	9.36	12.77	3.29	2.04	0.77	0.58	15.82	16.12	16.23	15.73
SD	4.24	4.12	0.90	1.61	0.89	0.77	2.28	2.18	2.09	2.03

Note: T = treatment group; C = comparison group

and reported fewer perceived barriers to the career development process.

Students' ratings of more knowledge about the world of work and reports of more information seeking thoughts and behaviors in Study 2 support a conclusion about the course's effectiveness for increasing knowledge about the world of work. The findings of a lower need for occupational information in Study 4 also supports that conclusion.

Finally, the increased decisiveness of students in the class (Study 1), higher self-reports of knowledge about job-search skills in Study 2, and the lower need for occupationally related information (Study 4) indicate that the course realized its goal of increasing job-search skills.

The descriptive findings from Study 3 were consistent with the quantitative findings in the other studies. The descriptive results also indicated that students thought the course helped them to reduce career-related anxiety, fear, and guilt.

Analysis of pre-course scores revealed characteristics about students who enroll in the course. The lower level of career maturity and higher level of vocational identity of students in Studies 2 and 4, respectively, revealed that students who took the course possessed needs that were consistent with the course. Thus, students who are less realistic and independent in career decision making and who have less clear and stable views of their goals, interests, and personality are more likely to enroll. Moreover, students who report a greater need for occupational information (Study 4) are likely candidates for the course. Finally, students who have a low evaluation of their job-search skills (Study 2) are more likely to take the course.

Collectively, the results reveal that there is some degree of self-selection among students taking a career development course. On the basis of these findings, however, program planners can feel encouraged that career programs attract students who need them. Additionally, one's colleagues can be alerted to the types of student who need and can benefit from a career course. Finally, a career development course may be an efficient way to provide the necessary services for students who might not choose to use nor have access to the services of a college or university counseling center. Career development courses, however, may not serve the needs of all students, and individual counseling may be required in some cases. In those cases, the instructor can serve as a credible referral source.

Another implication from the analysis of pre-course Vocational Identity scores (Study 4) is the need to re-emphasize the objective of increasing self-knowledge. A survey of psychology majors at Creighton University (Ware, 1983) revealed that they assigned the lowest priority to the importance of increasing knowledge about one's self. The findings of this research program demonstrate that students entering the course needed more than information about the world of work and job-search skills. Restricting one's efforts to providing information about work and job skills may limit students' career development by failing to establish a foundation in interest, value, and ability exploration and clarification.

Readers may also be interested in additional indices of the course's effectiveness. The Psychology Department at Creighton University has offered the career course to junior and senior psychology majors at least once a year since spring 1977. The course has established itself as a stable offering by the department. Student demand for the course has required that it be offered up to three times a year. The student demand for and response to the course confirms and extends the results of the quantitative evidence.

Suggestions

I have taught the career course at least once a year since spring 1980. The course has provided experience that might be useful to those who would like to develop a similar course. The following statements reflect concerns you may have about yourself, colleagues, and students.

• "I wasn't trained in the area of career development." Welcome to the club. My training at the master's and doctoral levels was in general psychology. My prerequisite credentials included: (a) a perception that students had a need, (b) a desire to do something about that need, (c) an absence of someone else to do it, and (d) an administration that was willing to give me a chance. I will discuss the issue of academic resistances later. Armed with the conditions just described, I proceeded to read, talk to others, read, and continue the cycle indefinitely thereafter. In the absence of the luxury of being retrained in a graduate program, you must be prepared to do it on your own. The time afforded by a sabbatical would be ideal, otherwise summer, weekends, and evenings are the likely times. Psychology colleagues in university counseling centers, as well as other college student personnel officials (e.g., the director of the placement office) can be of particular assistance.

• "What is a workable outline or framework for the course?" Perhaps my greatest frustration in preparing to teach the career course was the absence of structure. When I began, everything I read seemed equally important. I suggest that the course description presented earlier in this article provides one set of goals and arrangement of topics.

• "Will a career course have academic credibility?" I approached the career course as I would any other course. In general, academic courses require scholarly preparation and implementation. A career course is no different (Ware, 1982a). The career course, in particular, can be modeled after courses having a laboratory component. Thus, the course emphasizes both thinking and doing. Little is gained by arguing. The proof of the course's academic merit is in the product.

• "You can't assign grades in a course that emphasizes personal development." Although I have heard many individuals argue that grading is not possible in this type of course, I disagree. The basis for grading is the same as any other course. Once objectives are specified, grades are assigned according to the degree to which those objectives are achieved. I will admit considerable disappointment in assigning low grades, but as a once popular television commercial put it, "They earn it."

• "Won't students treat this course less seriously than others?" There is a genuine risk in teaching the career course the way that I have. The less pressure and more personal nature of the course often result in students assigning it a lower priority among the many demands in their schedules. However, I have found that a clear and formal structuring of activities, exercises, and assignments contributes markedly to maintaining student involvement. I set realistic deadlines and stick to them. I have discovered that most students respond favorably to such structure, particularly when they have trouble doing so themselves.

• "There should be few time demands on the instructor outside of class." My experience has been that a successful course will require considerable time outside of class. One must be prepared to spend time with students in individual conferences outside of class, to admit students who members of the class and one's colleagues refer, and to develop resource materials for majors who cannot or will not take the course.

I strongly recommend establishing a close working relationship with members of your school's counseling center. There will be some students whose problems exceed your skill level and time limitations. Be advised about seductive feelings such as, "I'm the only one who can help or understand this student," or "This student is too sensitive for referral," or "No one else can empathize with her the way I can." Such feelings are commonplace and making referrals can be one of the most important actions that you take.

The findings from this program of research were also consistent with results from previous research about the effectiveness of career development programs for freshmen and sophomores (Barker, 1981; Bartsch & Hackett, 1979; Cochran et al., 1980; Smith, 1981) and for upper-level college student (Babcock & Kaufman, 1976). A growing body of literature indicates that many upper-level college students need and can profit from programs in career development.

References

Aiken, J., & Johnston, J. (1973). Promoting career information seeking behavior in college students. *Journal of Vocational Behavior, 3,* 81–87.

Babcock, R., & Kaufman, M. (1976). Effectiveness of a career course. *Vocational Guidance Quarterly, 24,* 261–266.

Barker, S. B. (1981). An evaluation of the effectiveness of a college career guidance course. *Journal of College Student Personnel, 22,* 354–358.

Bartsch, K., & Hackett, G. (1979). Effect of a decision-making course on locus of control, conceptualization, and career planning. *Journal of College Student Personnel, 20,* 230–235.

Buckalew, L. W., & Lewis, H. H. (1982). Curriculum needs: Life preparation for undergraduate psychology majors. *Psychological Reports, 51,* 77–78.

Cochran, D., Hetherington, C., & Strand, K. H. (1980). Career choice class: Caviar or caveat. *Journal of College Student Personnel, 21,* 402–406.

Crites, J. (1973). *The career maturity inventory.* Monterey, CA: CTB/McGraw-Hill.

Evans, J., & Rector, A. (1978). Evaluation of a college course in career decision making. *Journal of College Student Personnel, 19,* 163–168.

Figler, H. (1975). *PATH: A career workbook for liberal arts students.* Cranston, RI: Carroll.

Figler, H. (1979). *The complete job-search handbook.* New York: Holt, Rinehart and Winston.

Gillingham, W. H., & Lounsbury, J. E. (1979). A description and evaluation of a career exploration course. *Journal of College Student Personnel, 20,* 525–528.

Goodson, W. D., (1982). Status of career programs on college and university campuses. *Vocational Guidance Quarterly, 30,* 230–235.

Haney, T., & Howland, P. A. (1978). Career courses for credit: Necessity or luxury? *Journal of College Placement, 39,* 75–77.

Harrington, T., & O'Shea, A. (1980). *The Harrington/O'Shea system for decision-making.* Moravia, NY: Chronicle Guidance.

Heppner, P., & Krause, J. (1979). A career seminar course. *Journal of College Student Personnel, 20,* 300–305.

Holland, J. (1974). *The self-directed search.* Palo Alto, CA: Consulting Psychologists.

Holland, J. D., Daiger, D. C., & Power, P. G. (1980). *My vocational situation.* Palo Alto, CA: Consulting Psychologists.

Holland, J. D., Gottfredson, G. D., & Nafziger, D. H. (1975). Testing the validity of some theoretical signs of vocational decision-making ability. *Journal of Counseling Psychology, 22,* 411–422.

Holland, J. L., Magoon, T. M., & Spokane, A. R. (1981). Counseling psychology: Career interventions, research, and theory. *Annual Review of Psychology, 32,* 279–305.

Powell, C. (1978). *Career planning and placement today.* Dubuque, IA: Kendall/Hunt.

Reardon, R., & Regan, K. (1981). Process evaluation of a career planning course. *Vocational Guidance Quarterly, 29,* 265–269.

Rogers, C. (1969). *Freedom to learn.* Columbus, OH: Charles E. Merrill.

Scrimgeour, J., & Gilgannon, N. (1978). Career development and life planning. *Journal of College Student Personnel, 19,* 575–576.

Smith, G. E. (1981). The effectiveness of a career guidance class: An organizational comparison. *Journal of College Student Personnel, 22,* 120–124.

Super, D., & Super, C. (1982). *Opportunities in psychology.* Lincolnwood, IL: VGM Career Horizons.

U.S. Department of Labor. (1977). *Dictionary of occupational titles* (4th ed.), Washington, DC: U.S. Government Printing Office.

U.S. Department of Labor. (1982). *Occupational outlook handbook* (1982–1983 ed.). Washington, DC: U.S. Government Printing Office.

Ware, M. E. (1981). Evaluating a career development course: A two-year study. *Teaching of Psychology, 8,* 67–71.

Ware, M. E. (1982a). Acknowledging the preparation of students for postgraduate life. *Teaching of Psychology, 9,* 40–42.

Ware, M. E. (1982b). *Providing perspectives and skills for career selection.* Omaha, NE: Creighton University, Department of Psychology. (ERIC Document Reproduction Service No. ED 210 595).

Ware, M. E. (1983, August). *Strategies at a smaller private university.* In J. Winer (Chair), *Managing and assessing students' career needs.* Symposium conducted at the meeting of the American Psychological Association, Anaheim, CA.

Ware, M. E. (1985). Assessing a career development course for upper-level college students. *Journal of College Student Personnel, 26,* 152–155.

Ware, M. E. (1987). *Career development and opportunities for psychology majors* (2nd ed.). Unpublished manuscript, Creighton University, Department of Psychology, Omaha.

Ware, M. E. (1987). *Pursuing graduate study in psychology.* Unpublished manuscript, Creighton University, Department of Psychology, Omaha.

Ware, M. E., & Beischel, M. L. (1979). Career development: Evaluating a new frontier for teaching and research. *Teaching of Psychology, 6,* 210–213.

Ware, M. E. (Producer), & Sroufe, P. G. (Producer-Director). (1984a). *Career development and opportunities for psychology majors.* [Videotape]. Omaha: Creighton University.

Ware, M. E. (Producer), & Sroufe, P. G. (Producer-Director). (1984b). *Pursuing graduate study in psychology.* [Videotape]. Omaha: Creighton University.

Welkowitz, J., Ewen, R. & Cohen, J. (1976). *Introductory statistics for the behavioral sciences* (2nd ed.). New York: Academic.

Woods, P. (Ed.) (1979). *The psychology major: Training and employment strategies,* Washington, DC: American Psychological Association.

Chapter 14

The Professional Psychologist: A course designed to introduce students to the profession of psychology

Stephen F. Davis, Emporia State University

This chapter describes an academic course that evolved directly from the questions and needs of my students. Several years ago I noticed that a number of students independently asked very similar questions: "What is a résumé and how do you put one together?"; "What is a professional network?"; "Who should I ask for references?"; "What kind of graduate program should I attend?"; and "What can I gain from going to a psychological association's convention?" In short, the students wanted to know about the profession of psychology. These questions typically are not asked in content-based courses.

For several years, I dealt with each student's questions on an individual basis. The next evolution was informal seminars involving several students. These seminars dealt with more specific topics such as résumé preparation, application to graduate school, and so forth. Ultimately, the seminars became weekly meetings, and then it was only a matter of time until an academic course was proposed, developed, and approved. That was several years ago. What follows is a description of the course as it is presently taught.

The Professional Psychologist: An Introduction is open to junior- and senior-level undergraduates and master's-level graduate students. The course is offered only during the fall semester each year, thus enabling students who will be applying for admission to graduate schools at the end of the semester or early in the spring to derive maximum immediate benefit from the material offered. Students receive one semester-hour credit upon successful completion of the course. (Specific course requirements are described later.) Hourly class sessions held weekly are of the discussion format. An annotated syllabus showing the major areas that are covered and the specific reading assignments follows.

Syllabus

I. Overview of the course

This section introduces students to the view that psychology is similar to a game with rules, different levels of proficiency, and different expectations associated with the various levels of proficiency. The instructor emphasizes the value of students making their own decision concerning the level they aspire to achieve and the need for a clear understanding of the degree of commitment that each level (e.g., bachelor's, master's, doctoral) normally requires.
• Sexton, V. S. (1983). The development of psychology as a profession in the United States. *Psi Chi Newsletter, 9,* 1–7. This article serves as an excellent introduction to the profession of psychology, past and present.
• McCain, G., & Segal, E. M. (1982). *The game of science* (4th edition). Monterey, CA: Brooks/Cole. This easily read book presents science as a game. It is written by two psychologists and is quite appealing to psychology majors. Particular attention is paid to chapter 8, "Scientists are People," which gives the students a clear idea of how one can choose to play the game.

II. Résumé preparation

If one believes that you can't tell the players without a scorecard, then this section of the course is most important. The psychologist's scorecard is the résumé. Students are given examples of good and bad résumés. Class discussion centers around the items that should be included in a résumé, who should be listed for professional references, the style and size of type to be used, the type of paper on which the résumé should be printed, and so forth.

• Shaffer, D. R., & Tomarelli, M. (1981). Bias in the ivory tower: An unintended consequence of the Buckley Amendment for graduate admissions? *Journal of Applied Psychology, 66,* 7–11. An excellent article that clearly indicates the advisability of maintaining a closed file containing confidential letters of recommendation. Certainly the effect of open versus confidential files can be generalized to other areas of professional contact.

• Ceci, S. J., & Peters, D. (1984). Letters of reference: A naturalistic study of the effects of confidentiality. *American Psychologist, 39,* 29–31. Replicates the basic findings reported by Shaffer and Tomarelli.

III. Becoming involved: Professional organizations and research

This course places a major stress on the importance of students' becoming involved in as many professional activities as possible, as soon as possible. Two of the most important activities that they can become involved in are research and professional conventions. The former is the foundation of the discipline, while the latter provides students with multiple professional opportunities, for example, meeting other faculty and students, hearing presentations, and making presentations. This is the section of the course where a discussion of the professional network, its establishment and importance, is best introduced.

Because professional societies will be the focus of considerable discussion, student membership (and its benefits) in such organizations as the APA, the regional affiliates, and state associations, is best introduced here. I always try to have applications for student membership in a variety of organizations available and encourage my students to take advantage of such opportunities.

If you have time, initiate a discussion encouraging students to develop or expand their professional library. In addition to receiving the *APA Monitor,* student affiliates of APA pay reduced rates for APA journals. Other inexpensive journals might also be suggested, particularly those offering a broad spectrum of papers.

• Kierniesky, N. C. (1984). Undergraduate research in small psychology departments. *Teaching of Psychology, 11,* 15–18. This is an excellent article to open a discussion on the topic of doing research. The article clearly

points out that quality research can be done at smaller institutions. If you are at a larger institution, so much the better.

• Tryon, G. S. (1985). What can our students learn from regional psychology conventions? *Teaching of Psychology, 12,* 227–228. This short, but effective article will tell you and your students why they actually should attend a regional psychology convention rather than relying upon others to bring the information back home.

IV. Graduate training? Where? What kind?

The flow of topics, from participating in the game, becoming involved in research, developing a résumé, to making a presentation at a convention seems to lead naturally to considering graduate training. As I teach both undergraduate- and master's-level students in this course, I cover a wide range of possibilities and types of graduate programs. It is important to explore the types of credentials, Graduate Record Examinations (GRE) scores, and laboratory and field experiences that various programs will most likely require.

• Couch, J. V., & Benedict, J. O. (1983). Graduate school admission variables: An analysis of 1980–81 students. *Teaching of psychology, 10,* 3–6. This short article is ideal for opening a discussion of what credentials will be required for admission to various types of graduate programs.

• Annis, L. V., Tucker, G. J., & Baker, D. A. (1978). What happens to PhD program applicants who have master's degrees? *American Psychologist,* July, 703–705. The authors presented data indicating that students with master's degrees face more difficulty gaining admission to doctoral (PhD) programs than do competent undergraduates. However, reductions in federal funds have reversed this trend. Now, many PhD programs appear to prefer well-prepared, skilled master's-level applicants. Certainly, a good discussion of the pros and cons of various types of programs will ensue from reading this article.

• Perlman, B., & Lane, R. (1981). The "clinical" master's degree. *Teaching of Psychology, 8,* 72–77. Many students, possibly a majority, picture themselves going into the area of clinical psychology. It is important that they realize the differences between master's- and doctoral-level clinical psychologists with regard to such issues as employability, certification and/or licensure, and eligibility for 3rd-party payment under Title XIX Medicaid.

• Walsh, J. (1979). Professional psychologists seek to change roles and rules in the field. *Science, 203,* 338–340.

• Henderson, D. B. (1982). On advising undergraduates about graduate school in professional psychology. *Teaching of psychology, 9,* 184–185.

• Smith, R. A. (1985). Advising beginning psychology majors for graduate school. *Teaching of Psychology, 12,* 194–198.

• Cole, D. L. (1979). Undergraduate preparation for admission to professional schools of psychology. *Teaching of Psychology, 6,* 179–180. These three articles introduce students to the possibility of graduate training in a professional school of psychology.

• Hodge, M. H. (1980). Prelims in experimental psychology at the University of Georgia. *Teaching of Psychology, 7,* 226–228. Most students are aware of the kinds of requirements for pursuing graduate training. This article is a good opener for discussing preliminary or qualifying examinations, thesis, or dissertation orals.

• Bloom, L. J., & Bell, P. A. (1979). Making it in graduate school: Some reflections about the superstars. *Teaching of Psychology, 6,* 231–232. This is one of my favorite articles. Here the students are presented with those factors that have enabled others to succeed in graduate school. The key consideration here appears to be intense involvement in the graduate program.

V. Employment? Where? What level? Strategies?

As not all students will want to, or should, pursue graduate training, a significant segment of the course is devoted to considering potential employment opportunities. This is another appropriate point in the course to emphasize that students need to become involved in as many professional activities as possible and to begin to develop a résumé that clearly conveys the individual's marketable strengths. With regard to the résumé, this is also a good time to discuss the importance of being able to adapt the résumé for a variety of purposes and needs, for example, application to graduate school, academic job application, business employment application, or research application.

• Woods, P. J. (Ed.) with Wilkinson, C. S. (1987). *Is psychology the major for you?.* Washington, DC: American Psychological Association. This book is required reading for this course. Specific chapters that are highlighted in class discussion of the course are chapter 8, "Are You Interested in a Business Career?"; chapter 11, "Emerging and Unconventional Careers for Psychology Majors"; chapter 13, "The résumé, cover letter, and interview"; and chapter 16, "A Survival Manual for New Hires."

The following articles help amplify the discussion concerning the variety of potential jobs that are available for qualified undergraduate psychology majors.

• Ware, M. E., & Meyer, A. E. (1981). Career versatility of the psychology major: A survey of graduates. *Teaching of Psychology, 8,* 12–15.

• McGovern, T. V., & Ellett, S. E. (1980). Bridging the gap: Psychology classroom to the marketplace. *Teaching of Psychology, 7,* 237–238. This article presents an excellent discussion of the need to acquire marketable skills, in addition to acquiring an appropriate academic background.

VI. The future of the field

The concluding section of the course attempts to put the training that our students receive into perspective. If this can be achieved, then the students will be better able to deal with and understand the field of psychology as fledgling professionals. The following articles definitely promote some excellent class discussions on this topic.

• Hettich, P. Lema-Stern, S., Rizzo, J. V. (1981). Dear student (and future professor). *Teaching of psychology, 8,* 156–158.

• Cole, D. L. (1981). Teaching tomorrow's psychology students: Who pays the piper? *American Psychologist, 36,* 506–513.

• Lunneborg, P. (1982). How are changes in graduate admissions affecting the teaching of undergraduate psychology? *Teaching of Psychology, 9,* 140–142.

Course requirements

During the semester each student is required to complete all reading assignments and contribute meaningfully to class discussions. Additionally, each student must complete:

1. An acceptable, typed résumé. In addition to content, particular attention is given to the physical appearance, (format, spacing, type size, etc.) of the finished copy.

2. An acceptable statement of goals and purposes. As with the résumé, this statement must be typed.

Several short-answer tests, taking 10–15 minutes of a class period, are administered during the semester. Given at the insistence of the student, the test's main purpose is to assist the students in achieving some integration of the material they have been covering. Apparently students feel that they gain more from the material when they are required to read it. A cumulative final exam is administered at the end of the semester. As with the tests, its major function is that of integration.

Of course, the choice of specific readings, activities, and grading format is, and should be, very flexible. Certainly many aspects of my course have changed, and continue to change, in response to student needs. For example, one recent addition has been to bring invited speakers, such as, mental health center administrators, graduate school representatives, other psychologists, and potential employers, to class to make a presentation and engage in a question-and-answer session. This addition has been exceptionally well received by the students.

Grading

All students are required to complete assigned readings and present an acceptable résumé and statement of purpose. Revisions of the résumé and statement of purpose may continue to be submitted until an acceptable version is produced. (If these are not presented before the end of the semester, a grade of *incomplete* is submitted.) The determination of specific letter grades for the course is based upon scores earned on the tests and the final examination. I have yet to find an acceptable format for assigning grades to either the résumé or goals statement. In the case of borderline grades, the amount of meaningful class participation is taken into account.

Course accomplishments

This course was specifically designed to introduce students to the professional side of the field of psychology. In this regard, a number of topics and issues that are covered in the course may be covered by a variety of other sources, including this text. What makes this course unique? First, this is a structured class having a regular meeting time and stated expectations. Hence, one should have greater confidence that the students will have acquired the appropriate information in a meaningful sequence. It is doubtful that such information would be as fully or meaningfully obtained by an individual following an uncoordinated approach. Second, the class-discussion format allows students to ask questions and hear answers that would not be possible in other settings. The intensity, naiveté, types of concerns, and sheer number of questions that are generated never cease to amaze me. Without hesitation, I firmly believe that the class-discussion, question-and-answer format results in the presentation of significantly more high-quality information than would be the case in a one-on-one situation. Third, the more organized class format enables a single faculty member to effectively reach far more students than would be possible otherwise.

All of these positive aspects suggest that this course should be quite effective. A comparison of the professional activity and poise of our students prior to the introduction of this course with that shown after the class had been taught several times indicates that this is the case. For example, our students are currently making a significant number of presentations at state, regional, and national conventions each year. Many of these presentations have resulted in the receipt of awards and other forms of recognition. Numerous students are listed as coauthors on journal publications. In short, they have accepted the challenge to become involved. Students are entering the workplace in a variety of appropriate job placements. Similarly, our students are viable in terms of admission to graduate programs and the receipt of graduate assistantships and/or fellowships. Numerous other positive instances could be cited.

However, I would offer a *caveat emptor* in closing; as faculty, if you undertake a class such as this, be aware that you will have to make a commitment. You are saying to the students that you are willing to be available and genuinely want to help them become involved. If the interest and commitment are there, then I feel that students and faculty alike will be richly rewarded.

Chapter 15

Field experience for undergraduate psychology students

Barbara C. Jessen, University of Evansville

Field experience has been included in the undergraduate psychology curriculum because of the student demand for pre-professional experiences in psychology and the recognition that students have skills to contribute to field placement settings. In addition, psychology departments are taking more responsibility for providing career guidance to undergraduate psychology students, especially to the approximately 85% who do not enter graduate psychology programs (Boltuck, Peterson, & Murphy, 1980).

Vande Creek and Fleischer (1984) found that two thirds of the 291 psychology departments they surveyed offered field experience, and they believe that "it is likely that no other undergraduate psychology course has grown as rapidly" (p.13). Eighty percent of these programs have been introduced since 1969. However, they conclude:

> Although practicum is frequently available, it is different things to different departments. The variety is more striking than the similarities, and there are few consistently found mechanisms of quality control. It has grown rapidly without any overriding sense of mission. What is needed is discussion about its purpose, its operation, and its evaluation. (p.14)

While field experience has many benefits, the primary purpose is to involve the undergraduate student in a relevant academic experience and, secondarily, to provide a useful service to the agency. Additional goals of guiding the process of developing and maintaining a field experience program are to clearly distinguish between the roles of the faculty supervisor and the agency supervisor, to minimize the extra work required of agency personnel in supervising a field student, and

to provide meaningful and interesting experiences to the student. Placements in which the student has direct involvement with clients and professionals are viewed most favorably by students. In addition, students prefer placements which provide structured experiences in well-organized training programs (Morris & Haas, 1984).

Benefits of field experience

Field experience has many potential educational and personal benefits for students. Students have the opportunity to apply theories and use skills learned through coursework, and to acquire knowledge and develop new skills in many areas: the practice of psychology, psychological problems, ways of helping people, agency functioning, other mental health professions, professional relationships, interviewing techniques, psychological testing, report writing, consultation, behavior modification, and group therapy. This experience often helps students explore their own attitudes and values through working with professionals and clients who may have backgrounds, attitudes, and values different from the students'. Students can learn how much they do not know and can become more aware of their personal and professional limitations. Field experience not only provides a bridge between their undergraduate work and a career or graduate school, but it can also motivate students to learn more. A direct benefit to the community is that students may learn about job and career opportunities available locally and remain in the community after graduation. For some students, field experience leads to a job with the placement agency.

Field experience benefits the placement agency, which gains a carefully selected and supervised student-worker. In addition, the agency supervisor has the opportunity to train and supervise the student. The university has an excellent means of enhancing community relations, through providing student-workers to agencies. The psychology department receives feedback about the education and training of its students, both through information from agency supervisors and through direct observation of the student. In addition, contact with community agencies allows the department to learn about job openings and employment trends. Finally, field experience allows the faculty supervisor to get to know students on a more personal level, to develop and practice supervisory skills, to contact and develop rapport with community agencies, and to develop opportunities for research and consultation.

A model for field experience

General guidelines

Field experience is an elective in 90% of the schools which have a field experience program. The total credit a student can earn varies from 2 to 24 semester-hours, with a median of 6. The mean number of hours per week required per semester-hour of credit was 3.1 (Vande Creek & Fleischer, 1984).

At the University of Evansville, a student earns one quarter-hour of credit for 30 hours of work in a community agency. Students register for 4 quarter-hours of credit per academic quarter and spend 12 hours per week for 10 weeks in the agency. Seniors majoring in psychology may elect field experience for one to three academic quarters. We encourage students to spend one quarter in one agency and two consecutive quarters in a second agency. This arrangement permits students both to have experiences in two different agencies and to become more involved in a single agency.

Settings for field experience can vary widely, from the traditional social services agencies (community mental health centers, centers for retarded people, and state hospitals) to day-care centers, schools, nursing homes, general hospitals, and to the police department, court system, and human relations commission. Students in our program are also allowed to earn credit for paying jobs they may already have, if the job is one which would otherwise qualify as an appropriate field experience and for placements outside of our geographical area. For example, students earned credit for summer jobs in residential facilities for the mentally retarded and for work done in England. Students may develop individual activities and earn field experience credit. One student earned field experience credit for planning and instituting an Awareness Day, during which administrators experienced our campus as a handicapped person might, by being blindfolded or placed in a wheel chair.

Selection and placement

Faculty supervisor interviews each student. Before the term in which the student will be earning field experience credit begins, the faculty supervisor interviews each student. The task of the faculty supervisor is to locate an appropriate placement for each student regardless of any limitations of the student. The individual interview allows the faculty member the opportunity to get the information she or he needs to make an appropriate placement. Useful information about the student includes interests, abilities, relevant coursework, relevant job and volunteer experience, learning and career goals, and personality characteristics such as maturity, flexibility, empathy, sensitivity, assertiveness, motivation, insight, and communication skills. This approach to placement is a humanistic one, in which faculty trusts students to know what they can and want to do. Not only does this method of placement require students to take some responsibility, it also prepares them for later interviews in the job market. Based on the faculty member's knowledge of the student and field placement settings, the faculty member and student agree on a possible field placement setting.

Faculty supervisor develops field settings. At the University of Evansville, the psychology faculty has found it efficient to arrange field placements in community agencies only after a student has expressed an interest that might be pursued in that agency. Because we do not approach an agency until we have an interested student, we do not develop unneeded placements or lead agencies to anticipate getting students we do not have. When a student expresses his or her preferences and interests through the pre-experience interview, we try to find an agency for that student. For example, students expressed an interest in the criminal justice system and developed placements in a presentence investigations program and a work-release program. We also had a student interested in personnel management and arranged a placement with the personnel director of a local hospital.

Many psychology majors are interested in the more traditional settings of community mental health centers and state hospitals. As interested students are likely to be continually available, so it makes sense to develop these placements. However, you must be cautious when establishing placements as it is inefficient to develop *many* potential placements for students who may not materialize. Furthermore, students and agencies benefit the most from careful selection of placements, which allows students to develop their interests, rather than fitting students into pre-existing slots.

Once we have an interested student, we try to locate an agency where the student can pursue his or her interests and goals and use his or her aptitudes and skills while making a contribution to the agency. We meet with an agency representative to talk about students' roles and responsibilities and about the particular student whom we want to place. We try to interest the agency representative in field experience by being honest about what we can and will do for them and what they can do for us.

Student contacts agency supervisor. After the faculty supervisor has contacted the agency supervisor to work out the requirements for field experience in the agency, the student must arrange an appointment with the agency supervisor. This meeting provides the student with another interview experience and allows the agency supervisor to meet the student. The agency supervisor has the prerogative of deciding if the student will work in the agency. If all goes well in this meeting, as it usually does, the agency supervisor and student also decide on the student's schedule and activities in the agency.

Some reports recommend establishing specific learning objectives for the students (Keller, 1979; Kramer & Harshman, 1979). Specifying goals, objectives, and activities at the beginning of the term maximizes the learning experience for the student, provides an effective method of monitoring each student, clarifies supervisor responsibilities, and minimizes problems.

The process of establishing learning objectives starts during the preplacement interview in which the faculty supervisor and student discuss the student's career goals, past experiences, and interests. When the student's placement is arranged, activities and expectations are specified. Soon after the student begins field experience, specific learning objectives can be specified by the student in consultation with the faculty and agency supervisors.

Managing a field experience program

Group supervisory sessions. Group supervisory sessions, in which the faculty supervisor meets weekly with all field experience students, are an extremely important aspect in the management of a field experience program. Wolfgang (1976) lists the purposes served by these meetings:

First, and perhaps most important, the teacher, by taking the time to supervise, and the school, by providing faculty time, convey to both the student and the agency an attitude which indicates that the internship is a worthwhile experience which merits faculty involvement. . . .
A second function of supervision is that of providing ongoing evaluation and monitoring of both the student and the agency, and providing appropriate feedback to both parties. . . . Related to this aspect of supervision is the function of assuring that neither the student nor the agency are exploiting each other or the school. There are some agencies which, rather than providing proper experiences, will attempt to use students as if they were clerical help. On the other hand, there are some students who may see such a non-academic course as a chance to earn credits for doing nothing. . . .
The third function of supervision is an extension of the second. Adequate supervision greatly facilitates evaluation of the student so that the grade given at the end of the course will be more valid. . . .
A fourth function of faculty supervision is to help the student relate the field experience to class work and to be a resource person providing guidance and reading resources. A closely related function is to give encouragement and to be available when problems arise, helping the student resolve the problem and/or letting the student ventilate. . . .
A sixth function of ongoing supervision is . . . counseling . . . specifically it means allowing the student to reflect on that experience. (p. 184)[1]

Student journals. Students are required to keep a journal or log of their activities in the agency. This encourages students to keep a record of their activities, to organize their thinking about their activities, and to share personal reactions.

Agency contacts. The faculty supervisor phones the agency supervisor at least twice, once after about 3 weeks and at the end of the quarter. Thus, the faculty member increases rapport with the agency supervisor and obtains information about the student's activities and performance. The agency supervisor is also encouraged to contact the faculty member whenever questions or problems arise.

Evaluation of students

Most field experience programs use traditional letter grades (Matthews, 1979). Final grades are assigned by the faculty supervisor, based on the actual amount of time spent by the student in the agency, the agency supervisor's evaluation of the student, the student's participation in the group supervisory sessions, and the student's journal.

Use of card file

We have found it useful to keep a card file to help organize field placements. The set of agency cards has a card for each agency or program with the agency supervisor's name and phone number, possible student activities, constraints affecting placements (times of day, days of week, gender of student, skills needed, etc.), and names of students who have been placed there.

A second set of cards includes a card for each student with a list of placements and notes from the phone contacts with agency supervisors. These cards provide useful notes for giving feedback to students and provide a record on each student for additional uses, such as writing letters of recommendation.

Faculty roles and responsibilities

Field experience makes demands on the faculty supervisor that are different from the demands of traditional psychology courses. These demands include (a) time needed to negotiate appropriate placements for students, to interview and place students, and to supervise students in placements; and (b) skills in interviewing and supervising students, and in working with agency supervisors. Kramer and Harshman (1979) view the demand for faculty time as a barrier to an effective program. However, the time demand is not significantly different from that required for a traditional psychology course, and, as they point out, a systematic approach to structuring field experience reduces the amount of faculty time required. Another way to reduce the time involved is to have all field experience placement arranged by a centralized university facility, such as a Career Planning and Placement Center (CPPC) at Saint Louis University (Kramer & Harshman, 1979), which assumes responsibility for developing community contacts and for placing all field experience students for the university. However, having a psychology faculty member develop placements and place and supervise students has advantages, including enhancing communication and rapport among the faculty supervisor, student, and agency supervisor.

Perhaps because the role of the faculty supervisor requires different skills and activities than those traditionally required of faculty, 40% of the 188 schools offering field experience in Vande Creek and Fleischer's study (1984) provided no load reduction for faculty supervisors. Unfortunately, limiting the faculty time spent in placement supervision and monitoring of students might undermine the academic soundness of field experience. Certainly, field experience, for which students are paying tuition and earning credits; which requires additional work such as journals, term papers, and class meetings; which is seen as an appropriate educational experience; and which benefits from increased faculty attention to developing placements, screening students, and monitoring placements, merits faculty release time.

Roles of the agency supervisor

Clear discrimination between the roles of the faculty supervisor and the agency supervisor is important to prevent confusion, cross-communication, and conflict from developing. The faculty supervisor also has ultimate responsibility for evaluating the student's performance, ensuring the educational value of the student's experience, and monitoring the usefulness of the student to the agency. With regard to ongoing supervision, the faculty supervisor is a consultant to the student, who provides the student with information, instruction, support, and assistance in problem-solving. The agency supervisor should be responsible for actual supervision of the student, including arranging, directing, and monitoring on-site activities. However, Hess, Harrison, Fink, Lilliston, Aponte, and Korn (1978) provided an excellent example of a situation in which it was appropriate for the faculty supervisor to become involved in the on-site supervision of the student: "One of my students was forbidden further contact by her client's husband who threatened the student. I forbade the student to make further contacts with the client. However, the agency kept pressuring her to continue seeing the client" (p.81).

Student role

Students in field experience may have difficulty with their roles and expectations. One problem is that the student's role is a unique one. The student is neither a volunteer nor a paraprofessional. Because the student is carefully screened and placed, brings knowledge and skills directly from the classroom to the agency, is closely supervised by a faculty member and the agency, is not a paid employee but is paying for the earning credit for the experience, and is usually committed for several hours per week for a limited period of time, the student and agency may be uncertain of the student's role in the agency.

Second, as Prerost (1981, p. 20) pointed out, "students develop an expectation that academic professors demonstrate frequent availability and easy access," an expectation which may not be met by an agency supervisor, because the student is now in the role of caregiver. Third, students may be "poorly equipped and unprepared for the stresses confronting them" (Prerost, 1981, p. 20) in field placements, such as the political realities of agencies and psychopathology in clients. Finally, unlike preprofessional programs such as nursing and teaching, in which "the students are involved in academic programs designed to develop specific skills and field practica are carefully designed as an integral part of the program's curricula," (Prerost, 1981, p. 20) psychology field experience is usually a completely separate course, often an elective, which is not always designed to let students acquire or develop specific skills or knowledge.

Use of contracts

Kramer and Harshman (1979) advocated a contract between the student and faculty supervisor. Wolfgang (1976) suggested that the faculty supervisor, agency supervisor, and student all sign a written agreement to "make supervision more systematic, providing a framework for evaluating, monitoring, and giving feedback" (p.183). While a written agreement might be useful for specifying the student's goals, activities, and responsibilities and for clarifying agency and faculty roles, such agreements tend to be time-consuming to develop. Other disadvantages of a written student contract are that student activities might be difficult to specify at the beginning of field experience, contracts can lead to inflexibility by constraining the participants,

and the negotiation of a contract can create additional and unnecessary work for the agency and faculty supervisors.

Insurance coverage

Vande Creek and Thompson (1977) pointed out:

> The vast majority of undergraduate intern programs with which the authors are familiar have limited insurance coverage or assume that a college or university blanket insurance policy covers all intern activities. Recent discussions with several insurance vendors who sell blanket policies to academic programs have elicited serious reservations about their company's intent to cover malpractice type problems . . . . Many academic personnel do not understand the nature of the malpractice risks involved in internships. (p.179)

This view is supported by a survey of 43 small liberal arts colleges' programs; none carried malpractice insurance. However, Cole (1977) reported that the agencies in his program "accepted legal responsibility for the work done by the students" (p.9).

Summary

Field experience is an important part of many undergraduate psychology programs. This experience has many potential benefits for students, community agencies, and psychology departments. However, field experience programs require planning and structure with careful planning of student placements, adequate supervision of students, and clear roles for agency and faculty supervisors. Additional issues, such as insurance coverage, must also be addressed.

References

Boltuck, M., Peterson, T., & Murphy, R. (1980). Preparing undergraduate psychology majors for employment in the human service delivery system. *Teaching of Psychology, 7,* 75–78.

Cole, S. (1977). Practicum in clinical psychology. In B. Caffrey, L. Berger, S. Cole, D. Marx, & D. Senn, Integrating professional programs in a traditional undergraduate psychology program. *Teaching of Psychology, 4,* 7–13.

Hess, A., Harrison, A., Fink, R., Lilliston, L., Aponte, J., & Korn, J. (1978). Critical issues in undergraduate training in various community settings. *Teaching of Psychology, 5,* 81–86.

Keller, P. (1979). Identifying goals for undergraduate internship. *Teaching of Psychology, ,* 240–241.

Kramer, T., & Harshman, E. (1979). A model for faculty supervision of interns. In P. J. Woods (Ed.), *The Psychology Major: Training and employment strategies* (pp. 249–259). Washington, DC: American Psychological Association.

Matthews, J. (1979). Undergraduate field placement: Survey and issues. *Teaching of Psychology, 6,* 148–151.

Morris, S., & Haas, L. (1984). Evaluating undergraduate field placements: An empirical approach. *Teaching of Psychology, 11,* 166–168.

Prerost, F. (1981). The feasibility of undergraduate field experience in child psychology: Program factors and suggestions. *Teaching of Psychology, 8,* 19–22.

Vande Creek, L., & Fleisher, M. (1984). The role of practicum in the undergraduate psychology curriculum. *Teaching of Psychology, 11,* 9–14.

Vande Creek, L., & Thompson, A. (1977). Management of undergraduate psychology internships. *Teaching of Psychology, 4,* 177–180.

Wolfgang, D. (1976). The psychology teacher and undergraduate field experience courses: The problem of supervision. *Teaching of Psychology, 3,* 183–184.

Footnotes

1. Reprinted from Wolfgang (1976) by permission from Erlbaum Publishers. Copyright 1976 by Erlbaum.

Chapter 16

Developing job-search skills: A training program for psychology majors

Janet Burke and Joan B. Cannon, University of Lowell

It is widely recognized that the majority of students graduating from liberal arts colleges have little experience in the job-search process. Psychology majors are no exception. For example, Woods (1979) cited the research of Gray-Shellberg, Keith-Spiegel, and Kornwasser that indicated that "only a relatively small percentage of the students surveyed could be said to have 'constructive and useful ideas' relating to how to go about looking for a job in their area of interest in psychology" (p. 11). Students lack experience in the preparation of introductory materials such as résumés, cover letters, and follow-up letters. Additionally, students may not recognize existing skills and talents, and their potential for possible employment. These points coupled with the lack of necessary polish in self-presentation, as evidenced in the details of dress, appearance, and demeanor, all contribute to the difficulty students have effecting a positive impression in the job interview and thus obtaining employment.

There are several references in the literature that students can utilize to overcome these obstacles and to enhance their chances for employment. Woods has edited two general references, *Career Opportunities for Psychologists* (1976) and *The Psychology Major: Training and Employment Strategies* (1979). In "Where To Look For Positions" Fretz (1979a) listed 22 work settings for psychologists. In another chapter, Fretz (1979b) offered information on self-presentation which highlights critical positive and negative behaviors for the job interview. There are numerous references to assist the student in developing and improving résumés, cover letters, and follow-up letters, including: Bolles, 1984; Bowser, 1984; Figler, 1979; and Woods, 1979. Students should also seriously consider obtaining professional help in developing these important materials.

The purpose of this chapter is not to provide detailed specific elements relative to a successful job search. Rather, the purpose is to describe a 2-day training program that has successfully helped students improve their skills in seeking and obtaining employment. This information should be of great value to the reader in two specific ways: (a) to assist you in establishing similar programs at your own institution and (b) to provide you with constructive and useful ideas concerning the ingredients of a successful search process.

Description of the program

Although there are challenging, exciting, and upwardly mobile job opportunities for psychology majors, the primary obstacle to securing such employment may rest with the students themselves and their lack of knowledge of employment opportunities and appropriate job-search strategies rather than the scarcity of employment. We designed the program described in this chapter to focus on the following (a) a belief that jobs do exist; (b) an understanding of how to begin searching, locating, and obtaining these jobs; and (c) an awareness of the fact that presenting oneself with respect to cover letters, résumés, and finally the interview itself, is crucial to a successful search process.

Objectives

The objectives of the training program in employment-seeking strategies are

- to help students identify potential work and career opportunities in fields related to psychology;

- to help students recognize their existing skills and talents, and the potential that these hold for possible employment.

- to help students prepare a professional résumé, cover letter, and follow-up letter; and

- to familiarize students with the process of the job interview and to improve their self-presentation.

These objectives are equally important in a successful search process.

Outline of activities

The authors contend that first impressions are extremely important in the search process. Because individuals possessing a well-organized and polished résumé, a firm handshake, and a sense of confidence clearly have the advantage over their competitors (all other factors being relatively equal), a substantial amount of time was devoted to videorecording and analyzing student behavior in simulated settings related to the interview process. On each day of the 2-day program, the four major objectives are addressed and integrated into the training activities.

Day 1

The participants were asked to bring a professional résumé to the opening session of the training program and to come dressed as they would for a job interview. A trainer greeted each participant at the door, shook hands with them, asked them to take a seat, and explained that someone would be with them shortly. Simultaneously, the other trainer videotaped the introductory exchange.

When all of the participants had arrived and were seated, individual and group discussions with suggestions for improving each participant's résumé took place. This discussion highlighted skills and talents suggested in the résumé and the participant's potential for employment. In addition, the group discussed the importance of a cover letter and the follow-up letter, as part of one's marketing strategy. The participants received several documents, covering résumés, cover letters, follow-up letters, job listings, and interviews, with samples of each. They also received a comprehensive publication, *The College Placement Manual* (Bowser, 1984), which contains and considers

lists of career opportunities for liberal arts graduates as well as information on and samples of résumés, cover letters, and follow-up letters. Students were asked to review the major area newspaper and to return the following day with an improved résumé and a cover letter appropriate for five jobs actually advertised.

While the program was in progress, parts of the sessions were videotaped and later played back to the group. Thus, participants viewed themselves and examined their demeanor at the initial encounter with the trainers, that is, shaking hands and introducing themselves. They also observed their behavior while engaged in a discussion with several other people. This experience appeared to be the most interesting and important for everyone. Extensive discussion of how each of the participants could improve their behavior, and what postures and mannerisms were most appropriate for a job interview followed. Participants then repeated their entrance and initial encounter with the trainers. Videotapes of this session demonstrated and marked improvement in the participants' initial presentation of themselves to the interviewer.

Day 2

The same program procedure was followed on Day 2: A trainer videotaped the students' entrance behavior and introductory exchanges with the trainers. The trainers and participants first reviewed the cover letters and improved résumés for the five actual jobs, making any necessary modifications and additional suggestions where appropriate.

Students spent the remainder of the second day on mock interviews. A trainer interviewed each student while the other students observed the exchanges and dynamics of the videotaped interview. Following the interview, the videotape was replayed and discussed in terms of how the student could have improved his or her performance in the context of the interview. Each student participated in two mock interviews, subsequent group analyses, and discussions.

The program officially terminated after all interview sessions had been analyzed and discussed. The trainers spent the remaining time with individual students, working with them to improve the final drafts of their résumés, cover letters, and follow-up materials. However, students were reminded of the importance of the résumé and were encouraged to seek professional assistance with the final draft.

Program evaluation

Four months after the completion of the training program, the authors conducted an evaluation of the program's impact on the student's employment. Participants were interviewed and asked to respond to a series of questions that assessed the training program and to provide suggestions for future ones.

Seventy-five percent of the students reported that they had obtained employment in an area related to their academic major. In general, the participants indicated that the training program was a positive and invaluable experience for them both personally and professionally. All agreed that the most valuable aspects of the program were the simulations and videotapes of the interview process.

This program demonstrates that students can be trained in job-searching skills in a relatively short period of time, and that such programs are valued by the participants in terms of helping them to successfully attain employment.

References

Bolles, R. N. (1984). *What color is your parachute?* (2nd.ed.). Berkeley, CA: Tenspeed Press.

Bowser, J. J. (Ed.). (1984). *The college placement manual.* Bethlehem, PA: College Placement Council.

Figler, H. (1979). *The complete job-search handbook.* New York: Holt, Rinehart and Winston.

Fretz, B.R. (1979a). Where to look for positions. In P. J. Woods (Ed.). *The psychology major: Training and employment strategies* (pp. 27–29). Washington, DC: American Psychological Association.

Fretz, B. R. (1979b). Presenting yourself. In P. J. Woods (Ed.). *The psychology major: Training and employment strategies* (pp. 30–38). Washington, DC: American Psychological Association.

Gray-Shellberg, L., Keith-Spiegel, P., & Kornwasser, H. (1979). In P. J. Woods (Ed.). *The psychology major: Training and employment strategies* (pp. 282–291). Washington, DC: American Psychological Association.

Woods, P. J. (Ed.). (1976). *Career opportunities for psychologists: Expanding and emerging areas.* Washington, DC: American Psychological Association.

Woods. P. J. (Ed.). (1979). *The psychology major: Training and employment strategies.* Washington, DC: American Psychological Association.

Suggested Reading

Figler, H. (1975). *PATH: A career workbook for liberal arts students.* Cranston, RI: Carroll Press.

Gould, C. A. (1983). *Consider your options: Business opportunities for liberal arts graduates.* Washington, DC: Association of American Colleges.

Moore, C. G. (1976). *The career game.* New York: Ballantine.

PART 4

Psychology majors in the workplace and school

Chapter 17

"How can I get into graduate school, and what do I do if I want a job?"

James A. Eison, Southeast Missouri State University

The two options that undergraduates most commonly explore upon completion of a bachelor's degree are whether to go to graduate school or get a job. Most students call upon their faculty adviser for helpful guidance and assistance. The adviser's challenging task is to locate information about each alternative and provide reasonable recommendations.

College and university faculty are highly trained experts in their respective disciplines; some have also studied instructional design and pedagogical technique. However, very few acknowledge expertise in academic advising and career counseling. Aware of the problems inherent in generalizing from anecdotal evidence or data based upon extremely small samples (such as using the previous year's graduates as a guide) and mindful that in a changing economy today's facts can quickly become tomorrow's falsehoods, many faculty rightfully confess ignorance about such matters.

While a few faculty may pass along personal intuitions, and some may offer sweeping generalizations about the "real" requirements for entry into graduate school or the labor force, few advisers can substantiate their recommendations with current evidence. Many assume that the measures of undergraduate success most useful for candidates seeking postbaccalaureate education opportunities are the same indicators of achievement that make job applicants attractive to personnel directors. The following chapter briefly presents research data that seriously challenge the accuracy of that assumption.

As part of a large national study Milton, Pollio, and Eison (1986) distributed a lengthy questionnaire to 751 faculty employed at 23 schools representing different geographic regions. They included community colleges, 4-year colleges, and large universities. Because they seldom are involved directly in decisions about graduate school admissions, the 158 faculty teaching at community colleges were not included in the statistical analyses that follow. While more detailed information about sampling procedures and other important methodological matters can be found elsewhere (Milton et al., 1986), it should be noted that 138 (or 28%) of the remaining faculty members taught in the natural sciences; 120 (or 24%) taught in the social sciences; 124 (or 24%) taught in the humanities; and 118 (or 24%) taught in preprofessional programs such as business, computer science, education, and engineering.

A similar questionnaire was completed by 362 representatives of business and industry who were actively involved in the interviewing and hiring of college graduates. The authors randomly chose business representatives (using a one-in-four selection procedure) from among the 3600 company officials listed in the directory of the College Placement Council. Among the positions represented by individuals in this directory were vice-president, personnel, personnel director, manager, campus recruiter, employee relations supervisor, and corporate recruiting supervisor.

Both groups of respondents assigned a number from 1 to 7 that indicated the value or degree of importance they placed on each of

15 possible pieces of information when reviewing materials submitted by recent college graduates for either employment in their firm or for admission to graduate school. The number *1* represented minimum value, and 7 represented maximum. Table 17–1 shows the results of this survey.

Several additional items regarding the use of grades by college recruiters appeared in the survey instrument; interesting findings from these items will be selectively highlighted in the section that follows.

Results

An examination of Table 17–1 provides two summary statistics for each of the 15 pieces of information: (a) the mean rating each item received, based upon a 7-point rating scale in which a score of 7 represents the maximum value; and (b) the percent of each sample that assigned a rating of 6 or 7 to each item. Statistical comparisons between the two groups of respondents were computed using *t*-tests applied to mean rating scores for each item.

T-test comparisons between data provided by faculty and business representatives re-

vealed significant group differences on 13 of 15 variables; the two items which failed to produce significant differences were (a) publications, awards, honors, and (b) reputation of school attended or of recommenders. These findings clearly suggest that entry into graduate school requires different skills than those sought by college recruiters.

Group means have little meaning or relevance, however, when an individual faculty member reviews a graduate school application folder or when a businessman interviews a job applicant. What does become salient are those individual pieces of information thought by the reviewer to be most useful. To provide a clearer picture of the actual selection criteria regarded as most important by each group, Table 1 summarizes the percentage of respondents assigning scores of 6 or 7 to each item.

Here we see that business representatives seldom attributed great significance to standard test scores (i.e., less than 7% of the group rated this item 6 or 7); nearly one third of the faculty respondents, however, rated this with scores of 6 or more. Equally notable is the fact that nearly 60% of the business representatives assigned a rating of 6 or 7 to personality; only 17.6% of the faculty did

Table 17-1. Degree of Importance Employers and Graduate Admissions Place on 15 Factors

	Mean ratings		t value	Percent assigning a rating of 6 or 7	
	Business (N=346)	Faculty (N=574)		Business (N=362)	Faculty (N=794)
Standard test scores (ACT, SAT, GRE, etc.)	2.7	4.9	19.84^2	6.3	34.6
Overall grade point average	4.7	5.0	2.55^1	32.3	34.4
Grades in major courses	5.1	4.6	4.31^2	51.9	64.3
Breadth of courses taken	4.6	5.0	4.44^2	27.8	36.6
Number of difficult courses completed	4.3	5.1	8.60^2	23.2	44.9
Letters of recommendation	3.6	4.9	12.10^2	11.7	40.4
Samples of student writing	3.8	5.0	10.84^2	18.0	44.2
Participation in extracurricular activities	4.5	3.6	−9.00^2	26.4	10.0
Nature of noncollege jobs held	5.0	3.6	−14.66^2	38.2	9.9
Breadth of personal life experiences	4.6	4.0	−6.46^2	27.5	18.0
Publications, awards, honors	4.7	5.0	2.32^1	25.4	39.5
Contributions to the school	4.0	3.7	−2.13	14.4	13.0
Personality of student	5.5	4.1	−15.29^2	59.3	17.6
Affirmative action needs	4.0	3.3	−6.82^2	15.9	9.6
Reputation of school attended or of recommenders	4.7	4.9	1.72	27.8	35.3

^{1} p < .01 ^{2} p < .001

likewise. Where 38.2% of the business representatives placed great importance on the nature of noncollege jobs held, only 9.9% of the faculty considered this important for evaluating graduate school applicants. Skill at written expression was rated as important by 44.2% of the college and university faculty; 18% of the business recruiters responded in a similar fashion. Both the business representatives and faculty members assigned great significance to grades in major courses with 51.9% and 64.3%, respectively, assigning ratings of 6 or 7 to this item; each group placed considerably less importance on overall grade-point average, 32.3% and 34.4%, respectively, assigning this item high ratings. Written letters of recommendation rated highly with faculty (40.9%), although only 11.7% of the business representatives reacted similarly.

To determine if faculty respondents teaching in four general discipline areas (i.e., natural science, social science, humanities, and undergraduate preprofessional) rated the various student characteristics differently mean ratings for each item were compared using one-way analysis of variance techniques. For 12 of 15 items no significant group differences were found. Duncan's multiple range comparisons were performed on the three items producing significant group differences. Faculty teaching in the natural science area placed significantly greater importance on letters of recommendation (F = 3.87, df = 3, p < .01) and significantly less importance on samples of student writing (F = 5.51, df = 3, p < .001) and breadth of personal life experiences (F = 3.80, df = 3, p < .01) than did faculty teaching in other disciplines. Thus, it appears that graduate school admission committees throughout the university are surprisingly homogeneous in the way they view the relative importance of the many pieces of information that applicants present.

Because the meaning and significance of college grades are frequently discussed by students, faculty members, and business representatives but have seldom been subject to empirical inquiry, several additional findings from a larger investigation (Milton et al., 1983) merit mention. When asked to indicate the extent to which grades and grade-point average (GPA) influence decisions made by their company (using the rating scale of little, slight, moderate, great, or crucial), 46% of the business sample reported grades to be of moderate importance for initial hiring; an additional 38% said the influence was great or crucial. Once this first hurdle (i.e., initial hiring) is passed, grades become significantly less important in determinations of (a) initial salary, (b) selection for special training programs, or (c) subsequent promotions. Thus, good grades may open the door to initial employment but lose their significance immediately thereafter.

In light of the importance grades have in initial hiring, it is interesting to note respondent replies to the question, "Does your company have a minimum GPA or cutoff for initial hiring?" Forty-five percent reported that there was no established minimum grade cutoff in their company. With companies that did have established minimums, only 28% required a B average or better (i.e., a GPA of 3.00 or more).

Both students and faculty may also be surprised to learn that when the business sample was asked, "Has your company conducted any studies relating college grades to on-the-job performance?", 89% responded negatively. Of the few studies (11%) that have been conducted, 34% responded that at best college grades were fair to poor predictors of success; approximately 25% reported grades to be excellent predictors of job performance.

Discussion and implications

The results of the 1983 study revealed clearly that two prominent sets of "gatekeepers" who control students' postgraduation opportunities, apply very different criteria for gaining entry to the fold.

Implications for job-seekers

Among the implications the data have for students seeking postgraduation employment is the realization that self-presentation is of upmost concern to interviewers; approximately 60% of the business sample assigned ratings of 6 or 7 to student personality. While the specific personality traits considered most desirable by business representatives were not considered in this survey, personal attitudes such as self-esteem and self-confidence are all but ignored in most college course curriculums and in graduation requirements. Perhaps this is related to the fact that information of this type is of little importance to graduate school admission committees. A second possibility is that this represents an instance of the college curriculum not mirroring a pervasive value system found in the business community. Advising students to enroll in public speaking courses and to practice their interviewing skills is strongly supported by these data.

Pilla (1984, p.19) reported that employers participating in a survey conducted by the American Management Society were asked to select from among nine traits the most important characteristic of candidates applying for an entry-level college graduate position. The percent rating each item as most significant was as follows:

enthusiasm/motivation	35%
education background	20%
communication skill	16%
scholastic performance	12%
intelligence	5%
work-related experience	2%
interpersonal/leadership skill	2%
maturity	2%
creativity	0%

While it is always difficult to compare findings from studies employing different survey instruments, enthusiasm/motivation which clearly ranked first among the choices listed above would appear similar to the Milton et al. (1986) finding that student personality was rated as most significant. Similarly, intelligence was selected as most important by only 5% of the respondents (Pilla, 1984); in Milton et al. 7% of the business representatives rated standard test scores of great importance. Other direct comparisons do not seem prudent. For example, it is impossible to determine precisely which of the Milton et al.'s 15 items are comparable to Pilla's variable of education background (i.e., breadth of courses taken, number of difficult courses taken, contributions to the school, reputation of the school attended, etc.).

Weinstein (1985) listed the following eight qualities, which were indicated as most important by college placement directors, company recruiters, and executive search consultants: decent grades, communication and interpersonal skills, enthusiasm, flexibility, leadership, problem-solving ability, high energy level, and maturity. The source and adequacy of Weinstein's data (i.e., anecdotal information, personal interviews, surveys, etc.) were not reported. It is also unlikely that many students or college faculty subscribe to *Business Week*'s "Guide to Careers"; thus, information of this type does not typically reach a large undergraduate audience.

Lunneborg (1985) reported a recent survey of members of the Pacific Northwest Personnel Management Association ($N = 55$) and an additional 61 college recruiters who used the University of Washington's Placement Center. These individuals indicated that among their favorite questions when interviewing liberal arts applicants were questions such as,

"Where do you see yourself in five years? In ten years?" and "What are your career goals?" Shingleton and Bao (1977) reported that 90% of a national sample of employers said their main reason for rejecting a candidate was a lack of motivation and goals. As such attributes are less likely to influence graduate schools admissions, faculty may be unlikely to realize their importance for students seeking postgraduate employment.

According to Milton et al. (1986), grades in major courses ranked second in significance for business grades in major courses representatives. It is noteworthy that this statistic (i.e., 51.9% rated the item 6 or 7) was judged more valuable than the student's overall grade-point average (i.e., only 32.3% rated this item 6 or 7). Thus, given the choice of repeating a course outside of one's major to raise a poor grade (and increase one's overall GPA) or attempting a new course from within one's discipline, the latter option seems more prudent and productive.

The nature of a student's noncollege jobs held ranked third in importance and received ratings of 6 or 7 from 38.2% of the business sample. This finding thus supports the general recommendation that students seek career-relevant part-time employment while in school.

It should be noted that two of these three dimensions (i.e., student personality and noncollege jobs held) are of very limited value to students seeking admission to graduate school. Conversely, standard test scores, letters of recommendation, and writing samples, which are relatively important to faculty when reviewing graduate school applicants, were judged to be far less relevant to potential employers.

Participation in extracurricular activities, which high school students are often told will enhance the attractiveness of their college applications, was ranked 9th in importance out of 15 by business representatives and 14th in importance by faculty. Extracurricular activities that enhance a student's personal presentation of self would seem especially useful to the job hunter.

Implications for graduate students

Advice for students interested primarily in attending graduate school reflects a very different pattern of concerns. In the faculty sample, 3 of 15 possible pieces of information produced mean scores greater than 5.00: (a) number of difficult courses completed, (b) breadth of courses taken, and (c) samples of student writing. (These were of rather low priority for the business representatives.)

Where skill at written expression appears essential for graduate school admission, speaking skills (certainly a major component of how one's personality is presented) are of greater importance to job applicants.

Rating just below these items among faculty respondents were (d) overall grade-point average, (e) letters of recommendation, and (f) publications, awards, honors, and so forth. The mean rating for overall GPA was greater than that of grades in major (i.e., 4.7 and 5.1, respectively) among faculty respondents. Examining the percentage of faculty rating these items 6 or 7, a dramatic shift in importance is noted—64.3% rated grades in major 6 or 7, while only 34.4% gave similar ratings to overall GPA. In this regard, faculty and business representatives appear more similar than different—both place considerable importance on grades in one's major.

Faculty also placed significantly greater importance on the letters of recommendation written by other college and university faculty than did business representatives. Similarly, a student's academic publications, awards, and honors appear to carry far greater weight with a graduate school admission committee than a job recruiter.

Conclusions

A few cautionary notes and suggestions for future research are appropriate. As is often the case with survey research, posthoc examination of the data revealed several interesting issues not addressed in the initial effort. For example, what specific dimensions of student personality are most likely to impress interviewers in a favorable, or in an unfavorable, fashion. Similarly, one can only wonder what characteristics of a student's writing are viewed most significant by graduate school admission committees? Future researchers would certainly want to examine these issues closely. It should be recalled that business representatives in this study evaluated employment materials without knowledge of the specific nature and type of job the applicant was seeking. Follow-up investigators might wish to identify several types of jobs and compare hiring criteria across positions. A surprisingly high degree of cross-discipline similarity characterized criteria used in graduate school admissions; whether this consistency is similarly true for business representatives remains to be seen.

The relatively large sample used in the study (593 faculty and 362 business representatives), and the rather striking group differences obtained, might tempt faculty advisers to substitute these data for prior personal intuitions and offer these findings to students as definitive advice. As with all survey data, readers are urged to exercise appropriate caution and restraint. Although the present data challenge seriously the assumption that graduate school admission committees view applicants in the same light as that found within the business community, it is premature to offer students simplistic prescriptive formulas based upon singular studies (however large their sample might be).

In summary, perhaps the best response a faculty member could offer the undergraduate who asks, "How can I get into graduate school, and what do I do if I want a job?," is an empathic smile and the recommendation that their question be addressed in two separate, and different, fashions.

References

Lunneborg, P. (1985). *Putting the liberal arts to work.* Seattle: University of Washington.

Milton, O., Pollio, H., & Eison, J. (1986). *Making sense of college grades.* San Francisco: Jossey-Bass.

Pilla, L. (1984). The job search—What college students say. *Management World, 13,* 19.

Shingleton, J., & Bao, R. (1977). *College to career.* New York: McGraw-Hill.

Weinstein, B. (1985). What employers look for. *Business Week Guide to Careers* [Special issue], pp. 10–13.

Chapter 18

Basic interest areas as a guide to undergraduate preparation for employment

Keith T. Checketts and Blaine R. Worthen, Utah State University

One of the things that almost all parents and even some students fear most is the possibility that, after 4 years of college education, the degree that is awarded will be of little utility in obtaining meaningful employment. The prime examples of undergraduate degrees with limited utility include philosophy and history, fields that are enjoyable to study but appear to be of limited practical value. The same criticism has been leveled at the bachelor's degree in psychology. College advisers have been known to advise students that if they major in psychology, the only way in which the degree will be of value to them is if they go on for graduate work in the field.

The faculty in the Department of Psychology at Utah State University (USU) faced the dilemma: Is a bachelor's degree in psychology only useful as preparation for a graduate psychology degree? If it is, then we may be justified in rethinking our undergraduate offerings. Conversely, if it is not true, what evidence is available to correct the image? Moreover, what careers are available where a bachelor's degree in psychology would be desirable or necessary, and what can be done with the undergraduate curriculum to make the degree even more attractive to prospective employers?

The practical utility of the bachelor's degree

We took several steps to examine the question of the usefulness of the bachelor's degree for preparing psychology majors for employment. We examined the existing literature to find any surveys or conceptual papers on the variety of uses of undergraduate psychological training. We surveyed graduates of the USU undergraduate psychology program to determine the extent to which their undergraduate education led to employment and prospective employers to determine if a job market existed and how the psychology baccalaureate's marketability could be enhanced.

An investigation of career dictionaries and newsletters from relevant organizations revealed that psychologists are or could be performing services in a wide variety and level of work settings. The list of job titles that could be filled by undergraduates is too large to be listed here, but among the major areas of employment reported for undergraduate psychology majors were: advertising, communications, education, personnel and industrial relations, marketing and sales, medical services, publishing, social services, and government. Within almost all of these major areas of employment, there is a need for counselors. Many of these positions, such as drug and alcohol counseling, are filled with people without graduate training.

As a part of a follow-up study of our undergraduate majors, we surveyed the graduates to determine the extent to which their preparation in psychology is being used in their current academic or employment status. The results of this survey indicated that nearly all of the graduates either go on to graduate school or take jobs which require or recommend training in psychology. Over half of the graduates went directly into the job market; a survey of their employers indicated that in the vast majority of these positions (a) psychology training was required, or (b) the effectiveness of the employee was enhanced by their preparation in psychology. The survey further indicated that the positions could be classified in the following broad categories: (a) applied behavior or analysis, (b) educational applications, (c) human services, (d) organizational behavior, or (e) scientific applications. These broad categories and examples of the types of employment available in these areas will be presented in a later section.

As a result of the rather surprising fact that so many of the students with undergraduate degrees obtained jobs where a major in psychology was a definite asset, the faculty of the USU Psychology Department studied the department's undergraduate program with a goal to modify it to prepare students more directly for positions in the five interest areas. A second objective was to develop a high-quality program that could be offered within the resources of the department. It became obvious that there was another significant group of students who majored in psychology, but were not going on for graduate training. These students studied psychology with the objective of self-improvement, without any immediate employment or additional education objectives. This category—personal development—added a sixth option for psychology majors.

The undergraduate degree at Utah State University

According to the 1984 USU catalog, "The aim of Utah State University is to provide a program designed specifically for each student. An individual program will depend on many factors. Four important ones are (1) the student's goal, (2) the nature of the major subject area, (3) past experiences, and (4) how fast an individual wishes to proceed" (p. 9). As this demonstrates, the University was philosophically oriented in the direction the Psychology Department wished to proceed. However, in contrast to this rather flexible statement, there are specific requirements for graduation, and any flexibility must take place within this set of constraints. The general structure of these requirements is listed below. As USU is on a quarter system, credit-hour requirements are listed in quarter hours with the equivalent semester hours in parentheses immediately following the quarter hours.

Total credits required for graduation	186	(124)
General education	46	(31)
Professional training	122	(82)

The 122 credits listed for the professional training component are the maximum that

can be required and include all requirements for the major, and where applicable, certification, and the minor.

The remaining 18 (12) credits are reserved for electives and cannot be proscribed by the department or college; however, there is a great deal of flexibility within the professional component. The Psychology Department requires a minimum 45 (30) credit hours, which are distributed as follows:

Total credits	45	(30)
Core requirements	21	(14)
Approved electives	24	(16)

The 21 (14) credit core consists of General Psychology, Human Development, Analysis of Behavior, Statistics, and History and Systems.

The 24 (16) credits of approved electives are to be selected from courses offered by the Psychology Department.

USU policy and Psychology Department requirements still leave the equivalent of approximately 2 years of the undergraduate experience free to individualize the educational experience. This large pool of credit that can be used by departments to individualize the student's program is paramount to provide the necessary flexibility to prepare some students for graduate school, others for employment in a variety of settings, and to allow some to major in psychology for personal enrichment.

At USU (not unlike many other universities), the Psychology Department lacked adequate resources to expand undergraduate offerings in any but the most meager way. Two significant resources available included the courses offered by other departments in the university and an advisor specifically hired to guide and individualize the preparation of undergraduate psychology majors.

To capitalize on these resources, the psychology faculty refined their definition of each of the six areas and examined the university course offerings in an attempt to collect a set of recommended courses that would prepare students in the areas that they elected. The psychology faculty labeled the areas undergraduate interest areas. While retaining the basic requirement for psychology, the faculty recommended additional courses to help students achieve their purposes for majoring in psychology. Students who wished to follow the outlined suggestions were free to do so. Some elected to complete the suggested course work in two or more interest areas, and then sample from the others.

Undergraduate interest areas

In the following sections the six undergraduate interest areas are defined, titles of the recommended courses are presented, and the practical impact of the interest area concept on undergraduate psychology majors is discussed.

Applied behavior analysis interest area

This area is concerned mainly with those areas of employment that require skills in the objective measurement and management of behavior. The major placement settings are in a mental health setting, educational institution, or psychology laboratory. Some of the types of positions available include aides in a psychiatric or psychological therapy unit using behavior modification, teacher's aides in mainstreaming students with maladaptive behavior, research aides collecting observational data, or research associates in a laboratory studying behavior modification.

Course work:

Psychology Core   21 (14) credits required
Psychology Electives 24 (16) credits required
  Some suggested electives
    Abnormal Psychology
    Behavior Modification
    Analysis of Behavior
    Techniques of Programmed
      Instruction
    Practicum in Child Psychology

  Suggested courses in other departments
    Biology
      Bioethics: Emerging Issues in
        Biomedicine
    Communication
      Persuasion
    Communicative Disorders
      Introduction to Communicative
        Disorders
      Clinical Process and Behavior
    Sociology
      Juvenile Delinquency
      Social Deviance
    Special Education
      Education of Exceptional Children
      Emotionally Handicapped Child,
        Introduction
    Secondary Education
      Practicum: Management of Student
        Behavior

The total number of credits for all of the suggested courses outside of psychology for this interest area is 30 (20).

Educational applications interest area

Students emphasizing this area of study would be prepared to seek employment as teacher aides, day-care center workers, children's tutors, and other education-related positions that do not require a graduate degree or certification. (USU offers a specific major for those who wish to teach psychology in the schools.)

Course work:

Psychology Core   21 (14) credits required
Psychology Electives 24 (16) credits required
  Some suggested electives
    Thinking and Verbal Learning
    Educational Psychology
    Behavior Modification
    Personality Theory
    Analysis of Behavior
    Human Development: Adolescence
    Psychometrics
    Principles of Interviewing

  Suggested courses in other departments
    Communicative Disorders
      Introduction to Communicative
        Disorders
      Language, Hearing, and Speech
        Development
    Elementary Education
      Foundation Studies in Teaching
      Early Childhood Education
    Instructional Media
      Instructional Media Communication
        Theory
      Instructional Media in Education
    Philosophy
      Philosophy of Education
    Secondary Education
      Current Problems & Future Trends
      in   Education

The total number of credits here for all suggested courses outside of psychology is 30 (20).

Human services emphasis area

The courses in this area relate to skills for providing human services in mental health, family services, child care, and so on. Students prepared at a bachelor's level usually are not able to deliver direct psychological services, but would be able to take employment related to the delivery of these services. Some relevant job titles would be psychologist's assistant, ward attendant, home visitor, staff interviewer, welfare organizer, case aide, foster care worker, social worker assistant, and test administrator.

Course work:

Psychology Core   21 (14) credits required
Psychology Electives 24 (16) credits required
Some suggested electives
    Child Abuse and Neglect
    Abnormal Psychology
    Social Psychology
    Behavior Modification
    Personality Theory
    Human Development: Adolescence
    Introduction to Counseling &
        Guidance
    Psychometrics
    Principles of Interviewing

Suggested courses in other departments
    Social Work
        Introduction to Social Work
        Social Welfare Among Minority
            Groups
        Social Work Practice
        Child Welfare
        Mental Health
        Protective Services for Children
        Service to the Aged
        Legal Obligations Within the Family
        Public Social Policy
    Sociology
        The Sociology of Aging
    Family and Human Development
        Practicum in Agencies Servicing
            Children

The total number of credits for all courses
outside of psychology is 30 (20).

Industrial/organizational behavior interest area

Almost all large organizations have continuing
needs in the industrial/organizational behavior area. Because the scope of industry, business, government, and consulting is so broad,
job opportunities are favorable. Some representative job titles that are available in this
interest area are performance evaluation specialist, job analyst, personnel selection and
placement officer, job evaluation specialist,
training and development specialist, and industrial tester.

Course work:

Psychology Core   21 (14) credits required
Psychology Electives 24 (16) credits required
Some suggested electives
    Educational Psychology
    Behavior Modification
    Personality Theory
    Introduction to Counseling and
        Guidance
    Psychometrics

Psychology of Business and Industry
Principles of Interviewing
Suggested courses in other departments
    Business Administration
        Management Concepts
        Leadership Training/Group Dynam-
            ics
        Behavioral Dimensions of
            Management
        Business and Society
        Employment Practices
        Wage and Salary Administration
        Problems in Personnel & Industrial
            Relations
    Communication
        Public Relations
    Sociology
        Social Institutions
        Group Dynamics
        Human Relations in Industry
        Community Organization &
            Leadership

The total number of credits suggested for all
courses outside of psychology is 39 (26) for
this interest area.

Scientific applications interest area

The intent of this area is to provide the
student with a broad base of knowledge of
scientific studies, which could lead to opportunities for employment in positions such as
lab assistant, data analyst, science writer, or
public relations specialist for science-oriented
industries.

Course work:

Psychology Core   21 (14) credits required
Psychology Electives 24 (16) credits required
Some suggested electives
    Thinking and Verbal Learning
    Perception and Psychophysics
    Physiological Psychology
    Social Psychology
    Educational Psychology
    Behavior Modification
    Analysis of Behavior
    Psychometrics
    Practicum in Child Psychology

Suggested courses in other departments
    Biology
        Biology and the Citizen
        Human Anatomy
        Human Physiology
        Evolution, Ecology, and Man
        Human Genetics
    Chemistry
        Principles of Chemistry

Communication
    Introduction to Communication
        Theory
    Introduction to Symbolic Processes
Computer Science
    Introduction to Computer Science,
Philosophy
    Introduction to Problems of
        Philosophy
    Ethics
    Theories of Knowledge
    Concept of Mind
    Philosophy of Science
Physics
    Introductory Physics
Sociology
    Introductory Sociology
Honors
    Frontiers of Research
Wildlife Science
    Animal Behavior
    Animal Behavior Laboratory
Anthropology
    Introduction to Anthropology
    Language and Culture
    Comparative Value Systems
    Comparative Family Systems
    Comparative Religious Systems
    Psychological Anthropology

The total number of credits suggested for all courses outside of psychology is 90 (60) credits for this area. Most students interested in this option would pick and choose to find the combination of course work most congruent with their individual needs and desires.

Personal development interest area

Electives in this area include courses selected to help students learn about themselves, their relationships with others, and ways to improve their personal skills. The intent is to provide students with a suggested curriculum that may serve as a guide to self-awareness, interaction with others, and participation as an effective member of society.

Course work:

Psychology Core   21 (14) credits required
Psychology Electives 24 (16) credits required
    Some suggested electives
    Issues in Human Relations
    Career Exploration
    Personal Study Efficiency
    College Reading and Listening
    Co-op Education Work Experience
    Behavior Modification
    Undergraduate Research Creative
        Opportunity
    Human Development: Adolescence

Principles of Interviewing
Analysis of Behavior: Adult

Suggested courses in other departments
Biology
    Biology and the Citizen
    Personal Health
    Family Health
Business Administration
    Law and the Consumer
    Leadership Training/Group Dynamics
Communications
    Communication: Public and
        Interpersonal
    Public Speaking
    Interpersonal Communication
English
    Great Books and Ideas
Family and Human Development
    Marriage and the American Family
    Update in Quality Parenting
Health Education
    Health and Wellness
    Alcohol, Tobacco, and Drugs
    Consumer Health
Home Economics and Consumer
    Education
    Design in Everyday Living
    Family Finances

The total number of credits suggested outside psychology is 60 (40) credits for this area. This high number suggests that students interested in this option select from among the suggestions.

The practical impact of the interest areas concept

The presentation and implementation of the interest areas concept did not change the graduation requirements for the USU Psychology Department. Nor did the number and scope of undergraduate courses offered by the Department change. What did change was the relationship of the Psychology Department with other departments. Many other departments were pleased to have the Psychology Department recommend courses in their departments. Suggested patterns of courses gave focus and direction to the students' curriculum, while allowing students to design custom-fit programs themselves.

The pattern of course work suggested here is not prescriptive nor all encompassing. Rather, it provides a framework within which the students may fit their personal interest, match it with the employment possibilities, and create a program that has focus and direction. The professional adviser in the psychology department also finds these guidelines to be of significant practical utility in directing students in their desired goals.

One way that students who are planning to go to graduate or professional schools have employed this concept at USU is to choose the interest area closest to their desired area of graduate preparation and use the suggested course work to complete their undergraduate preparation. As examples, a student interested in medicine may rely heavily on the science interest area, while one who is thinking of law may select courses from the organizational interest area.

One concept of career guidance is to help students to arrive at plateaus, which may serve as a foundation for the ascent to even higher levels of educational and vocational preparation. The interest areas concept is consistent with that concept. If students choose elective course work carefully, they develop valuable skills and knowledge for a career or for employment to help provide financial support while they are gaining graduate training.

At most institutions, there is a component of free electives that can be effectively used to enhance the basic preparation of a major. The titles of the courses may be different, but the principle remains the same. Motivated students working with a well-informed, caring adviser can significantly enhance their undergraduate preparation by carefully focusing on one or two interest areas and exploring the entire university curriculum for creative enhancements to the psychology program. The development of the interest areas discussed above, which has served USU well may stimulate similar productive efforts in other institutions concerned with enhancement of their undergraduate major in psychology.

Chapter 19

What skills and knowledge do potential employers value in baccalaureate psychologists?

John Edwards and Kerry Smith, Loyola University of Chicago

Undergraduate students, as well as their parents, friends, teachers, and others, commonly ask what one is able to do with a bachelor's degree in psychology. There are several answers to this question; one is to point out the great diversity of opportunities for graduate and professional training in psychology and related fields and for paraprofessional jobs available to baccalaureates.

Ample evidence (e.g., Davis, 1979; Titley, 1978; Ware & Meyer, 1981) indicates that the majority of students with undergraduate psychology degrees do not pursue advanced formal education, but enter the job market and are often successful in finding work relevant to their undergraduate work. An inspection of the types of jobs undertaken reveals that many of them involve the direct delivery of service to some type of client, for example, youth counselor, recreation assistant, or rehabilitation adviser. This emphasis may be an indication of the clinical bias of psychology students that has been reportedly manifested in other ways (Babarik, 1980; Korn & Lewandowski, 1981). One result of such a bias may be growing frustration on the part of the students who face graduate schools and job markets glutted with competitors seeking human service delivery careers.

Another answer to the question—What can one do with a BA in psychology?—involves identifying the skills and areas of knowledge that distinguish psychology students from other liberal arts and sciences graduates. Although the increasingly popular career development programs and courses (e.g., Haney & Howland, 1978; McGovern, 1979; Ware, 1981) have stressed the need to clarify and sharpen students' marketable skills, as yet there has been little rigorous effort to accurately identify these skills. However, some information on

this issue can be gained by simply reviewing the content material provided in typical undergraduate courses. Such a review makes it very clear that the content areas are not limited to those directly related to human services delivery careers. Rather it appears that students have considerable opportunity to learn valuable skills that are relevant to other types of careers, particularly those involving research of either a basic or applied nature. The reputed clinical bias may be blinding students (and their advisers) from options in the "other side" of psychology, that is the side which seeks to promote human welfare by applying psychological principles and research methods to generate socially useful information.

But what do we know about the abilities of psychology students as researchers, and are these abilities useful in obtaining and performing jobs with a bachelor's degree? Most faculty members probably have extensive experience in observing and developing the research competencies of undergraduates. Moreover, results from several studies (Evans, Rintala, Guthrie, & Raines, 1981; Norcross & Wogan, 1982) indicated that, with proper supervision, psychology majors can perform very well as researchers in nonacademic settings—even before graduation. Students with appropriate course backgrounds proved they can apply and extend their abilities to gather, analyze, and report data. They are advised (e.g., Fretz, 1976) to promote these skills in their job searches; however, it is not known how marketable such skills might be. In contrast to the information available about the types of skills and knowledge desired for human service providers (Boltuck, Peterson, & Murphy, 1980; White & Lindquist, 1982), very little has been done to discover the specific research and related areas of knowledge desired by employers of researchers with bachelor's degrees.

Purpose of the study

The main purpose of the investigation reported here was to conduct a needs assessment that would help identify some of the skills and knowledge areas that employers might be seeking when hiring a person whose duties would include research. Further, we aimed to learn whether these needs varied according to several characteristics of potential employers such as what kinds of research are done in their organizations, their experience with psychology students as undergraduate interns and employees, and the nature of the organization in terms of ownership and function. Regarding this latter characteristic, it is our impression that the largest proportion of psychology baccalaureates who find work related to their training do so in government agencies and profit or nonprofit organizations whose primary function is delivering some type of human service. In an economic climate with declining financial support for such services, psychology students need to consider alternative markets—particularly corporate business. This includes not only private corporations whose primary business is research, but also producers of goods and services engaged in a variety of types of research for which psychology students may be well suited. Fernald, Tedeschi, Siegfried, Gilmore, and Chipley (1982) suggested that psychology students entering corporate business may encounter barriers including misperceptions about their skills. Comparative data are needed to determine whether the need for psychology students and their skills vary among types of organizations.

We surveyed several types of organizations to elicit their felt need for and interest in baccalaureate-level psychology graduates and some of their skills and expertise. We hoped to provide information bearing on the following questions:

- In designing curricula or career development programs and courses, what content areas might psychology teachers emphasize if they wish to enhance their students' preparedness to fill research jobs?

- In conducting public relations efforts to expand the marketplace for bachelor's-level students, what practical skills can organizations such as the APA or individual departments advertise as possessed by psychology graduates?

- In planning their course work and other experiences, what types of expertise should students seek in order to help improve their employability?

- In applying for volunteer work and pre- or postbaccalaureate jobs, what areas of knowledge and skill should students emphasize in their application materials?

In addition, we expected to gather information that would form the basis for answering other questions: What is the correspondence between the skills needed and those actually, or at least potentially, possessed by psychology students; and what differences, if any, might exist between psychology majors and other liberal arts and sciences graduates that make the former better equipped for certain types of work?

Method

We conducted brief telephone interviews to gather information from representatives of the several types of organizations that we felt to be appropriate settings for employing psychology majors as researchers. In addition to eliciting perceptions of the importance of certain skills, knowledge, and personal qualities, other questions examined the organization's experience with and interest in interning or employing psychology baccalaureates.

Respondents

The initial step was to identify a reasonable number of organizations in the Chicago metropolitan area that seemed relevant to our research aims. Thus, we defined the population as those organizations that seemed sizable enough (i.e., more than 10 employees) and engaged in the type of activity (e.g., marketing, advertising, consulting) that would justify some interest in psychological research. We obtained names of places through several means including the telephone directory, the authors' experiences, lists of large corporations from library references, and the suggestions of other contacts. As we did not seek a representative sample in the strict sense, these purposive methods were appropriate. Using them, we developed a list of 130 organizations of which 118 were contacted. These were about evenly divided among four types: nonprofit agencies engaged in action, advocacy or service delivery such as charitable or community organizations; government agencies at the federal, state, and local level concerned with such matters as welfare, law enforcement, environmental quality, and education; commercial organizations that sell home appliances, clothing, food, petroleum, or other products; and other for-profit corporations that sell services such as banking, marketing, advertising, and management consulting.

The respondents who provided the data in this study held positions ranging from receptionist to chief executive officer but were typically department (e.g., personnel) heads. They presented their own views which may or may not represent the corporate position of their organizations. As we did not request any personal information about the respondents, it is not possible to identify what effect other characteristics (e.g., a background in psychology) had on their answers.

Interview instrument

The structured interview we used consisted mostly of closed-ended questions, although some open-ended follow-up items were also included. The first page of the instrument contained a standard script for the interviewers to follow when explaining the study's purpose and when identifying, to the person answering the phone, what type of individual within the organization we wished to interview. Once this individual was contacted, he or she was given a fuller explanation of our purposes from a prepared script.

The initial questions asked about the organization's recent history of receiving applications from and hiring people with bachelor's degrees in psychology and about any types of research in which the organization routinely engaged. The next sections asked for the ratings of the usefulness of 11 skills and 13 areas of knowledge. After hearing each item read to them, respondents rated how useful these would be to their organization: *very useful, somewhat useful, not at all useful,* or *not sure.* They were also asked to describe any other research skills, knowledge areas, or personal qualities that they would look for or find valuable in an employee.

We asked respondents about a number of skills and knowledge areas (listed in the Results section) which were somewhat diverse in their level of specificity. Although neither mutually exclusive nor exhaustive, we considered them to be representative of some types of expertise potentially possessed by psychology majors. That is, we selected items partly on the basis of their informativeness in related research (Edwards & Holmgren, 1979), but largely from reviews of course descriptions and a survey of psychology department faculty members about the topics to which students are exposed in our courses.

The final parts of the interview questioned the organization's history of and interest in having undergraduates as field-study interns. We sought this information for the dual purposes of identifying potential internship sites and providing a characterization of the organization that might influence the ratings of skills and knowledge.

Procedure

Ten students conducted the interviews; eight of whom were undergraduates who volunteered for this project to gain research experience. All interviewers underwent a training session that entailed going over the instructions for and the purpose of each question, discussing ways of dealing with possible problems, and simulating interviews. Each interviewer received a supply of interview booklets, call disposition cards, and a list of names and telephone numbers incorporating all four types of organizations. The students conducted interviews during regular business hours over two extended time periods: March to May and October to December, 1982. These periods coincided with the mid-to-late portions of the spring and fall semesters, when the student volunteers were available to make calls.

We instructed interviewers to make up to five callbacks if an appropriate respondent was not available at the initial contact. Of the 118 organizations contacted, interviewers obtained complete or nearly complete interviews from 68 organizations, a response rate of 57.6%. More specifically, the rates for the four types of places were: non-profit, 63.0%; government, 51.6%; corporations specializing in goods, 63.0%; and service corporations, 48.7%. The reasons for nonresponse included: (a) The organization was too small (in some instances the places we called were regional offices of U.S. federal government agencies or large corporations that conduct research but only at their headquarters); (b) the respondent (or sometimes the interviewer) felt that the nature of the organization was really not appropriate for the population in which we were interested; (c) the unavailability of an appropriate respondent during the times when the interviewers could call; and (d) some organizations had a policy against giving interviews or preferred to respond by mail.

Results and discussion

Before reporting the findings regarding the rated usefulness of skills and knowledge, it is necessary to consider some other factors revealed by the interviews, as these identify some characteristics of the organizations that play a role in interpreting the ratings. One set of questions asked about the types of research engaged in by the organizations. The percentages reporting involvement in the three types of research are: organizational studies on worker morale and productivity, 64.7% yes, 33.8% no; evaluation of the effectiveness of their activities such as marketing, advertising, and program evaluation, 69.1% yes, 27.9% no; and other research such as testing for personnel selection, 58.8% yes, 35.3% no. (In these and some other results, totals may not equal 100% due to "don't know" answers or missing data.) Although, overall, about two thirds of the organizations reported engaging in one or more of these types of research, the percentages varied somewhat with type of place; government agencies were most likely to be involved in all three types and nonprofit groups were least likely—especially in the personnel selection type category.

Other sets of questions delved into the organization's experience with psychology majors as job applicants, employees, and interns. When asked if any people with bachelor's degrees in psychology had applied for work at the organization within the past two years, 70.6% said *yes*, 16.2% said *no*, and 11.8% *did not know*. The percentages of those who responded *yes* varied among types of places from a low of 56.2% for government agencies to a high of 78.9% for corporations providing services.

Those who responded affirmatively were asked to indicate an approximate number of applicants, the number hired, and what type of work they were doing. Of the 48 respondents who reported that psychology majors had applied, only half were able to estimate the number of applicants. These estimates ranged very widely from 1 to 100 or more with a median of 15.5. When asked if any of these applicants were hired, 22 said *yes*, 16 said *no*, and the rest did not know (or were not asked this question because of their previous answer). Of those giving a *yes* or *no*, the percentages saying they had hired psychology graduates were higher for nonprofit and government agencies (both 80.0%) than for goods (55.6%) or service (35.7%) corporations. Those who responded affirmatively were asked to report the number hired, but only 13 could give a specific number. These numbers ranged from 1 to about 30 with a median of 2.3. The most frequently mentioned type of work done by those hired was personnel. All of the other replies were idiosyncratic to the particular organization. Some seemed very relevant to a

background in psychology (e.g., entry-level caseworker, evaluation research, psychological technician) while others were less relevant (e.g., store manager, sales, trust administrator).

The small number of respondents precludes drawing any reliable conclusions about the probabilities of seeking and finding work by students with baccalaureate degrees in psychology. However, it is noteworthy that the 22 organizations that reported hiring some psychology graduates represents 18.6% of the organizations that we contacted, 32.3% of the organizations that agreed to be interviewed, and 45.8% of the organizations reporting that they had had some psychology students applying for jobs in recent years. Our findings also suggest that the number of applicants far outstrips the number hired, although other information such as the number and type of positions available would be needed to properly interpret these figures. Again, the main reason for asking these questions was to allow comparisons between organizations that have versus have not had much experience with psychology graduates.

Interns

Several other questions asked about the organization's experience and interest in undergraduate interns (i.e., students taking a field study course). Forty-two (61.8%) of the respondents indicated experience with undergraduate interns. Of these, 10 reported that the interns were psychology students, 20 said they were not, and the rest did not know. Less than one fourth of the organizations with interns reported using psychology students. Experience with interns varied somewhat among types of organizations from a low of 50% for companies providing goods to about 70% for the other three groups. The type of work reportedly done by these interns seemed relevant for psychology students and included such activities as collecting and coding data, administering tests, using canned statistical programs, counseling children, engaging in public relations, observing, and interviewing. Other reported activities were not relevant and varied as a function of the nature of the organization, for example, engineering and legal assistance. On the question of whether their organization would be an appropriate setting for an undergraduate psychology student internship, 42.6% said *yes* and 41.2% said *no*. The percentages of respondents who answered *yes* varied markedly among organizations from 82% for nonprofit agencies, to 50% for government and service corporations to only 29% for corporations providing goods.

Some of the organizations ($N = 38$) were asked if they would be able to use a field study student. A plurality (44.7%) replied, *don't know*, while 15.8% said *no*, and 39.5% said *yes*. The latter were asked what type of work the field study students would be doing and what they would learn. The few replies mainly referred to research activities (e.g., data collection and analysis), service (e.g., personnel, counseling), and learning about work in a real world setting.

Again, due to the small number of respondents involved, it is unwise to draw conclusions about the prospects of psychology students in gaining internships, especially those that are research related. The 10 organizations that specifically indicated having had psychology interns represent about 8% of the organizations we contacted, 15% of the organizations that completed an interview, and 24% of the organizations that had some type of interns. In response to other questions, about 40% of the organizations reported they would be an appropriate place for or would be able to use a psychology undergraduate student intern. In addition, organizations with experience in receiving job applications from and hiring psychology students were somewhat more likely than other organizations to have had psychology interns or to feel their organization was an appropriate place for them.

All of these factors—type of organization, history of having psychology students as applicants, employees and interns—contributed to the organizations' appreciation of various skills and knowledge that might be embodied in persons with bachelor's degrees in psychology.

Ratings of skills

Table 19-1 lists the 11 skills we asked about along with the percentage of respondents who rated them as *somewhat* or *very useful* (combined), the percent saying *not sure,* and the mean and standard deviation of the ratings (excluding the *not sure* respondents). Overall, the more highly rated skills included some conceivably possessed by any college graduate (i.e., writing proposals and being able to apply knowledge to identifying and solving problems) and some perhaps more likely to be found among psychology students (i.e., conducting interviews and statistical analyses). Administering standardized tests was the least useful item in this list, and test construction and observing behavior were also seen as useful by only about half the respondents. Notable percentages were unsure of the value of several skills, especially job analysis and using canned computer programs.

We further analyzed these ratings to see if they varied according to type of organization. In general, the mean ratings combining all 11 skills were similar (about 2.2) for all four groups, indicating no tendency for one type of organization to give more extreme ratings than the others. Differences among organizations on specific skills were examined by conducting both chi-square analyses of

Table 19-1. Ratings of the Usefulness of Skills

	% Somewhat or very	% Not sure	Mean	SD
1. Writing proposals and reports	89.7	2.9	2.62	.63
2. Being able to identify problems and suggest solutions based on research findings or knowledge of human behavior	79.4	5.9	2.44	.75
3. Conducting interviews	83.8	0.0	2.40	.76
4. Doing statistical analysis	83.9	4.4	2.37	.70
5. Knowing how to design and conduct research projects	70.6	8.8	2.26	.81
6. Job analysis	69.2	13.2	2.17	.75
7. Coding data	75.0	5.9	2.11	.72
8. Using canned computer programs to analyze data	60.3	11.8	2.05	.82
9. Systematically observing and recording people's behavior	51.4	5.9	1.84	.86
10. Constructing tests and questionnaires	55.9	4.4	1.82	.79
11. Administering standardized tests	30.9	7.4	1.43	.66

Note: The skills are listed here in decreasing order of mean usefulness rating, not in the order in which they were presented in the interviews.

frequencies and one-way ANOVAs of means. Between-group differences were generally non-significant. However, nonprofit agencies gave somewhat higher ratings to methodological skills (research design, conducting interviews, job analysis, and observation), government agencies and service corporations gave higher ratings to data processing skills (coding, statistical analysis, computer usage), while corporations producing goods gave some of their higher ratings to a mixture of skills (interviewing, job analysis, and computer usage). The only statistically significant differences by either or both types of analysis were for items 8 and 9 with the patterns of means and percentages suggesting that nonprofit agencies placed less value on computer skills and more value on observation of behavior than did the other three groups. Another indication of the degree of comparability in rated usefulness of skills among the four groups was obtained by computing the rank order correlations of the mean ratings. All six of these intercorrelations were positive; the highest similarity (Rho = .83) was between government agencies and service corporations, while the lowest correlations (Rho = .46) were between nonprofit agencies, and both government agencies and service corporations. Some group differences might have been more apparent with larger samples. However, the present findings suggest that, despite some uniquenesses, the relative usefulness of the skills is rather similar across organizational types.

We explored the possible differences in the rated importance of skills in terms of responses to the aforementioned three questions about research activities within the organization. Those organizations reporting that they did conduct one or more of these types of research tended to give higher ratings to nearly all the skills than did other organizations, although this trend was statistically significant only for "doing statistical analyses." We also examined if skill ratings were correlated with an organization's having received job applications from or having hired psychology graduates. Ratings of all the skills (except job analysis) tended to be higher for those who reported receiving job applications from psychology majors than for those who had not; however, this difference was significant only for skill in writing proposals and reports. Comparing those who responded affirmatively to hiring psychology majors with those who responded negatively revealed that the former rated most of the skills higher (this difference was significant for observing behavior and job analysis), but the latter gave slightly, but nonsignificantly, higher ratings to

four skills (items 4, 5, 7 and 8 in Table 19-1).

Comparisons were also made between organizations with or without prior experience using undergraduate interns. Skills were generally rated higher by the former, and for five of the skills (i.e., coding data, statistical analysis, observing behavior, designing research, and writing proposals) the differences were significant to at least the .04 level. Finally, we compared the skill ratings according to whether or not the respondents felt their organization would be an appropriate place for psychology interns. Again, those who answered *yes* gave higher ratings for nearly all the skills than those answering *no*; these differences were statistically significant to at least the .02 level for three skills (i.e., constructing tests, conducting interviews, and observing behavior).

After completing the skill ratings, respondents were asked if they could think of any other research-related skills that might be valuable to their organization. Seventy-five percent answered *no*, while those answering *yes* had only a few suggestions which either reiterated previous ratings (i.e., statistical analysis) or were unique to one respondent (e.g., programming).

Ratings of knowledge areas

Table 19-2 lists the 13 knowledge areas we asked about along with descriptive results. The more highly rated areas included attitudes, information processing, personnel selection, and small groups while areas receiving lower ratings were mental illness, human development, needs and motivation, personality, and organizational behavior. Only a small percentage indicated uncertainty about the value of any of the knowledge areas.

Intergroup comparisons revealed that, over all areas, corporations producing goods tended to give somewhat higher ratings (about 2.2) than did government agencies (about 1.8) with the other organizations falling in the middle. Statistically significant differences among the four groups were found for five of the 13 areas using both the chi-square and one-way ANOVAs. These effects appeared largely due to the nonprofit agencies giving higher ratings to the areas of personality differences, human development, attitudes, and learning and memory, and lower ratings to personnel selection. The rank order correlations of the mean ratings among the four groups confirmed this difference in priorities by showing negative correlations between ratings given by nonprofit agencies and those of the other three groups (Rho ranged from −.24 to −.60), while the correlations among the

Table 19-2. Ratings of the Usefulness of Knowledge Areas

	% Somewhat or very	% Not sure	Mean	SD
1. Formation and change of attitudes and opinions	75.0	0.0	2.19	.75
2. Principles and techniques of personnel selection	72.0	1.5	2.19	.78
3. How people think, solve problems, and process information	77.9	2.9	2.16	.68
4. Structure and dynamics of small groups	75.0	2.9	2.08	.68
5. Effects of the physical environment on people's feelings and actions	66.2	4.4	2.06	.79
6. Organizational development	69.1	2.9	2.05	.75
7. Principles of human learning and memory	63.3	2.9	2.03	.81
8. How people sense and perceive their environment	70.6	0.0	2.00	.71
9. Theories and research about individual personalities and differences	63.2	1.5	1.98	.79
10. Principles of human needs and motivation	61.8	4.4	1.92	.74
11. Theories and research about organizational behavior, work and productivity	67.6	2.9	1.89	.65
12. Theories and research about human development and stages of life	50.0	0.0	1.69	.75
13. Symptoms, causes and treatment of mental illness, abnormal behavior	36.8	2.9	1.51	.69

Note: The knowledge areas are listed here in decreasing order of mean usefulness rating, not in the order in which they were presented in the interviews.

other three were all positive (Rho ranged from .41 to .83).

The usefulness of the knowledge areas varied according to whether or not the organizations engaged in one or more types of research. In general, those who conducted research gave higher ratings than those who did not, but this difference was significant for only three of the areas: small groups, needs and motivation, and personnel selection. Knowledge ratings varied somewhat with the organizations' experience in receiving job applications from and hiring psychology graduates. Organizations that received applications tended to give higher ratings to most of the areas than those who had not; this difference was significant for the topics of human development, abnormal behavior, and sensation and perception. Organizations that had hired psychology majors gave higher ratings to nearly all the areas than organizations who had not; this difference was significant for the topics of human development, abnormal behavior, and learning and memory. The ratings also tended to be higher among organizations that had interns, but this difference was significant only for the areas of human development, physical environment effects, and learning and memory. Finally, organizations indicating that they would be appropriate sites

for internships tended to give higher ratings to most of the areas, although none of these differences reached statistical significance.

When asked if they could think of any other areas of knowledge that would be valuable to their company, 55.9% answered *no*. Of the 33.8% who answered *yes*, they mentioned administrative/motivational skills, analytical skills, helping skills, group dynamics, and knowledge of business terminology, and practices most frequently. The open-ended answers to this and other questions indicated that the respondents were skeptical about the knowledge and skills of psychology students and preferred students with at least some business background.

Desired personal qualities

In the initial interviews conducted for this study, we included a short list of personal qualities to be rated. Because they were all being rated very highly, we changed our strategy to an open-ended approach to elicit what might be the most salient characteristics employers say they are seeking. The traits most frequently mentioned (in decreasing order of frequency) were the ability to work with others in a team, the motivation to work hard, a positive attitude toward the work and the organization, leadership, maturity, flexibility, ability to communicate well, intelligence, problem-solving ability, integrity, and tolerance for stress or ambiguity. A few individuals mentioned other desirable characteristics such as honesty, responsibility, and organization.

Conclusions

Perhaps the primary finding of this study is that nearly all of the skills and knowledge areas we asked about were seen as at least somewhat useful by the majority of respondents. A comparison of the upper portions of Tables 19-1 and 19-2 suggests that research skills might be seen as more valuable than knowledge. This may be because the nature of the skills and their applications are more clear-cut and visible than are the knowledge areas and their application. Stated differently, it might be concluded that it is not just knowledge, but (as indicated by the high rating of item 2 in Table 19-1) the ability to apply knowledge that is valued.

These findings also show that some skills and knowledge are more highly and broadly regarded than others. The ability to write, to apply knowledge in solving problems, and to employ certain methodological skills such as interviewing, coding, and statistical analysis of data received more favorable ratings than other method skills such as behavioral observation or the construction and administration of tests. In general, knowledge in the social and organizational areas of psychology received higher ratings than others such as personality, developmental, or abnormal psychology. On the other hand, the priorities given to many of the skills and knowledge areas varied somewhat with the organizational characteristics that we took into account. When examining all the comparisons made, it is clear that the perceived usefulness of some skills and knowledge areas varied more as a function of organizational characteristics than others. The one skill that varied the most in these comparisons was observing and recording behavior; the skills whose perceived usefulness varied least were administering standardized tests, constructing tests, and identifying problems and suggesting solutions based on knowledge of human behavior. The knowledge areas that showed the most variation due to organizational factors included human development, learning and memory, abnormal behavior and personnel selection; those varying the least were effects of the physical environment, sensation and perception, and organizational behavior and development. The number of statistically significant

differences due to type of organization, extent of research activity, and their experience and/or interest in psychology students as interns and employees were few relative to the number of comparisons made. The clear tendency was that organizational representatives who were presumably more familiar with psychology students, for whatever reason, placed higher value on their abilities. The advantages of enhancing this familiarity by field study experience are obvious.

We also suspect that the perceived usefulness of psychological knowledge and skills varied with characteristics that were not taken into account here. Just as others have found in obtaining ratings of other types of knowledge (Boltuck et al., 1980), the open-ended answers and other comments made by our respondents implied that the importance of some abilities is highly idiosyncratic to an organization, its specific functions, and the types of people it serves. In many cases, the acquisition of the desired expertise would require students to go beyond the offerings of their psychology departments.

Limitations of the study

The favorable evaluations of the knowledge and research skills reported here should be pleasing to teachers and students. However, these findings must be tempered by the limitations of this study. First, this study reflects selection biases as we deliberately contacted only those organizations that initially seemed appropriate to our aims, and some of those selected themselves out of our sample because they deemed themselves irrelevant. It is unlikely that the ratings would have been as high if a random sample of organizations had been obtained.

Second, social desirability or other response sets may have contributed to the high ratings. The interviewers identified themselves as undergraduate psychology students, which may have caused respondents to avoid devaluing the interviewer's presumed interests. This may partly account for the notably high ratings given to the skill of "conducting interviews." Although trained and supervised, the interviewers' lack of experience may have produced responses that are invalid to an unknown degree. However, the large number of interviewers involved helps to rule out any particular systematic bias.

A third category of limitations has to do with the numerical, geographical, and temporal boundaries of this study which restrict the generalizability of the results. It would be hazardous to project whether the observed tendencies for subgroup differences would be enhanced or eliminated in a larger sample. It is also conceivable that the relative priorities of certain skills would be different in other regions of the country. Although the data collection took place over a fairly extended time period, in a larger sense the period is quite narrow. As new skills and knowledge areas are developed, the items studied here may fade in importance. Still, it should be noted that the data collection period occurred during a time of economic recession marked by record unemployment levels, which may have reduced the desirability of psychology students.

A fourth limitation is that the nature of the items on the interview schedule may have produced misleading results. The restrictions imposed by the telephone interview precluded the use of a more comprehensive list of items, as well as more thorough explanations of the items that were included. Perhaps slightly different descriptions of these same topics would have yielded markedly different ratings of usefulness. Similarly, respondents may have had a different conception than the investigators of the meaning of a particular item. For instance, by "conducting interviews," we were referring to a method used as a research tool, while some respondents may have construed it to mean a diagnostic procedure. Additionally, such terms as information processing, sensation and perception, and abnormal behavior could have meant something to our respondents that is quite different from what is typically presented in undergraduate courses on these topics.

Finally, the respondents may simply have been wrong in their perceptions of what is and is not useful to their organizations. Some items may sound relevant, but in fact are not. Conversely, others may be quite valuable, but are just not recognized as such. These possibilities are partly due to our ignorance of "meta-knowledge." That is, we may not be cognizant of the specific skills and bits of knowledge we are applying or how we learned them. The perspective afforded by a broad background in psychology, including courses on topics not rated highly or even not incorporated in our lists, may be what is most valuable for psychological researchers even though they (and their employers) do not realize it.

Despite these limitations, we hope that these results have contributed to answering the questions raised in the introduction to this chapter. The data in Tables 19–1 and 19–2 may afford some guidance to those who are designing curricula, new courses, and career development programs; conducting

public relations efforts to expand awareness of what psychology graduates can do; planning what courses to take; and applying for research positions. Regarding curricular changes, we recommend the creation of more opportunities for field experience in research. In recent years there has been rapid growth in field study/internship courses for undergraduates (Gold, 1980; Matthews, 1979; Prerost, 1981b; Ross, Hughes, & Hill, 1981; Vande Creek & Thompson, 1977) and numerous evaluations revealing their benefits such as favorable student evaluations, being accepted into graduate school, obtaining psychology-related jobs, and job satisfaction (e.g., Keeley & Kreutzer, 1981; Lunneborg & Wilson, 1982; Prerost, 1981a; Sherman, 1982). However, most of the current field study opportunities seem to involve providing help to individuals in settings that deliver some type of mental health service. Our findings add to the evidence that there are opportunities for other types of field study, especially involving research, in other types of settings including those in the corporate world.

Other than providing some encouragement for the development of opportunities to obtain nonacademic research experience, our findings do not and should not imply revisions in what courses are offered by psychology departments or taken by students. Instead, we concur with Costin (1982) who has defended the merits of general education in psychology as opposed to strict concentration on career preparation. This is not to say, however, that the manner in which courses are presented and undertaken should ignore the practical relevance of the material. In the present context, this includes attending to how the acquisition of skills and knowledge is necessary for careers, not just in human service, but also in research. If teachers can make more salient the marketable value of what they are teaching, then students may be more motivated to learn it, and better equipped to explain to employers (and others) what indeed they are able to do with a bachelor's degree in psychology.

References

Babarik, P. (1980). "What do they really want?": A survey of undergraduates' preferences and aversions in psychology. *Canadian Psychologist, 21,* 84–86.

Boltuck, M., Peterson, T., & Murphy, R. (1980). Preparing undergraduate psychology majors for employment in the human service delivery system. *Teaching of Psychology, 7,* 75–78.

Costin, F. (1982). Some thoughts on general education and the teaching of undergraduate psychology. *Teaching of Psychology, 9*, 26–29.

Davis, J. (1979). Where did they all go? A job survey of BA graduates. In P. Woods (Ed.), *The psychology major: Training and employment strategies* (pp. 110–114). Washington, DC: American Psychological Association.

Edwards, J., & Holmgren, R. (1979). Some prerequisites for becoming a "really" applied social psychologist. *Personality and Social Psychology Bulletin, 5*, 516–523.

Evans, R. I., Rintala, D. H., Guthrie, T. J., & Raines, B. E. (1981). Recruiting and training undergraduate psychology research assistants for longitudinal field investigations. *Teaching of Psychology, 8*, 97–100.

Fernald, C. D., Tedeschi, R. G., Siegfried, W. D., Gilmore, D. L., & Chipley, B. (1982). Designing and managing an undergraduate practicum course in psychology. *Teaching of Psychology, 9*, 155–160.

Fretz, B. R. (1976). Finding careers with a bachelor's degree in psychology. *Psi Chi Newsletter*, p. 5–9.

Gold, M. (1980). Training for off-campus psychology: A cautionary tale and some elements of a model. *Academic Psychology Bulletin, 2*, 309–319.

Haney, T., & Howland, P. (1978). Career course for credit: Necessity or luxury? *Journal of College Placement, 39*, 75–77.

Keeley, S. M., & Kreutzer, J. S. (1981). A follow-up evaluation of an undergraduate community mental health worker training program. *Teaching of Psychology, 8*, 28–31.

Korn, J. H., & Lewandowski, M. E. (1981). The clinical bias in the career plans of undergraduates and its impact on students and the profession. *Teaching of Psychology, 8*, 149–152.

Lunneborg, P. W., & Wilson, V. M. (1982). Job satisfaction correlates for college graduates in psychology. *Teaching of Psychology, 9*, 199–201.

Matthews, J.R. (1979). Undergraduate field placement: Survey and issues. *Teaching of Psychology, 6*, 148–151.

McGovern, T. (1979). The development of a career planning program for undergraduate psychology majors. *Teaching of Psychology, 6*, 183–184.

Norcross, J. C., & Wogan, M. (1982). Undergraduates as researchers in mental health settings. *Teaching of Psychology, 9*, 89–91.

Prerost, F. J. (1981a). Post-graduation educational and occupational choices of psychology undergraduate practicum participants: Issues for the psychology profession. *Teaching of Psychology, 8*, 221–223.

Prerost, F. J. (1981b). The feasibility of undergraduate field experiences in child psychology: Program factors and suggestions. *Teaching of Psychology, 8*, 19–22.

Ross, S. M., Hughes, T. M., & Hill, R. E. (1981). Field experience as meaningful contexts for learning about learning. *Journal of Educational Research, 75*, 103–107.

Sherman, A. R. (1982). Psychology fieldwork: A catalyst for advancing knowledge and academic skills. *Teaching of Psychology, 9*, 82–85.

Titley, R. (1978). Whatever happened to the class of '67? *American Psychologist, 33*, 1094–1098.

Vande Creek, L., & Thompson, G. (1977). Management of undergraduate psychology internships. *Teaching of Psychology, 4*, 177–180.

Ware, M. E. (1981). Evaluating a career development course: A two year study. *Teaching of Psychology, 8*, 67–71.

Ware, M. E., & Meyer, A. E. (1981). Career versatility of the psychology major: A survey of graduates. *Teaching of Psychology, 8*, 12–15.

White, G. D., & Lindquist, C. U. (1982). Survey of mental health agencies in curriculum development of a Master's-level psychology training program. *Teaching of Psychology, 9*, 212–215.

Authors' Notes

We wish to extend our gratitude to the following volunteer interviewers without whose assistance this study would not have been completed: Don Allen, Sarah Brotherton, Susan Froula, Anne Herron, Pat Jorgenson, Kathy Kadlec, Joe Steffo and, especially Mary Pat Fowler and Jack Lamey. We also thank Dr. Fred Bryant for his helpful comments.

Chapter 20

Beyond the bachelor's degree

Vicki M. Wilson and Patricia W. Lunneborg, University of Washington

This chapter focuses on the strategies to be applied by that minority of undergraduate psychology majors seeking acceptance into psychology graduate programs. Because the myth that one cannot do anything with *just* a bachelor's degree is widespread, it may be surprising that those planning to enter graduate school constitute only a small proportion of psychology graduates. In Kulick's (1973) review of undergraduate education in psychology, departmental chairpersons estimated that only from one fourth to one third of their students were oriented towards graduate school. From 1975 to the present at the University of Washington, fewer than 20% of each class have applied to graduate school.

Why, then, should there be any need for strategies for admission? Remembering the fairly uncomplicated transition from high school to college, many students think that a similar transition takes place between undergraduate and graduate study. Not so! The competition for acceptance is incredibly keen. At some schools the acceptance rate is less than 2% of applicants (APA, 1986). The competition is similar to that for medical school with one important difference. If one wants to continue in psychology, is willing to take the time needed for preparation, and develops a reasonable application strategy, one will probably be accepted in a graduate program, although not necessarily at one's first- or even second-choice school.

Jobs in traditional settings for psychologists are diminishing. Opportunities in colleges are declining slowly but steadily, as are those in hospitals and clinics. The major positive change is an increase in opportunities with state and local governments (Cuca, *1975*). Wood's (*1976*) *Career Opportunities for Psy-chologists* with its emphasis on expanding and emerging nontraditional areas is testimony to this changing market, as is Zambrano and Entine's (*1976*) *Career Alternatives for Academics.* So there is a good market for psychologists, but it's a different market, and fresh PhDs will have to seek new settings and work activities in which their training and expertise can be fully utilized.

The decision then to attend graduate school should really be a function of the desire to study psychology because it is the area in which one wants to become educated. Students should ask themselves where becoming a psychologist falls in their priority list. If other goals or obligations have higher priority, these may limit their chances for acceptance into graduate study. For example, if one decides to remain in San Francisco, such a decision reduces one's chances for advanced study, as one must apply to schools of varying geographic location to maximize the chances of acceptance. Not everyone who would like to continue in psychology wants it more than anything else in life; there may be other things of more importance, depending on the individual. However, the fewer restrictions one puts on becoming a psychologist (i.e., I must live *here*, I must attend school *there*), the higher the probability that one will make it.

A bright spot—after asking the above question many students might look at alternative ways of meeting their career goals and discover that psychology might not be right for them after all. They may find that a program in social work, educational psychology, business, public affairs, guidance and counseling, law, nutrition, occupational therapy, or special education may be more appropriate to their needs and desires and less difficult to enter.

After making the decision to continue in psychology, what should one do? There are three keys to achieving acceptance into a graduate program: persistance, preparation, and application know-how.

Persistance

Webster's defines persistance as resolute or stubborn continuance, in spite of opposition, importunity, or warning. No matter what obstacles appear and regardless of pessimistic advice received, one must maintain dedication to one's academic goals and career objectives and refuse to be deterred. Schools look favorably on those who demonstrate decisiveness. One student, against our advice, decided that there was only one school for her. After applying there for 3 consecutive years she was finally accepted. Each time she was rejected, she found out the reason for the rejection and worked to correct the deficiency. Her dedication and willingness to work hard was finally rewarded.

Preparation

Preparation is an easy word referring to a not-so-easy task. In this context it means using one's undergraduate years (not necessarily 4 years but possibly 5 or 6) to build attractive credentials. As a potential graduate student one will be judged on a number of criteria that vary in weight depending on the orientation of individual departments: cumulative grade point average, psychology grade point average, Graduate Record Examination (GRE) scores, general academic coursework, science background, research experience, letters of recommendation, and clinical experience. If a department has a strong research orientation and is heavily funded by grants, it will favor people with strong science, laboratory, statistics, and research backgrounds. For those interested in clinical or counseling psychology, research is still important, but field experience is also necessary. It is critical to be able to offer a graduate program proof that one has experience in the field of clinical/counseling psychology and knows what is involved. In summary, a student with a solid background in the "hard" sciences (math, biology, chemistry, etc.) and laboratory work statistics, research, and fieldwork (if appropriate) is well on the road to graduate acceptance.

Academic background

Once students know what is needed, they usually want to know how much is needed. There is no one, right answer. How much of any one element is needed to make you attractive as a candidate for a graduate program depends on the emphasis of individual graduate departments. A general rule is that a minimum of 10 quarter credits each of math, physical sciences, and biological sciences is necessary. As part of the psychology major one should take at least two solid courses in laboratory and statistics, and a minimum of 1 year of research. Add to this a year of clinical work if appropriate. Combining all of these courses with desired electives, one can see why the undergraduate career may stretch to 5 years, particularly if one's decision to go to graduate school is not made early in the college career.

We came up with these numbers from our experience in advising thousands of students. We routinely examined the backgrounds of our undergraduates who have applied to hundreds of different programs to see which schools accept what types of backgrounds. We concluded that the best approach is a conservative one—excellent preparation in all areas. Of course, exceptions, both by students and programs, can be found. One student accepted into graduate school did not major in psychology, another refused to get involved in research, and another had a science background consisting only of oceanography. These people are to be congratulated, but not modeled. Schools can also prove to be exceptions. Although this chapter concerns preparation for the typical traditional graduate program in psychology, there are humanistic and clinical programs that place less emphasis on science and research as undergraduate requirements.

Research and fieldwork

Research experience as an undergraduate can be obtained by linking up with faculty in one's department and working as a research assistant. Eventually one may progress to doing one's own research and possibly even coauthor some publications; graduate schools are extremely impressed by such activities. Some institutions have undergraduate-research or independent-study courses that provide research experience. However, it is not the accumulation of credits that is important. What is critical is to perform research over an extended period of time and to develop a close professional relationship with faculty members.

Students who need clinical field experience, but whose schools have no practicum programs, can contact local mental health agencies, hospitals, or other agencies of interest and volunteer. One should make clear to the agency the type of experience desired—counseling, interviewing, testing, or research—and keep looking until one finds it. This process is much easier than it sounds, as half of most mental health agencies' staffs are volunteers.

Letters of recommendation

One cannot expect to come up with three strong letters of recommendation without having cultivated a few sources. For students attending small colleges where the normal class size is less than 30, finding faculty sources is usually not a problem. However, for those attending a university where even upper-division courses can have as many as 200 students, getting to know faculty becomes a real challenge. In such universities, faculty the student has worked with on research are the best sources of letters. These professors are able to evaluate the student in terms of research ability, critical scholarship, written communication, professional identification, emotional stability, effective energy, and interpersonal relations. They can also provide an overall judgment of the student's probability of success. For clinical/counseling students, fieldwork supervisors are another excellent source for letters of recommendation.

What kinds of letters should applicants have? In general, the applicant should have at least three solid academic references—these are the most impressive. For clinical/counseling students, two academic references and one fieldwork reference are a good base. Some schools are now asking for four letters. However, as a courtesy to reviewers, we advise that applicants send no more than five letters.

Graduate Record Examinations

The finale in the preparation is the Graduate Record Examinations, which consists of two separate tests, the General Test and a Subject Test, and is required by essentially every graduate program in psychology. The General Test contains three sections measuring verbal, quantitative, and analytical ability and results in three sources. The Subject Test in psychology, not required by all programs, is designed to measure knowledge and understanding of psychological principles and facts from basic to advanced study and yields an overall score as well as experimental and social subscores. The verbal and quantitative scores are commonly viewed as most important. To determine if a school requires both the General and Subject Tests, consult *Graduate Study in Psychology and Associated Fields*, published an-

nually by the American Psychological Association.[1]

The GRE was administered five times in 1987-88 with test dates in October, December, February, April, and June (General test only). The General test is given in the morning on test dates and the Subject test in the afternoon. The testing office at one's college or university should have copies of the most recent *GRE Information Bulletin* (including the test application form and sample questions) published by the Educational Testing Service (ETS).[2]

Should one study for the GRE? Yes! The consensus of our advisees over the years has been that studying is critical. There are two basic purposes for studying: to increase speed and reduce anxiety. One may not learn any new material by studying, but reviewing will bring to mind material once learned but not recently used. Becoming familiar with the nature of the material will also increase one's speed and reduce the accompanying anxiety; one will know what to expect when walking into the testing room.

To study for this important exam students should buy a GRE study guide at a local bookstore. These guides aim primarily at preparation for the verbal and quantitative sections of the General test. Although study guides are available, we have found that reviewing as many new-edition introductory texts as possible is the best method of studying for the test in psychology. What about timing? The GRE should be taken in October of the year preceding the fall one would like to start graduate school. Some program application deadlines are as early as December, but most cluster around January and early February for admission the following fall. Completing the test in October leaves ample time for distributing test scores and for solving any problems that may arise.

How important is the GRE? *Very important,* but it is one of several criteria evaluated. One's attitude toward the GRE should be one of acknowledging its importance, studying hard for it, doing as well as possible, and then following through with an application strategy consistent with one's test scores. Poorer-than-expected test scores may mean toning down one's list of prospective graduate programs. In addition, the GRE should be viewed as a one-time endeavor. Even though the test can be retaken the ETS reports all scores, and the first scores are generally regarded as the most valid. There is also a 50–50 chance for getting a poorer second score; most students we have known did not do significantly better on a second try.

Application schedule

Appendix A is a suggested schedule for the undergraduate (Scott & Davis-Silka, 1974). This schedule for applying to graduate school represents an ideal. Unless the decision to attend graduate school is made during the first year of college, one will not be able to follow the schedule exactly. For example, if the decision to major in psychology is not made until the junior year, it is next to impossible to become a viable candidate in one year. With imagination, however, the schedule can be adapted to meet individual decision-making plans. Students applying to graduate school for the fall (when the majority of programs accept students) following June graduation should apply almost a year ahead of the anticipated admission time. Therefore, the most impressive course work must be completed by approximately December of the senior year. This does not apply to those delaying graduate study—such students will be able to submit their entire records.

Résumé and letter of intent

Two important elements mentioned in the suggested schedule are the résumé and the letter of intent; copies of both should be sent to prospective schools. The résumé outlines one's educational background, work and field experience, and research. A résumé should be no longer than one page—*never* more than two. A guide to preparing such a résumé can be found in Appendix B.

The letter of intent is a description of (a) the development of one's academic interests; (b) research experience; (c) clinical/counseling interests and experience (if appropriate); (d) unique abilities and skills relevant to psychology (e.g., experience as a computer programmer); (e) graduate goals; (f) reasons for wanting to attend a particular graduate school; and (g) professional goals. It is not an autobiography. If particular programs want other information, this will be specified in their application materials.

The letter of intent has some standard parts and some that are specific to particular programs. Applicants should be aware that even a qualified individual will probably not be accepted into a program whose specific emphasis is not clearly reflected in the individual's application materials. One must be very sure of one's direction and area of specialization and build the letters of intent around them. The goals stated must be compatible with the prospective program.

Application know-how

The final key to acceptance by a graduate school involves knowing the mechanics of applying—where to get information on prospective programs, how many programs to select, strategy in selection, financial aid, and timing. Three excellent sources of information are available. First, and most comprehensive, is *Graduate Study in Psychology and Associated Fields*, published annually by the APA. Along with general advice on graduate study application, it provides specific information (including departments and addresses, programs and degrees offered, application procedures, admission requirements, student statistics, degree requirements, tuition, and financial assistance) for hundreds of graduate programs in psychology in the United States and Canada. This book is a must!

A second source of application information is psychology department faculty. Professors aware of students' interests and abilities can use their knowledge of various programs to advise students on the most appropriate schools to which they should apply. A third source is the library. By going through relevant journals, students can find out who is writing articles and doing research of interest to them and where these authors are affiliated. The result of this research should be a list of from 20 to 30 prospective programs. If catalogs from other colleges are available, students can probably eliminate some programs from the list immediately. For those programs remaining, a typed postcard should be sent to the chairperson requesting information on the program, a catalog, an application, and financial aid forms. This information can then be used to trim the list down to the finalists.

How many and what type of schools should be on that final list? The list should consist of not less than 10 schools, representing a range in quality, geographic location, and level of degree offered. There are two main reasons for this distribution: competition and limited control over selection procedures. The keen competition has already been discussed; one simply cannot count on getting into any one program.

Even though an applicant can exercise partial control over graduate acceptance, there are some aspects of the process that are impossible to control. For example, an applicant may be rejected because a department decides not to take anyone in a particular area of specialization. A number of objective criteria including GRE scores, cumulative and psychology grade point averages, and science background are weighted according to a graduate department's orientation and combined to predict the success of each applicant. However, once a final group of top candidates exists, it is often difficult to choose from among them in an objective fashion, and subjective opinion may play a role. For example, a selection committee might choose a candidate who impressed them by making the trip to the department and being interviewed.

Another reason for applying to a wide range of schools is the problem of interpreting admissions criteria. In APA's *Graduate Study in Psychology and Associated Fields,* schools rate the importance they place during selection on nonobjective criteria such as letters of recommendation and work experience. While each department knows precisely what it means by these ratings of high, medium, or low, how does an applicant know? Even with objective admissions criteria there can be a substantial difference between meeting stated minimum requirements and being competitive. Thus, in order to allow a margin of safety for what cannot be controlled, one should apply to as many programs as possible (10 at a minimum).

Doctoral programs are harder to get into than master's programs. Thus, we advise all students to apply to some "master's only" programs. "Master's only" refers to schools that specialize in master's programs and do not offer the PhD. (Generally, if a school reports that it grants both master's and doctorate's degrees, it is really in the business of producing PhDs.) As a guideline for choosing the 10 schools to which to apply, it is wise to include three or four PhD programs that the candidate would *like* to attend, another four or five PhD programs one would not mind attending, and two or three "master's only" programs.

Many students are confused by this application strategy because they have been told that if they cannot attend a prestige institution, they might as well not go to graduate school. Others may wonder about applying to master's programs when they really want a PhD. First, it would be great to be accepted by one of the top schools in the country; however, there are only so many top programs, and they take only so many people. In considering other schools, students should remember that the decision to continue in psychology was made because it is the area in which they want an education; they should be willing to get that education anywhere possible.

Second, master's programs are another excellent way to work toward the PhD. They are less difficult to enter, and, if one's undergradu-

ate record is less than glowing, the master's program may be the path to the doctorate. After completing the master's degree, one can apply to PhD programs with a much better chance of admission because acceptance will be based on graduate-level work, rather than one's undergraduate record.

What about costs—the time and money to apply? Costs are a minimum of $300–400, depending on the number of applications sent. The average application fee is $25; add to this the cost of official transcripts (which must come from every college attended), duplication costs (for recommendations, résumés, letters of intent, etc.), postage, and even long-distance phone calls. Second, hundreds of hours are needed for the application process.

If students need financial assistance while in graduate school, they should routinely ask for financial aid forms along with applications and apply for it. Graduate school is a full-time job which leaves little time for part-time jobs. Programs with a tradition of supplying financial aid are still providing it, although they are not as committed in their initial letters of acceptance. In addition, stating that financial support is not needed will not necessarily help one get accepted, unless the reason is that one has a scholarship or funding from another prestigious source.

Finally, to avoid frustration, students should get started early, because it will be necessary to apply essentially a year prior to entering. Faculty must encourage students to begin to meet faculty early in one's undergraduate career, complete the most impressive coursework as soon as possible (statistics!), start selecting prospective programs early (not 2 weeks before deadlines), and when asking for letters of recommendation allow time for procrastination on the part of faculty writers (definitely follow up on requests to make certain starting a month after request).

For those who do not want to continue their education right away, everything mentioned still applies. By graduation students should have letters of recommendation and GRE scores on file. Sadly, faculty disappear for a variety of reasons, and if one returns in one or two years to ask for a letter, a particular faculty member may be gone. One may never use these letters, but if needed the original letters will be there. In addition, students not planning to go to graduate school immediately should take the GRE while still undergraduates or within a few months of graduation. Students out of school for any extended period get out of the habit of taking exams, and their exam-taking ability also decreases. GRE scores remain valid for five years, so students delaying their graduate education should plan accordingly.

There is no indication that not going on to graduate school immediately is detrimental to one's chances of acceptance. Factors that correlate with maturity—employment, postbaccalaureate studies, years of research and clinical experience—are gaining weight in the selection process. What would be detrimental would be disconnecting oneself from psychology: One should always keep a foot in the door as an indication of commitment to the field. If employment in psychology cannot be found, recommend that graduates at least do volunteer research or related fieldwork. The stronger one's continued commitment to psychology, the higher one's chance of future acceptance into graduate school.

Postscripts

Here is the parting advice of our most recent successful applicants.

1. Start the application process early (like early summer before the fall you apply). Writing your résumé and letters of intent is very, very time-consuming. You must take a light course load the fall quarter you apply.

2. If you blow the GREs, spend your time on the areas of life where you have control. Get good grades, do excellent and lots of research. Impress faculty with your reliability and creativity so they will write good letters.

3. Choose prospective schools based on the match between their training goals and your professional goals. Success and pleasure in graduate education come only from a good match. Anything less will be a disaster.

4. A positive attitude is important. It shows in your applications, letters, and résumé. Don't apply to graduate school until you are ready and know you will get in. Then confidently go for it.

References

American Psychological Association. (1986). *Graduate study in psychology and associated fields* 1986 ed. Washington, DC: Author.

Cuca, J. M. (1975). Placement report: 1973 and 1974. *American Psychologist, 30,* 1176–1179.

Kulik, J. A. (1973). *Undergraduate education in psychology.* Washington, DC: American Psychological Association.

Scott, W. C., & Davis-Silka, L. (1974). Applying to graduate school in psychology: A perspective and guide. *JSAS Catalog of Selected Documents in Psychology, 4,* 33. (Ms. No. 597)

Woods, P. J. (Ed.). (1976). *Career opportunities for psychologists: Expanding and emerging areas.* Washington, DC: American Psychological Association, 1976.

Zambrano, A. L., & Entine, A. D. (1976). *A guide to career alternatives for academics.* New Rochelle, NY: Change Magazine Press.

Appendix A: Suggested Schedule for Career Planning and Applying to Graduate School

SOPHOMORE YEAR

After completing most of the general education requirements in the first year of college, work on the basic psychology-major requirements, including statistics, laboratory, and science courses.

Become acquainted with several faculty members in the department.

Write a preliminary résumé.

Attend departmental colloquia.

JUNIOR YEAR

Continue, and try to complete, basic requirements.

Begin research with faculty and continue throughout junior year.

Think about letter of recommendation resources (e.g., research supervisors, professors of small classes).

Explore opportunities for joining professional organizations (e.g., obtain faculty sponsorship for a student membership in the American Psychological Association).

Redraft the preliminary résumé.

Attend the state's annual psychological meeting.

Keep attending departmental colloquia.

Do fieldwork if interested in clinical or counseling psychology.

Begin work on a paper on one's previous research for possible publication or presentation. (Start in spring of junior year.)

SUMMER BETWEEN JUNIOR AND SENIOR YEARS

Buy study guides for the GRE and begin studying.

Begin to investigate prospective graduate programs (consult with faculty and use library resources).

Do third draft of résumé.

From research work, write paper(s) for publication or presentation.

SENIOR YEAR

Complete, as much as possible, all impressive degree requirements, research, and fieldwork by December; continue the research and fieldwork, however, because they may be helpful later on.

September: Buy the current issue of APA's *Graduate Study in Psychology and Associated Fields* and write to prospective schools for application materials. Register in September to take the October GRE. Begin requesting letters of recommendation.

Through application materials find out about any additional requirements or tests needed by individual programs.

November: Have letter of intent written and a polished résumé completed. Have a faculty member or adviser check them for grammar, spelling, and content.

December: Send completed applications to schools way ahead of deadlines. Request transcripts to be sent from all colleges attended. If not continuing on to graduate school immediately, continue research, fieldwork, and faculty affiliations as long as possible.

Appendix B: Résumé Guide

Name
Address
Phone number (area code)

EDUCATIONAL GOAL
Degree sought and ultimate degree goal.

PROFESSIONAL OBJECTIVE
Professional work desired after completion of the degree (research, teaching, clinical practice?) The professional objective should match the training goal of the school applied to. If a school's goal is to train research clinicians, it will not be inclined to take a person with a private-clinical-practice orientation.

EDUCATION
Degree(s) earned or expected and dates. Also, the emphasis in psychology (ethology, development, personality, etc.) and any emphasis outside the department if it is impressive (e.g., a strong biology background). Mention honors, scholarships, fellowships, and awards earned.

RESEARCH EXPERIENCE
Elaborate on research background—whom one worked with and *exactly* what one did. Be very specific. This should be a big section.

WORK AND FIELD EXPERIENCE
Highlight those experiences related to psychology. Other nonrelated experience should be mentioned but emphasis should be on accomplishments and abilities demonstrated that will make one a more attractive candidate.

PAPERS AND PRESENTATIONS
Any publications or related professional presentation.

PROFESSIONAL AFFILIATIONS
Example: student membership in the American Psychological Association.

REFERENCES
Names, addresses, phone numbers of persons who have written letters of recommendation.

Footnotes

1. Students interested in this book should consult their bookstore or library; or for current price and ordering information, they should write to the Order Department, American Psychological Association, P.O. Box 2710, Hyattsville, MD 20784.
2. A copy of the *GRE Information Bulletin* and a test application form can be obtained by writing to Graduate Record Examination, CN 6000, Princeton, NJ 08541-6000.

PART 5

Preparing the psychology major for specific careers

Chapter 21

The psychology major as biofeedback therapist

Avie James Rainwater III, City of Faith Medical and Research Center, Tulsa, OK

One of the most exciting things about the science of psychology is the progressive stance it takes in encouraging new developments, both applied and conceptual. The psychology being studied by undergraduates today is quite different from the science studied 10 or 20 years ago, and will be different in another 10 years. The psychology major can take advantage of this growing change by becoming involved in one of psychology's newest developments, biofeedback.

Both as a field of study and as an applied technique, biofeedback has progressed rapidly. As a science with roots in psychophysiology, biofeedback experienced such rapid growth because of the extensive experimental attention it started receiving in the mid-to-late 1960s. The concepts of biofeedback have been more clearly defined and the applied techniques more clinically refined because research has continued to increase over the past 20 years. Biofeedback is now a leading area of study in the field of behavioral medicine and one of the most used clinical techniques of health psychology. On a daily basis, psychologists use biofeedback techniques to help patients learn how to relax and reduce the negative effects of stress, tension, and anxiety in their lives (See Appendix for a listing of problem areas treatable with biofeedback).

What is biofeedback?

Many people have questions about biofeedback because it is still a relatively new form of health care. The term *biofeedback* is a combination of two words: *bio*, which relates to biology or body; and *feedback*, which means giving information back. Although it is a new therapy technique, the principle of biofeed-

back has been in use throughout the history of health care. The thermometer is a good example. The thermometer gives information back to the user about the temperature of the body. Without the thermometer you could only guess that you have a fever, but with this simple instrument, you can know your exact temperature. The thermometer increases your awareness of your temperature and eliminates guessing. Awareness is the key.

When biofeedback is used as a therapy, it helps the patient become aware of body functions (e.g., muscle tension, heart rate, etc.) by using an electronic instrument or monitor. This biofeedback instrument provides patients with information (feedback) about their bodies (bio) about which they were previously unaware. Awareness increases; and once awareness is achieved, learned control becomes possible.

By using the biofeedback instrument to become aware of how tense muscles are, patients literally see or hear the need to relax and decrease the effects of stress and tension. By combining biofeedback with relaxation techniques, patients quickly learn to relax deeply. Once they are confident in their ability to relax, they will be able to apply the relaxation to reduce their symptoms.

Training

There are few colleges or universities offering formal undergraduate training or coursework in biofeedback. In fact, few graduate programs include the full range of necessary training. Training is obtained through independent work in four basic ways. The best way to obtain training is through volunteer work at an area psychological clinic or with a psychologist in private practice who uses biofeedback extensively. Most practitioners are happy to work with undergraduate volunteers to help them gain experience and exposure. Arrangements can be made for volunteer work to be accepted for course credit as a directed study or an internship.

A variation of the volunteer option is for the undergraduate to become involved with a psychologist practicing biofeedback as a research assistant. Many biofeedback practitioners have on-going clinical studies and would welcome an assistant. This opportunity affords the student good insight into the empirical aspects of biofeedback and might be performed for academic credit as an honors research project.

The third avenue requires active involvement in a state biofeedback society, the Biofeedback Society of America (BSA), or the American Association of Biofeedback Clinicians (AABC).[1] Professional societies such as these help students become knowledgable of biofeedback research and clinical application on a state and national basis. The national organizations both have student divisions which allow students to take advantage of the student-training experiences at their meetings and workshops.

Finally, as mentioned above, there are many excellent workshops. Most are weekend experiences, thereby allowing full-time students to participate. There are also extended training meetings of 1 to 2 weeks. The best way to find out about these training opportunities is by reading the *APA Monitor.* Announcements are also made by direct mail to many psychology departments and in the two national societies' newsletters' listings.

Certification

Licensure is not available to psychologists without a PhD. Thus, the psychology major working as a biofeedback therapist will want to gain certification as a biofeedback provider. Certification assures the patients that the biofeedback therapist has achieved a position of clinical expertise that is recognized at the national level. This is also becoming a credential standard that insurance companies are requiring for 3rd-party payments, if the biofeedback therapist is not a licensed psychologist or other health care provider. Both of the national professional societies offer certification, although in different forms.

One avenue for certification is through the Biofeedback Certification Institute of America (BCIA), which is an outgrowth of the BSA and recognized by the National Commission for Health Certifying Agencies. They offer a two-part certification process with both a written and a practical portion to the examination. The exam is offered twice a year, once in conjunction with the BSA's annual meeting and once at various locations across the nation at a different time of the year. Some state biofeedback societies, affiliated with the BSA, are approved to offer the BCIA exam.

Differing from the generic certification offered by the BCIA, graduated levels of certification are offered by the American Board of Clinical Biofeedback, which is associated with the American Association of Clinical Biofeedback: the Diplomate in Clinical Biofeedback, Certified Professional in Clinical Biofeedback, Certified Associate in Clinical Biofeedback, and Certified Technician in Clinical Biofeedback. The American Board of Clinical Biofeedback exam covers the theoretical, applied, and instrumentational aspects of biofeedback practice and is offered in conjunction with the AABC's annual meeting.

There are many review programs that are available to help the biofeedback clinician prepare for the certification process. Review courses are usually offered in an intensive 3-to-5-day format. However, there are several correspondence review programs and cassette type courses. The offerings for these courses can be found in the *APA Monitor,* as well as the BSA's and the AABC's newsletters. Only certifications which require assessment of the practitioner's intellectual and applied skills in biofeedback are acknowledged as valid professional credentials, although certifications without thorough assessment are available.

Technician or therapist?

In electronics and industry, *technician* is used to describe someone with extensive technical expertise. In health care, technician describes someone who has only entry-level ability, that is, someone who performs the basic aspects of a particular health-care service. Electroencephalograph (EEG) technologists can correctly record brainwave activity and care for the EEG instrument. They do not, however, have the credentials to interpret the EEG tracings or make recommendations based on the EEG study findings. Because the psychological therapy process is an active part of any biofeedback therapy course, a technical level of skills is unacceptable for providing unsupervised biofeedback therapy ("Ethical Principles," 1985). Individuals functioning as biofeedback technicians must work in conjunction with a psychologist, who supervises the technical (physiological) aspect of treatment and solely provides the therapeutic (psychological) aspect of the therapy course. For this reason, individuals without an academic background in psychology can only function at the technician level because they do not have an adequate understanding of the psychological process of biofeedback therapy or an appreciation for the psychological issues involved in the psychophysiological recordings.

Approximately 80% of the professionals involved in biofeedback are psychologists (Biofeedback Society of America, personal communication, March, 1985). Baccalaureate psychology majors are the only professionals with adequate academic credentials to function above the technician level without doing graduate work. Psychology majors can enter the field of psychology as biofeedback technicians once adequate training has been completed. As their skills increase they will be able to combine their specialized training in biofeedback with their undergraduate training in psychology to become biofeedback therapists. Having achieved this level of skill they can function effectively in conjunction with a licensed psychologist for consultation on difficult cases and provide insight into therapy problems. For the majority of cases, the biofeedback therapist will solely provide the health-care, initiate the therapy course, and carry it through to discharge and follow-up.

Employment

One of the best methods for achieving gainful employment as a biofeedback therapist, once the bachelor's degree in psychology and the biofeedback internship are completed, is to have a résumé that shows a substantial amount of productive field experience. The steps that the psychology major takes to become a biofeedback therapist provide part of the experience the employers want to see. The more training opportunities the psychology major utilizes, the better his or her chances will be for prompt employment. In fact, the number of well-trained entry-level biofeedback therapists, who have already received their training and are prepared to assist in a biofeedback practice without additional training, is so small that the psychology major with this level of training should have little difficulty in finding a meaningful psychology position. The best employment strategy is to be very well trained and appropriately credentialed.

With the growing emphasis on preventative health care and the heightened awareness of the need to control stress, the biofeedback therapist has several places to approach for employment. The best opportunity is often the place where the biofeedback practicum or internship was completed. An intern who performs well and shows promise is in a prime position to become an employee, if the internship site has a position opening.

There are four basic areas to investigate for employment opportunities, apart from cultivated employment contacts. The most obvious would be hospitals. The prospective employee must learn which department (e.g. psychology, psychiatry, neurosensory, electrophysiology, etc.) provides biofeedback services, and begin the application and self-marketing process. Second, all the area psychological, psychiatric, pediatric, neurological, substance abuse, weight reduction, smoking cessation, and family medicine services can be approached. Often these clinics make active use of biofeedback and may welcome an opportunity to expand their services. Third, Health Maintenance Organizations (HMOs) are prepaid insurance plans that emphasize preventative and self-help care, and usually encourage their insurees to take advantage of self-regulatory techniques such as biofeedback.

Finally, the job-seeker should survey professionals in private practice who might be using biofeedback. They will most commonly include psychologists, psychiatrists, general medical practitioners, and dentists. However, a thorough survey may reveal other health-care professionals who might offer a practice opportunity. If, however, the professional is not a psychologist or psychiatrist, the biofeedback therapist is ethically bound to make arrangements with a licensed psychologist or psychiatrist to provide adequate supervision. This is an easy arrangement to make; once the supervisory relationship is in place, a weekly meeting of 1 or 2 hours to review therapy cases is all that would be necessary.

Possibly, the biofeedback therapist is in a town that does not have a biofeedback practitioner. This is actually an excellent opportunity, because most health-care practitioners are aware of the benefits of biofeedback and would welcome a practitioner into the professional community. Furthermore, a biofeedback therapist can be a financially profitable member of the health-care team. Thus, creating a position in a hospital, clinic, HMO, or private practice is also a strong possibility for the biofeedback therapist.

Summary

The practice of biofeedback is a viable opportunity for involvement in the science of psychology with training at the bachelor's level.

Training opportunities for learning biofeedback skills are available in both formal settings, such as practicums or internships, or informally in workshops and seminars. Combining an academic background in psychology and specialized training in biofeedback, the psychology major is eligible for professional certification to practice biofeedback therapy. This practice can take place in a hospital, clinic, mental-health center, or under the supervision of a psychologist or psychiatrist in private practice. As a biofeedback therapist, the psychology major can enjoy working in the field of psychology as a valuable member of the health-care team and helping others through the practice of psychology.

References

Ethical Principles of Biofeedback. (1985). *Biofeedback-Newsletter of the Biofeedback Society of America*, vol. 13, p. 17.

Suggested Reading

Basmajin, J. V. (1983). *Biofeedback: Principles in practice for clinicians.* Baltimore: Williams & Wilkins.

Fuller, G. D. (1977). *Biofeedback: Methods and principles in clinical practice.* San Francisco: Biofeedback Press.

Hatch, J. P., Fisher, J. G., & Rugh, J. D. (1987). Biofeedback: Studies in clinical efficacy. New York: Plenum Press.

Olton, D. S., & Noonberg, A. R. (1980). *Biofeedback: Clinical applications in behavioral medicine.* Englewood Hills, NJ: Prentice Hall.

Waterman, D., Candy, B., & Peper, E. (1978). *Relaxation: A bibliography.* Denver: Biofeedback Society of America.

Appendix: Areas for Evaluation and Therapy with Biofeedback

A. Stress management

B. Chronic pain management
   1. Headache
      a. muscle contraction (tension)
      b. vascular (migraines)
      c. mixed, combined
   2. Back Pain
   3. Arthritis
   4. Causalgia
   5. Dysmenorrhea
   6. Myofacial pain dysfunction
   7. Nonspecific (diffuse)
   8. Specific (of unknown etiology)

C. Emotional disorders
   1. Anxiety
      a. chronic
      b. acute (panic attacks)
   2. Phobias
   3. Generalized tension (inability to relax)
   4. Impulse control (temper tantrums)
   5. Tics

D. Behavioral control
   1. Substance abuse
   2. Smoking
   3. Weight

E. Neuromuscular disorders
   1. Stroke (spasticity)
   2. Spinal cord injuries (spasticity)
   3. Cerebral palsy (spacticity and/or rigidity)
   4. Parkinson's tremors
   5. Torticollis
   6. Muscle spasms
   7. Tardive dyskinesia

F. Gastrointestinal disorders
   1. Irritable bowel syndrome
   2. Ulcers
   3. Spastic colon

G. Sleep disorders
   1. Insomnia (primary and secondary)
   2. Bruxism

H. Circulatory disorders
   1. Essential hypertension
   2. Cardiac arrhythmias
   3. Raynaud's disease
   4. Premature ventricular contractions

I. Dental disorders
   1. Tempromandibular Joint Dysfunction (TMJ)
   2. Bruxism
   3. Bruxomania

J. Respiratory disorders
   1. Asthma
   2. Hyperventilation

K. Voiding disorders
   1. Enuresis (diurnal)
   2. Encopresis
   3. Vesical sphincter dyssynergia
   4. Urinary retention

L. Speech disorders
   1. Slow reading due to subvocalization
   2. Stuttering
   3. Strained speech syndrome

M. Other
   1. Hyperactivity
   2. Tinnitus
   3. Dermatitis
   4. Blepharospasm
   5. Diabetes
   6. Epilepsy
   7. Writer's cramp
   8. Guilliam-Barre syndrome
   9. Hyperhidrosis
   10. Adjunct to Lamaze prepared childbirth
   11. Adjunct to psychotherapy

Footnotes

1. Biofeedback Society of America, 10200 W. 44th Ave., Suite #304, Wheat Ridge, CO 80033. American Association of Biofeedback Clinicians, 2424 Dempster St., Des Plaines, IL 60016.

Chapter 22

Employment in human service agencies located in rural areas

Frank J. Prerost, Western Illinois University

One factor often overlooked by psychology majors seeking employment in human services is the geographic location of the agency. Students typically concentrate their initial employment searches around urban areas where a high density of human service facilities exists. Unfortunately, this strategy places the baccalaureate in direct competition not only with others with BAs, but also with employment seekers with advanced degrees (Korn & Lewandowski, 1981). This competition puts the baccalaureate at a disadvantage in gaining the attention of prospective employers. Furthermore, the entry-level positions appear to be limited in terms of financial return, job responsibility, and potential for advancement. Since persons with advanced degrees are available in urban areas, agencies can fill a wide variety of professional positions with them. Although new baccalaureates can enter human services, they should expect positions with specific responsibilities, such as hotline worker or child-care worker, and pressure to obtain an advanced degree at the earliest opportunity (Prerost, 1981). Pressure exists on both covert and overt levels as new employees become aware of the tenuous prospects for continued and long-term advancement in human services. Unfortunately, many employees with a BA react to the expectancies of low salary, limited professional challenge, and restricted advancement by avoiding or dropping out of the human service delivery system soon after graduation.

To overcome some of these problems, baccalaureates might consider human service employment in a rural location. This chapter presents the advantages and disadvantages inherent in working at rural human service agencies in order to assist psychology majors in considering alternatives to employment in urban settings. After the relevant variables about rural agencies are presented, a survey is described, detailing hiring preferences among urban and rural agencies.

The human service field has traditionally concerned itself with urban and suburban populations, and seldom with rural communities. The reasons for this focus are related to the increased availability of qualified personnel and financial resources in urban areas (Jeffrey & Reeve, 1978). A greater number and variety of human service agencies have appeared in urban and suburban areas than among rural populations. Johnson (1980) noted that rural America is one of the remaining frontiers for providing psychological services to the populace. Jones, Wagenfeld, and Robin (1976) suggested that a health resource imbalance exists in rural areas due to the high rates of mental disorders, and a shortage of trained personnel and human services.

In the early 1980s U.S. government agencies attempted to reduce any imbalance between services and needs in the human service area. A number of new community mental health centers opened in rural areas together with numerous other human service agencies (Flaskerud & Kviz, 1982). The efforts in the mental health community to increase service to special rural populations led to the dramatic need for personnel to staff new agencies and provide services (Scheidt & Windley, 1982). The trend toward increasing the human services to rural locations opened an avenue of employment for baccalaureates. Seeking employment in the human service field can be expanded into rural settings. Graduates need to be aware of the opportunities in rural America, and of the demands that living and working in a rural setting places on the individual, both professionally and personally.

The rural context

A discussion of rural human service agencies requires a common definition of rurality. The U.S. Census Bureau adopted the concept of a Standard Metropolitan Statistical Area (SMSA) in 1959. An SMSA is defined as a county that contains a city with a population of 50,000 or more inhabitants, as well as adjacent counties that are socially and economically tied to the central city. Areas that do not meet these criteria are considered nonmetropolitan (rural). Farley, Griffiths, Skidmore, and Thackeray (1982) stated that characterizing communities as rural on the basis of population alone is inadequate. They suggested that three perspectives are needed in any conceptualization of rural: (a) ecological, (b) occupational, and (c) sociocultural. The ecological factor refers to the distribution of people and space in the community. Thus, the distance from urban areas must be considered when determining if a town is rural.

The second factor is occupation. Rural locations still have agricultural or nature-related production as a main economic base. Because of this, residents of rural communities are generally attuned to the slow rhythms of nature. The third perspective in a definition of rural is the sociocultural. This construct refers to a variety of descriptions associated with rural life style including conservative, traditional, natural, and independent (Hassinger, 1978; Larson, 1978). The sociocultural factor, combined with the ecological and occupational variables, produces a work environment in rural areas that is distinctly different from the urban human service workplace. Recent baccalaureates seeking employment in rural settings need to evaluate these factors to determine if they are consistent with their work and leisure life-styles.

These factors contributing to the uniqueness of rural communities, produce both positive and negative effects on the baccalaureate willing to pursue employment at rural human service agencies. Awareness of the potential adjustments needed to work professionally at rural facilities can greatly assist the job applicant. How recent graduates present themselves for a job interview at a rural agency can have an effect on obtaining employment.

Ecological factors

A number of writers have presented the advantages of living and working in rural communities. Ginsberg (1978) noted the simplicity of life styles, the security from crime and violence, the lower costs of living, the tranquility, the absence of pollution, the slower pace of life, and the opportunity to work near one's home as important ecological factors for working in rural towns. The rural community's distance from urban settings permits a generally peaceful atmosphere which is absent in highly populated areas.

Because of the smallness of the rural community, an open communication system typically exists. News travels quickly and allows residents to respond readily to information. Positive aspects of such a communication system include the willingness of residents to help one another and be aware of needs that arise among neighbors. Some new community members might initially feel in a "fish bowl" where everyone knows their actions. But a new resident can use the open communication system to personal advantage by integrating oneself into the community system.

The new resident should immediately feel the sense of community prevalent among rural residents. The rural community typically tries to take care of its own members. The isolation and stigma often forced on dysfunctional individuals in urban areas does not exist in the rural community. This sense of community usually requires new residents to demonstrate a willingness to become an active member of the town through involvement in church or social activities (Ordway, 1976).

Although the rural area provides an escape from urban pollution and crime, many new residents feel geographically isolated; the vast open space between rural communities augments this feeling of isolation. Because rural communities are spread out, the human service worker may have to travel over an entire county or cluster of counties. The new human service employee needs to develop creative and innovative ideas to fill the voids during travel between isolated areas. Personal interests, such as stimulating hobbies, can be used to diminish the sense of isolation during off-hours at home.

Occupational factors

The human service worker is in the minority when living in a rural community; the only other professionals may be school personnel and health professionals. Hughes and Clark (1981) have cited the lack of professional contact as a major concern of human service workers. The long distances from major sources of professional contacts, such as universities and conferences, preclude on-going communication with colleagues for support and stimulation. Other limitations include the negligible supervision some human service workers receive (Howe & Wilcox, 1983) and the lack of back-up resources available to the worker (Jerrell, 1983). The human service worker cannot expect to have a large career cohort to provide professional and social support.

To maintain and nurture a professional identity while living in a rural community, the human service worker must seek continuing education opportunities offered by universities, health centers, and professional societies. The employee must be willing to travel and sustain professional contacts outside of the immediate community. With the expansion of human service agencies into rural settings, opportunities for interagency contacts should increase. New human service agencies should be viewed not only as sources of additional services for clients, but also for the potential professional contacts these agencies can furnish.

Sociocultural factors

The new resident of a rural community may be startled by the essentially homogeneous nature of small town settings. Social class differences are less pronounced than in urban areas because the extremes of the social spectrum are not far apart (Rogers & Burdge, 1972). The social solidarity in rural areas is based on similarities of group members' personal interests rather than occupational similarities as in urban settings. The frequency and diversity of social contacts are much less frequent in rural settings. This professional segmentation and limited social contacts result in suspicion of outsiders and resistance when attempts are made to modify current practices.

The adherence to traditional values in rural areas has been confirmed by a number of investigators (e.g., Benson, Hanson, & Canfield, 1982). Holding traditional values influences how the community evaluates and accepts new members. The concern that traditional values may be attacked or disregarded fosters suspicion of new residents; the new resident must defray suspicion to enter the social structure of the rural community. Involvement in highly visible functions approved by the community can diminish the initial barriers of suspicion, and the assimilation process of the new resident can be facilitated

by careful selection of community activities, coupled with a willingness to be open and flexible.

Adjustments to rural agencies

The psychology major seeking employment in the rural human service delivery system should avoid certain pitfalls. First, a new employee should avoid criticizing past practices. The present workers at the agency should be viewed as having superior knowledge about the community. This is also true of persons outside of the agency. In rural areas many therapeutic functions are provided by nonmental health professionals (Jeffrey & Reeve, 1978). These might include lawyers, ministers, probation officers, physicians, school psychologists, or welfare workers. The recently hired employee may be taking away some of the counseling roles of these nonmental health helpers and is often seen as a threat by the person who traditionally provides the needed services. Such helpers are reluctant to give up their counselor roles, and care must be taken not to antagonize these community helpers who enjoy the acceptance of the rural residents.

Second, the new employee must adjust to the slower pace of the rural agency. The new worker must take the time to assess the agency's formal and informal power structure. Since a human service agency is part of the rural milieu, it reflects the slow pace and care for tradition apparent in the overall community.

Third, the new employee must avoid trying to impress colleagues by citing research studies or theories garnered during classroom study. The rural community does not place great value on book learning; personal trust supercedes the issue of competence (Wilkinson, 1980). Thus, the new employee must try to instill trust in coworkers and community clients. Good ideas and therapeutic insights can be rejected unless personal trust has been established. The employee must permit the community to assess him or her before offering suggestions or demonstrating superior knowledge.

Because rural agencies have fewer professionals with advanced training than do urban centers, the recent graduate may feel less intimidated to express ideas for change soon after employment. The new employee should gain acceptance and trust before attempting to initiate change. Initially, social activities with agency coworkers should be stressed. Attending a high school basketball game with a coworker may be more productive than displaying one's knowledge of psychology.

Advantages of rural agencies

Since job satisfaction is engendered by work that is varied, allows for autonomy, is mentally challenging, and expresses personal interests, potential careers in the human service field should be assessed for these criteria (Schultz, 1979). Does human service work in rural locations satisfy the conditions for a rewarding career? Jerrell (1983) stated that the rural human service worker can best be described as a generalist. Since a low supply of mental health professionals with advanced degrees exists in rural America, human service employees are expected to assume a wide variety of responsibilities and professional roles. Rubin, Katz, and Powell (1982) reported that baccalaureates in rural agencies typically have experience with case management, intake interviewing, assessment, counseling individuals, advocacy work, crisis intervention, group work, and consultation. Urban agencies were found to pigeonhole baccalaureates into specialized roles. The generalist approach for rural mental health workers produced a high level of work satisfaction among mental health staff when questioned about their professional duties (Jerrell, 1983).

Rural practice offers widespread opportunities for accepting decision-making responsibilities and gaining exposure to many basic living problems as well as to severe psychopathology. The clients seen by rural human service workers repeatedly show an array of difficulties not seen by individual urban agencies because urban agencies restrict the clients they serve by using some selection criteria. Therefore, the rural worker has the opportunity to experience firsthand involvement with numerous types of problem behavior. Working at a rural agency permits the care giver to follow-up on clients and see the benefits of treatment long after treatment has ceased. This capability adds a further dimension of satisfaction for the worker.

If a psychology major is capable of developing the appropriate outlook, the rural setting can be an attractive alternative to a career at an urban service agency. To achieve success working in the rural human service delivery system, the employee must learn to function in the overall ecological, occupational, and sociocultural framework of the community.

Educational factors influencing hiring

With the increased number of courses available to psychology majors, questions concerning the value of specific courses for career preparation are relevant. Information concerning the value placed on specific course work by employers in the human service field can assist in the selection of electives for the psychology major (Boltuck, Peterson & Murphy, 1980). To obtain information on the factors influencing hiring at human service agencies, I surveyed a sample of facilities servicing either urban or rural locales to determine the extent to which specific courses are beneficial in acquiring entry-level positions at urban and rural human service agencies.

Procedure

One hundred and forty human service agencies serving either urban or rural populations received a questionnaire. The Chicago metropolitan area served as the urban locale for sampling 70 human service facilities. I drew the remaining agencies from agricultural communities with a ceiling population of 30,000. The sample provided a wide range of psychological and related services including diagnostics, individual and group psychotherapy, drug and alcohol rehabilitation, and inpatient care.

In addition, I collected data from 120 junior and senior psychology majors attending a medium-sized university in the Midwest. The student population ranged from ages 20–23. The sample included only upperclass students because I felt employment issues to be most relevant to them.

From the 140 agencies sampled, 111 responded with completed questionnaires (52 urban, 59 rural). The agency director or person in charge of hiring typically completed the survey. The respondents usually held a doctorate or terminal degree in social work. The rural agencies reported a significantly higher percentage of professional staff with terminal BAs than urban facilities. The questionnaire listed 32 psychology courses with brief catalogue descriptions. The respondents rated each course on a 5-point scale indicating importance in preparing students for entry-level employment at the agency: (1) not at all useful, (2) somewhat useful, (3) moderately useful, (4) definitely useful, (5) extremely useful. The list of psychology courses was an exhaustive compilation from a review of Midwestern university catalogues.

In addition to the courses, the agency questionnaire assessed the relative importance of the following when considering the hiring of new entry-level personnel: personal interview, letters of reference, volunteer and practicum experiences, undergraduate course work, workshops and seminars, and reputation of the student's college or university. Respondents used the 5-point scale described above to judge these factors. A sample of students rated the same material indicating the importance of each factor in helping them secure employment at human service agencies.

Results

Review of the ratings completed by personnel from the urban and rural agencies yielded dissimilarities in the perceived importance of undergraduate courses. Mean ratings of courses by the rural group of agencies demonstrated an interest in applicants who have completed coursework in the clinical and gerontological subject areas, namely, aging and old age, abnormal, adjustment, tests and measurements, field practicum, and psychotherapy. The course areas viewed as least beneficial by the rural agencies were statistics, research design, cognitive, learning, industrial/organizational, and motivation.

The most preferred courses for new employees in urban agencies were social, developmental, personality, field practicum, abnormal, and motivation. The courses receiving the lowest ratings were in gerontology, physiological, research design, statistics, industrial/organizational, and perception. Table 22-1 presents the mean ratings of the seven

courses perceived as most useful and the seven courses viewed as least useful in hiring entry-level personnel among urban and rural agencies.

Concerning the factors affecting an applicant's evaluation during the hiring process, both urban and rural agencies rated the personal interview of highest importance and usefulness (urban $M = 4.78$; rural $M = 4.63$). Rural agencies viewed the applicant's coursework as being more important for hiring decisions than did the urban group (rural $M = 4.29$; urban $M = 3.16$). Both groups considered letters of reference from the students' professors to be of minor usefulness in the hiring process (urban $M = 1.98$; rural $M = 2.24$). They rated practicum experiences as useful (urban $M = 3.75$; rural $M = 3.86$), but workshops (urban $M = 2.83$; rural $M = 2.48$) and the academic institution's reputation (urban $M = 2.89$; rural $M = 3.21$) were judged to be of moderate significance.

The mean scores of the student ratings of psychology courses showed a perceived importance of courses reflecting clinical and applied topics. The courses garnering highest ratings were: abnormal ($M = 4.75$); child psychopathology ($M = 4.63$); adjustment ($M = 4.51$); community mental health ($M = 4.33$); and counseling and psychotherapy techniques ($M = 4.39$). The courses with lowest evaluations were aging and gerontology ($M = 1.84$); psychobiology ($M = 1.66$); cognitive ($M = 1.47$); statistics ($M = 1.23$); and research design ($M = 1.15$). Students perceived letters of recommendation to be highly important in the hiring process ($M = 4.46$), as well as school's reputation ($M = 4.23$).

Table 22-1. Mean Ratings of Psychology Courses by Urban and Rural Agencies

| | Rural agencies | | Urban agencies | |
	Course	Mean rating	Course	Mean rating
Most Useful Courses	Old Age/Aging	4.41	Social	4.28
	Abnormal	4.37	Developmental	4.14
	Adjustment	4.19	Personality	4.01
	Tests & Measurement	4.06	Field Practicum	3.96
	Field Practicum	3.91	Abnormal	3.85
	Psychotherapy	3.83	Motivation	3.73
	Community Mental Health	3.71	Learning	3.62
Least Useful Courses	Perception	1.68	Clinical	1.84
	Statistics	1.55	Aging/Gerontology	1.79
	Research Design	1.52	Physiological	1.41
	Cognitive	1.31	Research Design	1.38
	Learning	1.28	Statistics	1.31
	Industrial	1.12	Industrial	1.19
	Motivation	1.08	Perception	1.10

Note: Ratings based on a 5-point scale with 5 equal to *extremely useful.*

Implications

Review of the results suggests that human service agencies in both locales rated psychology courses differently in their importance toward preparation for employment. Rural agencies appear to desire students prepared in specific skill areas related to the practice of psychology. Understanding psychopathology, its assessment and treatment, is the background entry-level employees need when applying at rural agencies. The high ratings given to the psychology of aging by rural facilities may indicate that the elderly are served extensively by these agencies. The rural agency may expect the entry-level employee to assume direct service activities with minimal on-the-job training. A shortage of personnel may be present in rural agencies to provide training and supervision. The new employee at a rural agency may be expected to assume a broad range of duties making practical knowledge and experience critical to employment.

The urban centers evaluated the non-clinically oriented courses as preferred for new employees and rated course background in social, developmental, and personality as useful. This may illustrate the urban agency's desire to train individuals who possess fundamental psychological knowledge for specific direct service functions, and perhaps indicate that urban agencies are more oriented toward training and supervision of new personnel than are rural facilities.

Since both rural and urban agencies placed minor usefulness on statistics and research design courses, minimal understanding of the usefulness of such topics for mental health workers may be present. Students shared the disdain for statistics and research design, rating them as being of minor importance in securing jobs at human service agencies.

Considering the limited number of entry-level positions in the human services, it seems important for academic institutions and students to be aware of the needs and preferences of agencies. Students might also benefit from selecting courses useful for employment in the geographic location of their job search. Because letters of reference from academic instructors are not highly prized as evaluation instruments by employers, students should focus attention on developing interviewing skills, securing practical experiences, and selecting appropriate coursework.

References

Benson, J. A., Hanson, D. P., & Canfield, J. (1982). Rural school psychology: A practitioner's view. *Communiqué, 10,* 1–10.

Boltuck, M., Peterson, T., & Murphy, R. (1980). Preparing undergraduate psychology majors for employment in the human service delivery system. *Teaching of Psychology, 7,* 75–78.

Farley, O. W., Griffiths, K. A., Skidmore, R. A., & Thackeray, M. (1982). *Rural social work practice.* New York: Free Press.

Flaskerud, J. H., & Kviz, F. J. (1982). Resources rural consumers indicate they would use for mental health problems. *Community Mental Health Journal, 18,* 107–119.

Ginsberg, L. (1978). *Social work in rural areas.* Knoxville: University of Tennessee.

Hassinger, E. W. (1978). *The rural component of American society.* Danville, IL: Interstate Printers and Publishers.

Hughes, J. N., & Clark, R. D. (1981). Differences between urban and rural school psychology: Training implications. *Psychology in the Schools, 18,* 191–196.

Howe, H. E., & Wilcox, T. (1983). The effects of increased information on intake decision making in a rural mental health center. *Community Mental Health Journal, 19,* 201–211.

Jeffrey, M. J., & Reeve, R. E. (1978). Community mental health services in rural areas: Some practical issues. *Community Mental Health Journal, 14,* 54–62.

Jerrell, J. M. (1983). Work satisfaction among rural mental health staff. *Community Mental Health Journal, 19,* 187–195.

Johnson, H.W. (1980). *Rural human services.* Itasca, IL: F. E. Peacock.

Jones, J. D., Wagenfeld, M. D., & Rabin, S. S. (1976). A profile of the rural community mental health center. *Community Mental Health Journal, 12,* 176–181.

Korn, J., & Lewandowski, M. (1981). The clinical bias in the career plans of undergraduates and its impact on students and the profession. *Teaching of Psychology, 8,* 149–152.

Larson, O. F. (1978). Values and beliefs of rural people. In T. R. Ford (Ed.). *Rural U.S.A.: Persistance and change* (pp. 91–112). Ames, IA: Iowa State University.

Ordway, J. A. (1976). Transference in a fishbowl: A survey of rural psychiatrists. *Comprehensive Psychiatry, 17,* 209–216.

Prerost, F. J. (1981). Post-graduation educational and occupational choices of psychology undergraduate practicum participants: Issues for the psychology professions. *Teaching of Psychology, 8,* 221–223.

Rogers, E. M., & Burdge, R. J. (1972). *Social change in rural society.* Englewood Cliffs, NJ: Prentice-Hall.

Rubin, A., Katz, A. J., & Powell, K. S. (1982). Mental health service priorities and the BSW. *Community Mental Health Journal, 18,* 159–168.

Scheidt, R. J., & Windley, P. G. (1982). Well-being profiles of small town elderly in differing rural contexts. *Community Mental Health Journal, 18,* 257–267.

Schultz, D. P. (1979). *Psychology in use: An introduction to applied psychology.* New York: Mac-Millan.

Wilkinson, K. P. (1982). Changing rural communities. In P. A. Keller & J. D. Murray (Eds.) *Handbook of rural community mental health* (pp. 20–28). New York: Human Services.

Chapter 23

Building a human service training component into the psychology major

John R. Shack, Loyola University of Chicago

In 1976, Loyola University of Chicago's large and traditional undergraduate Psychology Department developed a career-oriented Applied Psychology Program at its smaller city-center campus. This campus is located in a high density, commercial center of the city and draws a large number of older and working students. The new program was largely directed to an older, returning student population. The program was to be relatively small (80 majors), with an emphasis placed on a personalized approach to students and the experimental development of courses.

The survey

In anticipation of the program, the Psychology Department conducted a mail survey of the Chicago area's human service facilities to examine the market for baccalaureate human service providers. Responses from 150 agencies and institutions in the public and private sector indicated a healthy entry-level job market and provided the following information about personal qualities and experience sought by these employers.

1. Direct experience with the population being served by the respondent and with the particular methods employed in the setting were most desirable.

2. Personal maturity, as manifested in the ability both to work closely and intensely with others and the ability to work independently while accepting supervision, and adaptability to ambiguous and stressful working conditions, were also important.

Some employers, particularly psychologists, preferred for job applicants to have a background in traditional psychology rather than in "how to" or methods courses. Further, some respondents viewed the methods curriculum model to be less academically demanding than the traditional program and therefore popular with students with limited professional growth potential. The majority of respondents assume that their employees will eventually pursue graduate or certificate training. Finally, many of the respondents indicated that the academic setting should be the place where potential social service providers are screened.

The curriculum

The present curriculum of Loyola University's Applied Psychology Program is designed to respond to the needs discerned by our survey. Rather than attempt to provide background and training to meet the particular needs of all the prospective employers, the program's faculty identified knowledge and skill components considered basic to most human services and designed a series of courses to reflect them. The core of the major consists of six required courses, including statistics, research design, a research laboratory course, a structured interpersonal relations course, and an internship. Students are encouraged to balance their major electives between basic theory courses (e.g., developmental, psychology, personality, abnormal, social, physiological) and newly designed courses emphasizing foundation assessment and intervention skills.

The skills training courses are sequenced to build upon one another. The first course,

Interpersonal Relations: An Experiential Approach, systematically leads the student through a series of interpersonal awareness exercises in small groups aimed at increasing awareness of self and others while developing basic skills in listening, confronting, empathic responding, and group dynamics. Following this course, students take Counseling I, a combined counseling theory and basic training course, in which small groups of students work in pairs to systematically develop basic skills in exploring and interpreting the various levels of another's experience together with their own interface experience. Next, students may take two unique advanced skill development courses. Principles of Psychological Assessment seeks to refine the student's ability to discriminate behavior and infer motives from another's behavior and experience for the purpose of generating a useful written report. Skills developed in this course include abstracting themes and patterns from a developmental history, applying clinical inference thinking strategies to different types of psychological assessment devices, and psychological report writing. In Principles of Behavior Change, the student is introduced to methods for assisting others in overcoming resistance to change and learning alternative cognitive and behavioral formulations. This course, in its didactic component, abstracts common behavior change strategies from the various models of psychological intervention. Students subsequently apply these basic strategies, under close supervision, in a peer counseling laboratory.

A fifth skills course, Group Dynamics, allows students practical practice in leading groups with process supervision while they provide leadership for the small group training in the earlier skills courses. Finally, students enter their internship in their last semester before graduation. The internship involves a contract with the site supervisor for supervision and evaluation of the application of skills developed in the skills courses, and includes a career development workshop through which students develop a résumé and career strategy.

Other program dimensions

Additional features of the program include weekly informal faculty and student lunch meetings during which graduate school and career information are discussed. Students publish a newsletter which is sent to students and program alumni to disseminate informa-tion about jobs and special program events. Graduating seniors, who will be entering the job market, collaborate to telephone prospective employers to extend our original survey. Agencies and institutions are asked about current employment needs for our database, and the surveyors gain valuable job-search information at the same time.

Each spring a reunion for all the program's graduates is held. Seniors are also invited to this networking event. An alumni directory of students willing to share information with others from the program is updated yearly. As graduates succeed in their careers, they are invited back to campus to share their experiences with current students. Student volunteers produce these events.

Problems

Program image within the university

In a private university strongly committed to liberal arts, a career-enhancing program is highly suspect. The tendency on the part of the psychology faculty identified with the traditional major was to view the Applied Psychology Program as a vocational school alternative for students who were academically weak. Consequently, such students were often counseled to consider the applied psychology alternative. Actually, because of the personalized style of the program, these students often improve their motivation and performance.

Disparity in maturity and ability levels

Initially, the applied Psychology Program attracted a large number of older, experienced students and the faculty formed the skill courses around the mature abilities of these students. Many younger students, especially those with weaker academic abilities, lacked the quality of conceptual thinking necessary for the social inferential aspects of skills training. Also, the internship sites learned to expect a high level of performance established by the more mature students. With the subsequent influx of less mature students, the program faculty faced a choice of changing program standards, discouraging less able students from transferring into the program, or developing tracking levels within the program. Only the latter alternative was acceptable.

Solutions

The Human Service Skills Competence Certificate

The faculty designed a skills competency certificate program using the existing skill training courses. Each of these six courses, described above, focused on discrete skill dimensions that could be observed and rated by the course instructor. Any student who has previously taken a college-level introductory psychology course can attempt the Certificate. Students pursuing the Certificate indicate their intent at the beginning of each skills course and receive a special packet of information outlining the training expectations. In some courses these students then receive special training attention. At the end of each course, certificate students receive a profile sheet of skill competencies with a narrative explanation for each rating. Students are required to achieve an 85% competency rating average over all six courses to earn assignment to one of the prime internship sites that provide close supervision. An overall 85% competency average for all six courses earns the Certificate.

Certificate objectives

The long range objective of the Certificate course sequence is to establish a standard of basic skill competency for entry-level social service work. Most human services providers have relevant theoretical course work but minimal systematic training and documented direct service competency. Knowledge of theory is not the same as clinical skill. Skills competency in professional preparation is sadly overlooked at all academic levels. The competency certificate concept provides a start in rectifying this problem.

A corollary objective of the Certificate is to provide a personal maturity and interest screening for those planning to directly and professionally influence the development of others. The Certificate courses create a mechanism to improve on the natural selection of career choice for those planning social service careers. A demanding series of evaluation-intense courses, which are rich in self and other confrontation, will serve to help students realistically appraise their strengths in being able to deal directly and intensely with others in a helping role.

It seems most timely to address these basic skills dimensions at the undergraduate level before students disperse to various graduate programs or jobs. The body of preprofessional skills developed in the Certificate sequence should be a foundation for the advanced skills learned in subsequent graduate or on-the-job training.

Primary prevention mental health should be a goal of every applied social science course. Giving away the skills and insights of clinical psychology to the lay person is the most effective way of developing personal and interpersonal strengths. Even if a student only is able to take one course in the sequence, that student should have gained intra- and interpersonal skills necessary for improved psychological functioning.

The fundamental skill components underlying competent human service and how these skills interrelate are not yet fully understood. How individuals best learn these skills is also unclear. An important objective of the Certificate sequence is to conduct ongoing research and evaluation in response to these questions, at both the course and program level.

Finally, continuing efforts will be made to expand the meaning and reputation of the certificate concept in the community. Through professional workshops, consultation to educational establishments and social service agencies, published expositions, textbook material, and videotapes, the certification process and purposes will be advanced.

Chapter 24

Undergraduate preparation for a career in human factors

Daryle Jean Gardner-Bonneau, Kearney State College

The purpose of this chapter is to provide information to college faculty and counselors concerning undergraduate preparation for a career in this field.

For many students, their knowledge of the human factors field is confined to one paragraph in general psychology texts. Beyond that, there are very few references to human factors in most psychology curricula, and few undergraduate courses are offered in this area (Scheirer & Rogers, 1985). This is somewhat ironic since human factors is a growing area, and many of the professionals in the field are psychologists. Human factors provides a viable choice for psychology departments interested in expanding their curricula, particularly if those departments have a strong experimental orientation and exist in an environment where interdisciplinary programs are welcomed.

Although the main purpose of this chapter is to introduce you to an undergraduate program in human factors which currently exists within a psychology department, I would first like to offer a brief overview of the field and some examples of research topics of current interest to human factors professionals.

Overview

Human factors, also known as human-machine systems, engineering psychology, human factors engineering, and ergonomics, as well as a few other names, is a multidisciplinary field which links industrial engineering and psychology and interfaces with architecture, industrial and environmental design, and other engineering specialties. Chiefly concerned with the relationship between human beings and technology, human factors, at-tempts to apply what we know about the way in which humans think, process information, and behave to the design of the products, processes, equipment, and systems people use. As such, this field requires one to be knowledgeable in psychology, but also to have some education in engineering, computer science, mathematics, statistics, and the physical and life sciences.

The goals of human factors are many, including the design of equipment and products to promote their safe use, efficiency and productivity in the work environment, as well as the welfare of the worker. The human factors expert, however, is not necessarily a designer, per se; he or she is involved with discovering the information necessary for the design of a system, product, or process and providing it to the designer. Thus, the human factors expert serves as a designer advocate or ombudsman (Fisher, Bell, & Baum), 1984) with respect to the design process. Additionally, human factors professionals may become involved with product or system evaluation, as well as the development of procedures and instructions for carrying out processes and using products or equipment. Finally, some are concerned with the training of personnel and organizational design and management.

Applications

Human factors specialists work in many settings, and individuals who desire diversity and variety in their work should find this field fascinating.

Since the Three Mile Island (TMI) nuclear power plant incident, there has been a great demand by the public and by the industry for better design of reactor facilities to prevent future incidents of this nature. Operators in nuclear power plants, overloaded and not provided with information in an appropriate manner, nearly failed to avert a major catastrophe. As a result of the TMI incident, human factors professionals have become involved in all phases of nuclear power plant operation, from the training of operators to the design of controls and display and the development of adequate systems for warnings and alerts. Although engineers design the system, human factors professionals provide sound design recommendations based on the knowledge we have concerning information processing, perception, learning and human performance.

Another area of interest to human factors professional concerns the new technology for automated speech recognition. Engineers in the aerospace and aviation industries, in particular, are considering the use of this technology in the design of sophisticated aircraft, but they need to know more about the limitations of the technology and the limitations of the human being. All this requires the expertise of individuals who have knowledge of speech perception, speech recognition, the human capacity for information processing, and the growing technology developments in this area.

Very recently, professionals in the human factors field (Gould & Boies, 1984) tackled a problem for which many athletes at the Los Angeles Olympics were grateful—a problem which serves to show the depth and breadth of the field. All of these athletes need to communicate with their families, friends, and other athletes, despite the language barriers between them. Human factors professionals made this possible, through the design of the Olympic Message System (OMS), which served all the athletes, was simple to operate, and provided the vital communication network necessary. Although the OMS may be considered a product of this research, Gould and Boies were concerned with the process by which this mass communication could be achieved.

Finally, human factors professionals may be concerned with problems relating to everyday products and behaviors. If you have ever had to put together a toy whose package stated "assembly required," you have probably encountered the problem which occurs when a designer who already knows the workings of the toy, writes the instructions for its assembly. Beginning human factors practitioners are hired to devise instructions that match the way humans think in these instructions. The human factors professional may function,

within the same environment, to assure that the toy in question can be safely used by the children for whom it was designed. To a great extent, the sign of good human factors design is the total invisibility of the human factors work. If the product functions properly, safely, and easily, there will be few complaints; the human factors professional has done the job. In summary, human factors is noticed most when it has been excluded from the design process.

Curriculum

This should give you some idea of the scope of the field of human factors, and, hopefully, has further aroused your interest in the field. Now, it would be appropriate to provide you with some information about human factors education in the field of psychology. This information is provided not only for the students, but for the college faculty who might be interested in developing programs in this area and counselors who are advising students with respect to career development.

Ironically, over half of all the members in the Human Factors Society, the primary U.S.-based professional organization for human factors specialists, are psychologists (Knowles, 1985). Yet, most of the undergraduate and graduate degree programs in this area are housed in industrial engineering departments (Pew & Small, 1973). In addition, there has been relatively little attention given by psychologists to undergraduate preparation. As a result, many psychology graduates are placed at a disadvantage when they enter graduate programs in the human factors field.

Pearson (1976) noted that human factors is not industrial engineering; nor is it psychology. Rather, it is an interdisciplinary field. I believe that training should begin at the undergraduate level through an interdisciplinary major developed in either a psychology or an engineering department. Kearney State College has an undergraduate degree program in human factors, and a number of psychology departments at other institutions are considering one. Currently, Wright State University has an interdisciplinary program in human factors housed within the School of Engineering.

The Human Factors Society has wrangled with the problem of what constitutes an appropriate graduate human factors education, and there is some agreement with respect to the content of undergraduate training and preparation, as well. Parsons (1988) noted the student should have a firm background in experimental psychology, particularly in the areas of research methods, sensation and perception, learning, statistics, and human factors. In addition, the student needs to take a number of courses, which will help to provide the tools necessary to work in the field. Among the subject areas involved are mathematics (particularly calculus), physics, computer science, electronics, statistical methods, and technical writing. The development of oral presentation skills is important, as well. Finally, students should try to take some courses in engineering, which relate specifically to human factors, including occupational safety and health, operations research, simulation, environmental and industrial design, quality control, and transportation systems.

At Kearney State College, there were no engineering degree programs, but we were able to substitute material and course work from other areas within the college to develop our interdiscplinary program. An outline of the program is provided in Table 24-1. Our program is not an ideal program, because it lacks a specific engineering component, but many institutions have the resources to develop programs involving engineering.

Programs can also be individually tailored to meet the needs and interests of the student, precisely because the field is diverse and interdisciplinary. At the 1984 annual meeting of the Human Factors Society, I presented a paper with respect to the human factors program at Kearney State College (Gardner, 1984), and the reaction was positive from both psychologists and engineers. If I had to account for this positive reaction, I would say that the quantitative emphasis of this program was the reason. In general, engineers have been skeptical of psychologists working in the field, because many have come unprepared in quantitative areas. They have the knowledge of psychology, but are weak in calculus—a necessary tool for their work—and have not placed enough emphasis on the "hard sciences" (Pearson, 1976).

Another important aspect of human factors education is work experience and research opportunity. Research productivity is encouraged in our program in several ways: (a) All laboratory courses require completion of an independent research project; (b) students must take 3 hours of independent research in either safety or psychology; and (c) the practicum, offered as an elective, requires the completion of a research project in most instances. Students should have the opportunity to work in the field and to conduct applied research at the institution or outside of it in

Table 24-1. Kearney State College Comprehensive Major in Human Factors

Required Courses (47 hours)

PSY 250 – Research Methods
PSY 270 – Experimental Psychology
PSY 372 – Cognitive Psychology
PSY 312 – Sensation and Perception (with Laboratory)
PSY 371 – Environmental Psychology
PSY 410 – Industrial Psychology
PSY 425 – Human Factors and Safety
COMP SCI 109 – FORTRAN Programming
COMP SCI 375 – Operations Research
STAT 375 – Applied Statistics I
STAT 448 – Regression Analysis
MATH 115 – Calculus I w/Analytic Geometry
MATH 202* – Calculus II w/Analytic Geometry
PSY 499 – Research in Psychology
or
SAFETY ED 499 – Individual Research in Safety

Electives (15 hours)

PSY 313 – Physiological Psychology (with Laboratory)
PSY 311 – Human Learning and Memory (with Laboratory)
PSY 499 – Research in Psychology
or
SAFETY ED 499 – Individual Research in Safety
SAFETY ED 435 – Occupational Safety and Health
SAFETY ED 436 – Organization, Administration, and Supervision of Safety Programs
COMP SCI 400 – Computer Simulation
COMP SCI 201 – Assembler Languages
COMP SCI 418 – Advanced FORTRAN
COMP SCI 441* – Artificial Intelligence
STAT 445– Applied Statistics II
IND ED 382 – Applied Electrons
IND ED 483 – Digital Electronics
PHYSICS 426* – Computer Architecture
PHYS ED 360* – Human Anatomy and Kinesiology
PSY 475 – Practicum

Notes: Students are advised to take physics, biology and/or chemistry courses for the 12–hour science component of their general studies program.
* Courses pending formal approval for inclusion in the program.

industry, at research and development centers, or with federal government agencies. Industries are often willing to support students in practicums or internships which can mutually benefit the industry and the student. Such internships also help address another criticism which engineers have of psychologists, that we graduate with little appreciation got "real world" problems and have a lack of experience working in applied settings (Pearson, 1976).

The individual pursuing a career in human factors should be interested in experimental psychology, but should enjoy science and mathematics in general. Many human factors majors at Kearney are students who originally entered the institution in majors other than psychology, some from computer science and some from physical science. The degree program consists of a comprehensive major in human factors, meaning that no minor is required, but many of our students finish with enough hours to achieve a minor in computer science or statistics, along with the major.

Job opportunities

Of importance, naturally, to prospective human factors students are employment opportunities upon graduation. At this point in time, it is difficult for me to provide you with precise information for a number of reasons. First, there are only a handful of undergraduate programs in the field; most human factors professionals have a master's degree at least. (However, it is my understanding that students graduating from the Wright State Program, in engineering, have had no problems finding employment in the field. Second, the KSC program was developed in late 1982 and saw its first graduates in 1986. It is my understanding that, of the seven people graduating thus far, four are pursuing graduate degrees in human factors; the other three are working, but I have no information on the nature of their employment. Thus, the sample size is still too small to accurately assess the potential for immediate employment in the human factors field with the baccalaureate degree.

Nevertheless, I am guardedly optimistic that there will be job opportunities available for students graduating from undergraduate psychology programs such as the one described here. I have received inquiries, in fact, from a number of employers as to the availability of graduates from our program. There may be entry-level positions available in the computer industry in areas such as software development, instruction manual preparation, and workspace design. There may also be entry-level research positions available requiring skills in data analysis, computer programming, and experimental design and execution. For further advancement in the field as a researcher or a practitioner, students should consider obtaining a master's degree. My own advice for students graduating from psychology programs is to consider an interdisciplinary master's degree or one in engineering to acquire the depth and breadth of education needed for more advanced work. The master's degree will open a number of doors that a bachelor's degree will not.

As a human factors professional, particularly one with a master's degree, there are many settings in which the psychologist may work. Human factors professionals are employed by government agencies, such as the Federal Highway Administration and the Consumer Product Safety Commission, as well as the military Private industry also employs human factors professionals; some of the largest employers are IBM, Hewlett-Packard, Boeing, General Dynamics, Lockheed, Westinghouse, AT&T, and Eastman Kodak. Finally, there is the opportunity for private consulting or work with a human factors firm. Completion of the PhD can increase the opportunities available in industry and government, as well as provide the graduate the option of a position in academia. An academic career can offer research and consulting opportunities, as well as the fulfillment gained through teaching.

Human factors is becoming more and more important, as technology development increases. For the psychology student whose desire it is to help others, this field provides great opportunity. Human factors professionals can enhance the quality of work, as well as the quality of many aspects of our lives, and the need for individuals in this discipline should increase along with the complexity of the world in which we live.

References

Fisher, J. D., Bell, P. A., & Baum, A. (1984). *Environmental psychology* (2nd ed.). New York: W. B. Saunders.

Gardner, D. J. (1984). Undergraduate human factors programs: The need, the problems, the outlook. *Proceedings of the Human Factors Society 28th Annual Meeting,* 170–172.

Gould, J. D., & Boies, S. J. (1984). Human factors of the 1984 Olympic message system. *Proceedings of the Human Factors Society 28th Annual Meeting,* 547–551.

Knowles, M. G. (Ed.). (1985). *The Human Factors Society directory and yearbook.* Santa Monica, CA: The Human Factors Society.

Parsons, H. M. (1988). Psychology and modern technology. In Paul J. Woods (Ed.), *Is psychology for them? A guide to undergraduate advising* (pp. 140–144). Washington, DC: American Psychological Association.

Pearson, R. G. (1976, March). *Economics education—Towards the 21st century.* Paper presented at the NATO Symposium on University Curricula for Ergonomics/Human Factors Engineering, Berchtesgaden, Federal Republic of Germany.

Pew, R. W., & Small, A. M. (Eds.). (1973). *Directory of graduate programs in human factors* (2nd ed.). Santa Monica, CA: The Human Factors Society.

Scheirer, C. J., & Rogers, A. M. (1985). *The Undergraduate psychology curriculum: 1984.* Washington, DC: American Psychological Association.

Suggested Reading

Kantowitz, B. H., & Sorkin, R. D. (1983). *Human factors: Understanding people–system relationships.* New York: Wiley.

Sanders, M.S., & McCormick, E. J. (1987). *Human factors in engineering and design.* New York: McGraw-Hill.

Wickens, C. D. (1984). *Engineering psychology and human performance.* Columbus, OH: Charles E. Merrill.

Author's Notes

Colleagues who are interested in developing programs in human factors or counselors interested in more information about this area may contact me at Ohio University, Department of Industrial and Systems Engineering, 278 Stocker Center, Athens, Ohio 45701-2979. Colleagues may also contact Dr. Albert Kai Y. Ton, who serves as the Administrator of the Kearney State College Program.

Chapter 25

Psychology and modern technology

H. McIlvaine Parsons, Essex Corporation, Alexandria, VA

How interested are undergraduate psychology majors in modern technology? More to the point, how interested might they become in what its processes and products do to human behavior (and, in turn, what people do to technology)? Some undergraduates do not like machines, shun them, perhaps even fear them, so they want no part of technology and its human-related problems. They may prefer to study human problems unrelated to technology.

Others to whom machines are not aversive—they might even use computers or Skinner boxes for psychological research—may hold technology in some disdain, perhaps in imitation of their mentors. They think that to engage in technology is not to engage in basic science, in studying behavior in some "pure" state, context-free. Planning ahead, however, some students may wonder where, as new PhDs or MAs, they will find employment if not in nonacademic environments involving modern technology. They may also come to realize that generalizable research may be conducted in such a context and may even be inspired by technology's human-related problems.

Still others may be intrigued primarily by the prospect of investigating human—technology interactions and applying what is known about these. Modern technology, after all, is an important aspect of our lives. If it has not been an important aspect of contemporary psychology, some students may want to help contemporary psychology catch up.

Human factors psychology

A relatively small branch of contemporary psychology has been bringing psychology and technology together, and it is growing. Within the APA, the members of this branch comprise Division 21, Applied Experimental and Engineering Psychology. Most of these are also members of the Human Factors Society, a multidisciplinary organization of about 4,500 men and women with a refereed journal, annual meetings, 17 technical groups, 31 local chapters, and 9 student chapters. Overseas this multidisciplinary field is called *ergonomics.* The International Ergonomics Association is composed of societies in the United States, England, Japan, West Germany, Scandinavia, France, the Netherlands, Poland, Czechoslovakia, and other nations. The growth of the field is worldwide.

That growth has been stimulated in recent years by the increased use of interactive personal computers, which certainly exemplify modern technology. IBM, AT&T, and other companies have expanded their human factors groups, adding psychologists, programmers, and analysts who have become concerned with interactions between computers and end-users, with the performance of programmers, and with the design of commands, error management, and retrieval methods. Thus, human factors psychologists have gone into software, while still pursuing their interests in such hardware-oriented technology as aircraft and spacecraft, radar and sonar, highway and urban transportation, telephonic and radio communications, offices and postal operations, mining and nuclear power plants, and air traffic control and military command and control systems. Although this brand of psychology was largely a product of World War II, it had some roots earlier in printing, in manufacturing, and in highway safety, and today it provides opportunities in nonmilitary as well as military contexts.

As modern technology has become more complex and more information-based, so has human factors psychology (or engineering psychology, as it is frequently called). In its investigations of human capabilities and limitations, emphasis has shifted somewhat from motor skills and perceptual-motor considerations ("knobs and dials") to cognitive performance, that is, verbal and imagerial behavior and covert operations involving attention, memory, transformations, categorization, decision-making, and problem-solving. In applications to real-world problems, continuations of the earlier emphases now reflect technology's increasing complexity. For example, one of the earliest problems, four decades ago, was the design of the altimeter in an aircraft. How should it be designed so the pilot would not misread it and fly his plane into the ground as had too often happened? After the incident at the Three Mile Island nuclear power plant, human factors psychologists asked how the many control room panels in such plants should be designed to prevent operating errors from leading to similar incidents and risks.

With its increasing focus on information processing, human factors psychology as taught in some doctoral programs does not differ too widely from much of contemporary experimental psychology. Since the research in such programs is not likely to be conducted in a particular system or equipment context, its findings are highly generalizable. Outside academia, human factors psychology usually addresses particular human tasks of concern to those who pay the bill or suggests relevance to such tasks in addition to having generality. For example, much research has been devoted to "mental workload." If performance degrades when the mental workload is too great, what are its characteristics? Can methods for measuring mental workload developed in the laboratory be applied in the field? Such challenges enliven this branch of psychology, and a number of scientists working both in universities and in industry or government have risen to them.

Varieties of interests

To the present, human factors psychologists engaging in research have mainly studied human performance with such effectiveness measures as accuracy (error frequency or likelihood) and time (duration, rate, latency, or productivity) to reveal human capabilities and limitations. In applications of such knowledge, they participate in the design of equipment, environments, or computer programs (or even human-machine systems) which allow for the limitations or exploit the capabilities. (In this role a practitioner may be called a human factors engineer.) Human factors psychologists also formulate the procedures that go with the designs and test the outcomes of the designs and procedures. Of course, design engineers and programmers often try, through automation, to eliminate human performance entirely, but some always seems to remain, and it may be even more critical.

Alternatively, human factors psychologists as specialists in training or skill requirements develop training or selection techniques to adapt the operator (or maintainer) to the design. (The work of psychologists who specialize in training or selection often falls under the heading human resources.) They may be somewhat more person-oriented than those who help design and test equipment.

One can understand why performance effectiveness has been the main criterion of desired behavior. It contributes to commercial advantage or military success. Another criterion is safety. Equipment should be designed to make an error-induced accident less likely, certainly an admirable objective. Whether through design or training, human factors psychologists have also tried to reduce stress resulting from technology and to this end have investigated what causes stress. Similarly they have been studying what makes interactive personal computers "unfriendly," either in their software or their hardware design. Some psychologists have been measuring job satisfaction and increasing it by changing the composition or other features of jobs; more of this should be done by improving equipment design or training. Perhaps future psychologists will give increased attention to emotional variables and attempt to make performance more enjoyable as well as more effective.

Another prospect is for human factors psychologists to determine how to incorporate incentives for using equipment or software in its design or to exclude deterrents that induce an individual to forego its use. Such motivational variables have become especially important in commercial systems. Human factors psychologists investigate information feedback but seldom motivational feedback, positive or aversive. Such inquiry may appeal to students interested in operant psychology. They might also become intrigued with the training side of human factors psychology and the new technology that has evolved to support training and education including training and education required for modern technology.

Users of modern technology's processes and products often function in an organization—a business, a school, a government agency, a factory. Formal or informal social interactions are influenced by technology, although organizational and social psychologists have only occasionally studied its influence, and human factors psychologists even less often. The advocates of such research need recruits who have some orientation toward social or organizational psychology and are lured by human-machine systems.

To those interested in language (linguistics, verbal behavior), human factors psychology offers opportunities to become involved in new ventures in artificial intelligence called expert or knowledge-based systems. These systems are human-dependent and call for natural language interfaces, human knowledge extraction, and human-related reasoning—all matters that human factors psychologists have begun to investigate. Others are studying speech recognition and synthesis by machines, a development with vast potential.

Investigative techniques

What are the investigative techniques human factors psychologists use? Experimentation takes place in laboratories or in field settings, or in some mix of each. Experimental outcomes may be attributable to some human-machine combination or to the human only; the latter, of course, may be more generalizable and thus more in the mode of basic research. Some experiments can be extremely complex when they deal with an entire simulated system or major component. Some probe alternative display designs, environmental effects (noise, heat), skill requirements, maintenance procedures, or training techniques. Experiments that investigate interactive computing may assess how end-users differ, which menu design is superior, or what commands are most likely to cause errors.

Another investigative technique is direct observation of the operation or maintenance of a system or equipment or indirect observation through interview or questionnaire. Results may be incorporated in a computer model that can be manipulated to suggest what human-machine performance would become if some aspect of the system or equipment were changed, or if a somewhat similar system were developed. The more abstract the model, the more it can be generalized to suggest human performance in any related technological context. Predicting human behavior is a challenge.

Application

As an integral part of system or machine development, a human factors psychologist functioning as a human factors engineer performs task descriptions and analyses, which are essentially verbal simulations listing each action each operator takes or should take, the equipment or software used, the time required, and perhaps the error probability. This is a down-to-earth record of performance that guides design, procedure development, and training. If it seems an obvious requirement, there was a time when it did not.

Though such detailed description is a relatively mundane undertaking, obtaining the data for it is one of many activities that brings the human factors psychologist into contact with members of other disciplines who are primary data sources, and that requires intensive and detailed understanding of the equipment, software, environment, or system being examined. The time and error estimations add to the challenge. Of still greater interest is the need to help designers create or improve their products for human use and to help trainers optimize their instruction techniques and simulations. Such help consists of originating or altering design or training concepts and presenting recommendations or requirements frequently or continuously as team members. Though outcomes may not always be ideal, much satisfaction comes from the inclusion of human factors considerations in final products or processes.

For human factors psychologists conducting research, intrinsic reward takes the form of experimental findings and observational or survey data. Such findings or data may be directly applicable to some design or training problem, especially if they are obtained in the test and evaluation phase in system or component development or in the initial, conceptual phase to guide further development. Other findings or data may be more heuristic in nature, helping to establish principles or guidelines for future designs and techniques or simply extending knowledge about human behavior, especially human performance in the context of modern technology. A truly impressive amount of research by human factors psychologists is presented at a considerable number of technical meetings each year or published in technical reports and journals such as *Human Factors, Ergonomics, Applied Ergonomics, Behaviour and Information Technology, International Journal of Man-Machine Studies*, and the *Journal of Applied Psychology.* Many human factors psychologists are both investigators and practitioners. Applications work may call for some ad hoc research or consist of on-the-job or independent consultation.

Working with other disciplines

With what other disciplines does the human factors psychologist associate? Within engineering the psychologist comes into contact with industrial, electrical and electronic, and mechanical engineering for the most part, as well as aeronautical, civil, automotive, and manufacturing engineering. Human factors in computers ("software psychology") is taught in departments of computer science, and the human factors psychologist can expect to work with programmers, analysts, and computer scientists in studying end-user performance, programming, and artificial intelligence. Some human factors psychologists have become involved in environmental design, which brings them together with architects, interior designers, office designers, naval architects, acousticians, illumination engineers, and heating, ventilating, and air conditioning (HVAC) engineers. Those involved in consumer products will associate with industrial designers. Psychologists facing problems in anthropometry, biomechanics, and stress will collaborate with physical anthropologists, medical doctors, and physiologists. Individuals concerned with techniques of training may work with training specialists and educational psychologists. Organizational and personnel considerations may bring contact with industrial/organizational psychologists. Clearly, anyone entering human factors psychology should expect to collaborate to some degree with other disciplines, the extent being greater in applications than in research.

Effective collaboration is a skill. Many engineers, designers, and architects still have to be apprised of the value of human factors psychology, and psychologists must learn some of their technical jargon and methods. Fortunately, human factors research and application have received increasing acceptance, even respect, in the scientific and engineering community. For example, advertisements for IBM and General Motors have appeared in many major periodicals favorably mentioning human factors programs. Job vacancies have appeared in increasing number in the *Human Factors Society Bulletin*.

Preparing for a career in human factors

However, this surge of popularity does not mean that any undergraduate major in psychology can get a job in human factors psychology upon graduation. Some training in human factors or related work is a prerequisite but as yet undergraduate programs in this brand of psychology are rarities. A program established by Jefferson M. Koonce flourishes at the Air Force Academy. Another, at Kearney State College, is described by Gardner (1988); one hopes her lead will be widely followed. Wright State University has had an undergraduate human factors program (created by an engineering psychologist, Malcolm L. Ritchie) in its College of Engineering, and John G. Kreifeldt of Tufts University developed a program in the School of Engineering Design. A number of industrial engineering departments have undergraduate courses in human factors.

At the entry level, an undergraduate degree in psychology with substantial engineering or data processing may be acceptable to employers for some jobs, and an engineering degree may make employment a certainty. But due to the knowledge and skill needed, employers are likely to expect at least a master's degree for a person who will do applications work and additional graduate study for one who will engage in research. In short, graduate work is advisable, if not essential, whether in industry or business, consulting organizations, government laboratories, procurement agencies, or academia.

The aspiring undergraduate needs to know (a) the probable salary level of a job, (b) what to study as an undergraduate, and (c) where to get graduate training. Some courses will be particularly helpful to lay a skills foundation, in addition to or in conjunction with a psychology major. With respect to methodology, one should (a) learn to write (and speak) lucidly and succinctly; (b) be introduced to statistics (descriptive and inferential and perhaps calculus); (c) become fairly competent in computer programming in one or two languages; and (d) be instructed at an introductory level, at least, in research methods, such as experimental design and survey techniques. With respect to subject matter, the student should (a) take a course in human physiology or physiological psychology; (b) emphasize the study of the human senses and perception, learning, perceptual-motor skills, and cognitive processes; (c) acquire some familiarity with electronics and mechanics (physics could be a prerequisite), probably by venturing into the university's engineering school; and (d) study language semantics and structure, perhaps in introductory linguistics.

As indicated earlier, psychology courses in operant and social or organizational psychology may also be beneficial. Although human factors (or engineering) psychology is sometimes subsumed under industrial/organizational, it is a distinct discipline; a major in industrial/organizational might be appropriate only if the student gets the wider exposure indicated. In the absence of a human factors program in an undergraduate school, a student might be able to take some graduate courses in human factors if available. For example, seniors enroll in human factors graduate courses at California State University, Northridge.

Students face a more complex problem in proceeding to graduate training. Educational requirements differ between master's and doctoral levels. In a master's degree program, students' interests, capabilities, and aspirations may point them toward equipment and system design applications as practitioners in human factors engineering. Or, they may point students toward becoming practitioners in training or some related field such as job performance aids. In the first instance, students will want to take some engineering or computer science-related courses, perhaps in a human factors engineering program, in addition to advanced psychology and methodology courses. More of these human factors programs are now found in departments of industrial engineering; some are developing in other engineering departments and in departments of computer science. In the second instance, students may wish to place more emphasis on courses in human learning, cognition, and motivation, as well as computer software (e.g., for computer-assisted instruction and graphics).

For the doctoral degree, prospective human factors psychologists should be aware that opinion has been somewhat divided as to the most appropriate curriculum and, hence, the most favorable locations. Because human factors (engineering) psychology was started essentially by experimental psychologists who learned their specialty on the job, this progression is still feasible if not especially desirable from one current viewpoint. From another viewpoint, doctoral students should study engineering psychology in addition to experimental psychology, in an engineering psychology program or at least in an experimental psychology program which includes substantial engineering psychology emphasis.

From a third perspective, students should mix engineering (and computer science) and psychology coursework, regardless of an earlier concentration on psychology or engineering or computer science.

Surveys of graduate programs in human factors are compiled in a directory every few years (e.g., 1985 and 1988) by the Human Factors Society (Santa Monica, CA) and information is also collected by Division 21 of the APA. Such data can be obtained by University advisers or by students themselves. The APA also publishes a "Salaries in Psychology" every odd year which indicates what psychologists in various fields have been earning (medians, means, and distributions). The most recent edition appeared in 1987.

References

Gardner-Bonneau, D. J. (1988). Undergraduate preparation for a career in human factors. In Paul J. Woods (Ed.), *Is Psychology for them? A guide to undergraduate advising* (pp. 135–139). Washington, DC: American Psychological Association.

Pion, G., & Bramblett, P. (1985). *Salaries in psychology*. Washington, DC: American Psychological Association.

Suggested Readings

Kantowitz, B. H., & Sorkin, R. D. (1983). *Human factors*. New York: Wiley.

Parsons, H. M. (1976). Psychology for engineering and technology. In P. J. Woods (Ed.), *Career opportunities for psychologists: Expanding and emerging areas* (pp. 180–193). Washington, DC: American Psychological Association.

Parsons, H. M. (1984). Engineering psychology. In R. J. Corsini (Ed.), *Encyclopedia of psychology* (pp. 436–440). New York: Wiley.

Sanders, M.S., & McCormick, E. J. (1987). *Human factors in engineering and design*. (6th ed.) New York: McGraw-Hill.

Wickens, C. D. (1984). *Engineering psychology and human performance*. Columbus, OH: Charles E. Merrill.

Author's Notes

As a former president of Division 21 of the American Psychological Association (Applied Experimental and Engineering Psychology) and of the Human Factors Society, the author will welcome inquiries from faculty, counselors, or students addressed to him at the Essex Corporation, 333 North Fairfax Street, Alexandria, Virginia 22314. Information about Division 21 (as well as about this field of psychology) may be sought from its president, Dr. Michael A. Strub, 3309 Craigo, El Paso, Texas 29904.

Chapter 26

A survey of graduates from a psychology technician certificate program

Carol J. Erdwins, George Mason University

For a number of years, popular wisdom has held that the baccalaureate in psychology, along with most other liberal arts majors, is a poor career choice for anyone interested in finding well-paid employment after graduation. Several surveys of graduates reported in *The Psychology Major: Training and Employment Strategies* (Davis, 1979; Titley, 1979; Walsh, 1979; Woods, 1979) shed some factual light upon this matter and gave a somewhat more positive picture. The majority of graduates who sought work after obtaining their degrees found employment, and, over a period of several years, there may be considerable upward mobility in the kinds of positions held (Titley, 1979). At the same time it was also apparent that many graduates leave psychology either by taking jobs in other fields or by pursuing further training in other professions. For those who seek human service or paraprofessional positions, other data (Erdwins, 1980) indicated that these jobs frequently combine challenging and very responsible duties with a minimum of opportunity for career advancement. While people employed in these positions may report job satisfaction, they often do not view them as long-term career options.

The survey reported here focuses on a more specialized population of graduates, those who completed both a psychology major and psychology technician certificate program during their undergraduate education at George Mason University (GMU). The technician sequence includes fairly traditional academic courses in personality theory, abnormal and developmental psychology as well as skills-oriented courses in therapeutic communication, group dynamics, and behavior modification. In addition, there is a two-semester practicum placement in which students work one day a week in a community human service agency. This sequence was initiated by the GMU Psychology Department in an attempt to broaden the training offered to our undergraduates with course work that could be more readily translated into the human service job market. At the same time, the certificate program is seen as an adjunct to the psychology major, with the certificate being awarded only upon completion of the baccalaureate.

The sample

My research assistant and I surveyed psychology graduates from GMU in spring 1984. Of the 40 individuals who completed both the psychology major and technician sequence since its inception in 1978, we contacted 33 graduates, or 83%. Telephone interviews with each individual determined the jobs held since graduation and the duties, salary, and promotion opportunities involved in each one. A 7-point rating scale assessed satisfaction with job duties, salary, and relevance of the technician courses to their work tasks. Information was also obtained about any graduate training undertaken.

This sample included 30 women and 3 men with an average age of 33.1 years. While this group is representative of the 40 graduates, the respondents are older and more predominately woman than GMU's psychology majors in general. A number of re-entry female students elect to take the certificate program, which probably indicates both their greater motivation in completing the requirements for the major and certificate and their greater focus on acquiring specific job skills.

Career activities

While 20, or 61%, of these respondents held at least one paraprofessional or human service position since graduation, only 30% were employed in a paraprofessional position at the time of the survey. Thirty-six percent were currently working in other fields, and 15% had already completed a graduate degree and were now employed in professional positions in mental health programs. Four of the respondents, or 12% of the sample, were unemployed and attending graduate school, and two had just finished their graduate degrees and were seeking employment.

Paraprofessional and other employment

A total of 26 paraprofessional positions had been held by the respondents since graduation; however, almost half of these (42%) were part-time. Table 26-1 gives a summary of the job activities and client populations involved; these statistics appear to be fairly consistent with the findings of previous surveys on the characteristics of paraprofessional positions (Bartels & Tyler, 1975; Erdwins, 1980; Erdwins & Mendelsohn, 1979).

The work activities involved in all but two of these positions were rated as *slightly* to *extremely satisfying* with an average rating of 5.78 on the 7-point scale. The mean salary per year for the 15 full-time positions was $15,266; the hourly wage for the part-time positions was $6.24. The average rating of the paraprofessionals' satisfaction with these salaries was 3.14 (*slightly dissatisfied*). Forty percent of the positions provided no opportunity for promotion, while for another 35% only one promotion would be possible. This is consistent with the findings of the surveys cited previously.

Of the graduates employed in other fields, 83% held full-time positions in business and management. The reasons most often given for choosing their jobs reflect a focus on extrinsic considerations such as availability, higher salary, and convenient location, rather than on the actual duties. The average rating of satisfaction with their work activities was *neutral* to *slightly satisfied* (4.67), and their satisfaction with salary was very similar (4.33). The average yearly salary for the full-time positions was $19,600.

Although comparisons should be taken as extremely tentative because of the small sample size, *t* tests between the paraprofessional and business and management groups revealed significantly higher satisfaction with work activities on the part of the paraprofessionals ($t(33) = 2.58, p < .02$) with a trend toward significantly greater full-time salaries ($t(23) = 1.74, p < .10$) and satisfaction with salary ($t(31) = 1.73, p < .10$) for the individuals employed in other fields.

One third of the respondents also reported working as a volunteer on a regular basis, averaging approximately 6 hours per week. In all cases, this work was in the mental health field and, for the most part, involved direct work with clients, although two individuals were serving on the boards of community service organizations. All but two of the volunteers were employed as paraprofessionals.

Graduate school

More than half (52%) of the respondents were attending or had already completed graduate school. The majority of these continued in various areas of the mental health field, including counseling (24%), clinical psychology (24%), and social work (29%); and the remainder were all in related fields such as adult education, school psychology, and occupational therapy. The reasons given for pursuing a graduate degree centered around two themes: (a) There are more and better-paying positions available to persons with graduate baccalaureate degrees in the mental health field, and (b) the work that interested the individuals required advanced training.

Table 26-1. Characteristics of the Paraprofessional Positions

Job activities	%*	Client age group	%*	Diagnostic populations	%*
Individual counseling	88%	Child	12%	Neurotic	58%
Group counseling	77%	Adolescent	54%	Psychotic	35%
Family counseling	27%	Adult	54%	Antisocial	54%
Interviewing	81%	Elderly	19%	Drug/alcohol abuse	54%
Custodial care	54%			Mentally retarded	27%
Psychological testing	11%				

* Percentages > 100 because of multiple activities and client populations.

Relevance of the psychology technician program

The respondents rated the usefulness of the psychology technician sequence to their careers including both employment and graduate school. As one might expect, those employed as paraprofessionals found the courses fairly helpful (a mean rating of 6.16 on the 7-point scale). Surprisingly, the respondents employed in other fields gave an equally high rating (6.17), and those in graduate school rated the courses as even slightly more useful in their pursuit of a graduate degree (6.59). In each case, at least 75% of the respondents mentioned the therapeutic communication skills course as having been particularly valuable.

Beyond this similarity, differences appeared. About 75% of paraprofessionals felt the practicum experience had been helpful to them, while abnormal psychology, personality theory, and the practicum provided useful preparation for graduate school. Individuals employed in business and other fields listed considerably fewer specific courses, which suggests that while they may have positive feelings about the program, the coursework is probably less specifically applicable to their work.

Seventy-five percent of those with graduate training felt that the psychology technician sequence influenced their decision to pursue a higher degree. Their spontaneous comments most often reflected the theme of gaining self-confidence; the courses and practicum in particular gave them the opportunity to find that they enjoyed and could succeed at this type of endeavor.

Summary and discussion

The paraprofessional positions held by the respondents are very similar to those described in previous surveys. They usually involved direct client contact with an adolescent or adult population within the context of individual or group therapy or interviewing and information-gathering, as opposed to psychological testing. Thus, there appears to be considerable overlap between the activities of these paraprofessionals and their professionally trained colleagues. Divergence appears in the salary level and opportunity for advancement in the paraprofessional positions. In addition, many paraprofessional positions involve some custodial care of clients such as providing transportation and helping with meal preparation. While these paraprofessionals reported considerable satisfaction with their jobs, they were less satisfied with their prospects for advancement and frequent job changes.

An investigation of the individual career paths of these paraprofessionals yields some additional information. Only three left the mental health field entirely. The remainder moved into one of three paths: (a) better-paid full-time paraprofessional employment, (b) a combination of paraprofessional work and graduate school, or (c) full-time graduate study. Coupled with their volunteer work in mental health, this suggests that most of these individuals have made a long-term commitment to the mental health field. They view their paraprofessional employment as a phase in their career development rather than as a permanent occupation.

These data also suggest that an individual's priorities play a large part in shaping his or her career. The graduates working in other fields and voicing an original preference for a position in the mental health or human service area, pointed to pragmatic concerns such as availability of positions and salary levels as reasons for taking their jobs. Conversely, those in paraprofessional positions appear to place more weight on the intrinsic aspects of their work such as satisfaction derived from their duties. While they are not particularly satisfied with their salaries, they may be more willing to put this aspect of the job in a secondary position temporarily.

Ratings and spontaneous comments of the graduates indicated that the majority of the respondents were positive about the psychology technician program and felt it offered useful career training, even though some of them were not in the mental health field. Therapeutic Communication Skills, the course most frequently cited as having been useful, focuses on the development of constructive nonverbal attending behaviors, Rogerian or active listening, and the use of open-ended questions. While course work provides future paraprofessionals with the opportunity to develop and test their capabilities, it may also provide graduates who take jobs in other fields with the sense of being better equipped to deal with the variety of people with whom their jobs bring them into contact.

References

Bartels, B., & Tyler, D. (1975). Paraprofessionals in the community mental health center. *Professional Psychology, 6,* 442–452.

Davis, J. (1979). Where did they all go? A job survey of BA graduates. In P. J. Woods (Ed.), *The psychology major: Training and employment strategies* (pp. 110–114). Washington, DC: American Psychological Association.

Erdwins, C. (1980). Psychology majors in the paraprofessional role. *Professional Psychology, 11,* 106–112.

Erdwins, C., & Mendelsohn, M. (1979). A survey of paraprofessional positions in human service settings. In P. J. Woods (Ed.), *The psychology major: Training and employment strategies* (pp. 81–86). Washington, DC: American Psychological Association.

Titley, R. (1979). Whatever happened to the class of '67? Psychology baccalaureate holders one, five, and ten years after graduation. In P. J. Woods (Ed.), *The psychology major: Training and employment strategies* (pp. 103–109). Washington, DC: American Psychological Association.

Walsh, J. (1979). A Montana perspective on vocational opportunities. In P. J. Woods (Ed.), *The psychology major: Training and employment strategies* (pp. 115–119). Washington, DC: American Psychological Association.

Woods, P. J. (1979). Employment following two different undergraduate programs in psychology. In P. J. Woods (Ed.), *The psychology major: Training and employment strategies* (pp. 120–125). Washington, DC: American Psychological Association.

Chapter 27

Employment of bachelor's-level psychology technicians in the Veterans Administration

Edward J. Jordan, Jr, Veterans Administration Medical Center, Washington, DC

Psychology Services in the Veterans Administration (VA) employs persons with bachelor's degrees primarily under the position title *psychology technician*.[1] VA's hiring standards specify that psychology technicians must possess "a bachelor's degree from an accredited college or university with a major in an appropriate social or biological science, which included or was supplemented by 12 semester hours in psychology." The psychology technician must have "a practical understanding of some of the general principles, theories, methods, and techniques of psychology" but not the grounding in theory and the ability to apply it to practical problems which are expected of psychologists. The technician must know enough of the principles of psychology to be able to carry out effectively a plan devised by a psychologist in areas such as psychodiagnostic testing, behavior modification, or psychological research. Psychology technicians always work under the supervision of staff psychologists.

Baccalaureates are eligible for promotion each year for the first few years of employment, according to VA standards. The basic level is GS–5, which as of January, 1987, starts at $14,822 yearly. With additional years of experience, advancement is possible up to a career ceiling of GS–9, which starts at $22,458 (January, 1985).[2] Such advancement is only permitted, not mandated. Many psychology technicians remain at lower grades, principally because of the nature of their duties and their degree of responsibility on the job.

In qualifying for a psychology technician position, an applicant may substitute graduate education in psychology for the above-mentioned experience. One year of graduate education brings eligibility for GS–7, and 2 years brings eligibility for GS–9. This makes it possible for master's-degree holders to fill psychology technician positions by virtue of education for which baccalaureates are also eligible by virtue of experience. A multitude of local factors will determine, in any particular circumstance, whether education or experience will prevail.

Procedure

The psychology technician positions discussed above are located in the 172 health facilities nationwide, which are administered by the VA's Department of Medicine and Surgery. Thus, the most direct way of ascertaining job possibilities for psychology majors was to survey chief psychologists in these facilities about their hiring and utilization practices. Three questions were posed in this survey: (a) How many bachelor's-level psychology technicians do you employ? (b) What kind of work do they do?; and (c) What are the prospects for increase or decreases in their number? This was a repetition of the survey taken in 1977 (Jordan, 1979).

As in 1977, the survey was limited to those VA facilities whose Psychology Services reported having psychology technicians in the VA publication, *Psychology Staffing and Services*. The 1984 edition of this publication indicates 124 such VA facilities. A survey letter was sent to the chief psychologist at each of these facilities. Four facilities listed as having technicians did not in fact have them. Fifty-two written responses were returned, and the remaining responses were obtained by telephone. In all, 119 VA health facilities participated in the survey, an increase from 73 participating facilities in the 1977 poll.

How many bachelor's-level technicians are there?

Of the 119 facilities reporting, 62 (52%) stated that they had people with no higher than a bachelor's degree working as psychology technicians. These 62 facilities employed a total of 111 bachelor's-level individuals. Although a few of the positions represented were part-time, the majority were full-time. The 111 bachelor's-level technicians comprise about 43% of the 259.3 total full-time equivalent positions identified as psychology technicians in *Psychology Staffing and Services*.[3]

What kind of work do bachelor's-level technicians do?

Psychology technicians who are baccalaureates provide a wide range of services to patients and staff. By far the most frequently mentioned activity was psychodiagnostic testing. This activity was mentioned as a major aspect of work for 75 out of the 111 bachelor's-level technicians, almost 68% of the total. This includes a variety of cognitive, intelligence, and personality tests, as well as neuropsychological and vocational testing. Neuropsychological testing is the largest subgroup within the cluster of testing activities. It contains 31 individuals, 41% of the cluster, and 28% of all bachelor's-level technicians.

A second cluster of activities involved treatment or behavior change procedures, including biofeedback and various behavior modification techniques. This was mentioned as a principal activity 47 times or in 42% of the total group.

In 21 cases the predominant activity of the bachelor's-level technician was research. This is almost 29% of the total group. These positions tend much more than in other clusters of activities to be supported by outside grants and to be temporary in nature.

Still another grouping of relatively homogeneous activities among bachelor's-level technician was in the area of clerical and administrative support work. Included here are activities such as gathering program evaluation data, supervising equipment management, and a variety of paperwork duties. This was mentioned as a prominent type of activity 16 times or in 14% of the total. There was also a more diffuse cluster of activities involving administration of patients (as distinct from administration of supplies, equipment, or staff) in activities like vocational placement, outreach and follow-up, rehabilitation case management, and intake work. Twenty-six bachelor's-level technicians, or 23%, were represented in this grouping.[4]

Trends for the future

The third survey question, which concerned projections into the future, was purposely made very broad in order to best detect the overall chances of hiring at the bachelor's level. A 3-category analysis was used: (a) a *positive* response was one indicating that the chief psychologist employed bachelor's-level technicians and was willing and able to hire more; (b) a *negative* response indicated that the chief either employed no baccalaureates and had no plans to do so or that, whether employing them or not, he or she disliked the idea; and (c) a *neutral* response referred to situations in which a chief was neither for nor against the idea, employed bachelor's-level technicians but saw little likelihood of hiring more in the near future.

Responses to the third question were: 18% positive, 29% negative, and 43% neutral. Between one fifth and one sixth of VA chief psychologists were in a position to employ psychology majors directly from undergraduate school and would take advantage of that capability. A larger, though still small, number of VA psychology chiefs take a position in strong opposition to bachelor's-level technicians or, in some cases, to any technicians at all. The largest group of VA psychology chiefs were constrained by budgetary considerations from hiring technicians but accepted the idea of baccalaureates working for them.

Discussion

At the time of this survey, 111 psychology technicians holding only bachelor's degrees worked for the VA Department of Medicine and Surgery. This is almost exactly the number estimated in the (1977) survey. This is also about 42% of the approximately 260 full-time-equivalent (FTEE) positions occupied by all psychology technicians. Forty-two percent is a high estimate because the 111 total includes some part-time employees and would be lower if expressed as FTEE, the way the total number of technicians is expressed. Granting that the percentage of bachelor's-level personnel among all technicians would shrink if all terms were expressed as FTEE, it is still not conceivable that it would shrink below the approximate one third estimated in the 1977 survey. It is clear, then, that bachelor's-level psychology technicians still have substantial representation in VA Psychology Services.

When it comes to actual duties, 68% of all bachelor's-level psychology technicians are reported to have psychodiagnostic work as a principal activity. The comparable figure in 1977 was 60%. Although these figures are close to each other and might suggest a slight increase, there may in fact be fewer, not more, bachelor's-level technicians now administering testing exclusively. The survey reported here asked how many technicians administer testing as *an* important activity rather than as *the most* important, as in the 1977 survey. This change of emphasis may have added to the total a few technicians who are doing other important types of work and would not have reported psychodiagnostic work as their *most* important duty in the 1977 survey. Some loss of comparability between the two surveys in this regard seemed more than offset by the gain in information from categorizing in this new way. In any event, it can be safely stated that new graduates entering psychology technician positions in the VA most likely engage in psychodiagnostic work of a more or less traditional nature.

The fact that at least one third of VA psychology technicians have only a bachelor's degree should not be taken to imply across-the-board acceptance of a terminal BA. Acceptance of the baccalaureate varies from one VA health facility to another. Psychology chiefs' (usually the hiring authorities) reactions to baccalaureate candidates differ greatly—from delight at the prospect of training technicians to disappointment for their lack of preparation. However, there is general agreement that the education received in an undergraduate psychology program is not adequate preparation for the psychology technician's job, except rare cases where an academic institution has a program specifically designed for such preparation, usually as a result of close geographical proximity to a VA medical center. Technicians are encouraged to obtain more education while on the job, although this is done on a strictly informal basis, as the VA has no formal program to provide funds for this purpose. Often supervisors have provided influential recommendations for graduate school admission; and technicians have been able to qualify for master's, and even doctoral degrees, while continuing to work part-time.

Another factor clouding interpretation of the responses to the third survey question is the intrusion of attitudes about hiring psychology technicians at any academic level. Some chief psychologists prefer to hire only doctoral-level employees. Such attitudes effected the survey results by making rejection of bachelor's-level applicants part of a wider rejection. Although the effect is not large, confining the survey to facilities already employing psychology technicians did not automatically eliminate such wholesale disinclination toward technicians, because in several situations the technicians employed were holdovers from a previous regime and reflected the values of a departed chief rather than those of the present incumbent.

Despite the appearance of some possible decline from 1977 to the present in prospects for baccalaureates, the current graduate may find greater employment possibilities than are indicated in this survey in the near future. With considerable local and national pressure on personnel budgets in VA, many chiefs expressed that this may result in pressure to substitute technicians for staff psychologists as vacancies occur. This has apparently happened already in some facilities. At least one federal government initiative of this sort aims to reduce the number of employees from grade GS—11 to grade GS—15, the very range in which all VA staff psychologist positions occur. While the number of psychology technicians is inherently limited by the number of staff psychologists available to supervise their work, considerable expansion might be possible in many settings before that limit was reached.

Judging from this survey, the best advice for the new psychology baccalaureate is "Get more education." Opportunities for such applicants exist, but they are stable at best and may in fact be declining. It remains to be seen whether the possible decline could be overcome by an overall increase in hiring of psychology technicians.

References

Jordan, E. J., Jr. (1979). Trends in employment of psychology technicians in the Veterans Administration. In P. J. Woods (Ed.), *The psychology major: Training and employment strategies* (pp. 87–93). Washington, DC: American Psychological Association.

Nightingale, E. J. (Ed.). (1985). *Directory of psychology staffing and services in Veterans Administration medical centers, medical and regional office centers, domiciliary, outpatient clinics and regional offices with outpatient clinics* (4th ed.). (Not for circulation, Veterans Administration, Washington, DC).

Author's Notes

The author would like to express his deep appreciation to the 119 VA Chief Psychologists and designates who gave the time and effort necessary to complete this survey. Thanks also go to Dana Moore of VA Central Office and to Ann Wauben and Paula Thames, Personnel Service, VA Medical Center, Washington, DC, for their helpful suggestions and the access they provided to technical documents.

Footnotes

1. Psychology majors are sometimes employed by VA Psychology Services as *rehabilitation technicians.* These positions are not examined in this report since they do not require the baccalaureate, and they are typically filled by persons with less education. The bulk of the rehabilitation technicians do not seem to be employed in psychology services.
2. Federal salaries in the General Schedule (GS) are set yearly by presidential initiative with congressional concurrence or modification. Rates are based on such factors as change in the cost of living, comparability with similar positions in the private sector, and federal budget considerations. While confident prediction is not possible, the recent trend has been toward smaller increases yearly.
3. A change in the manner of reporting employment in *Psychology Staffing and Services* from number of people to full-time equivalent employees (FTEE) obscures the meaning of this percentage. The actual number of psychology technicians is somewhat larger than 259.3 because of part-time positions, and the percentage is therefore somewhat lower. The 1977 finding that bachelor's-level technicians made up about one-third of the total is probably not much changed by these new data.
4. The percentages given here total more than 100% because many technicians carry out activities in more than one cluster. The intent is to reflect all major components of the bachelor's-level technician's work.

Chapter 28

The psychology major as preparation for legal studies and the legal profession

Elizabeth V. Swenson, John Carroll University

The psychology major rarely appears on lists of the most popular prelegal undergraduate majors (Astin, 1984). In contrast, a recent assessment of the career paths of bachelor of science psychology majors of the past 15 years at John Carroll University revealed that 13% eventually found themselves in law school. Colleagues at other schools have noted similar findings. This raises the issues of (a) the conceptual relationship between the undergraduate psychology major and legal studies, and (b) the practical implications of this relationship for the student. These issues will be addressed in this chapter.

Of the surveyed psychology major-law students, approximately three fourths had waited several years after graduation from college to begin their legal studies. For the psychology major who had not immediately begun law school upon graduation, one evolution of this career direction was far more common than others. The typical graduate took an entry-level job providing direct service in a human services or a government agency. After the initial adjustment to and enthusiasm for the job had worn thin, the future began to look less promising. Because a number of baccalaureate psychology students often find their first jobs as probation officers, welfare caseworkers, institutional child caretakers, and psychiatric aides, many of their initial clients' personal concerns are inextricably related to their legal problems (Swenson, 1983). These include a number of possible legal entanglements: an abusive parent or spouse, trouble with the police, complex financial arrangements, welfare payments, and drug addiction. The frustration at being unable to effectively deal with or change the seemingly hopeless combination of life circumstances and bureaucratic red tape facing the client led many

graduates to consider the legal profession. Here they found what they believed would be the solution to their ineffectiveness: to be an advocate for the client with legal problems and, perhaps, to change the system in the process. Many psychology majors, consequently, are initially drawn to areas of law that deal with family issues, the juvenile justice system, and the rights of mental patients and the otherwise handicapped. Whether they remain in these areas after graduating from law school has yet to be determined.

Relevance of psychology to the study of law

A psychology major gives the student a unique empirical perspective on law. To study law is to study human behavior. " . . . law is preoccupied with human behavior and its implications." (ABA, 1980, p. 118) But the legal perspective focuses on logic, ethics, and precedent. The student of psychology should immediately recognize that speculation about behavior, particularly common in legal questions of intent and the prediction of future behavior, presents far from the total picture. Legal theories and legal decisions frequently contain statements about human behavior that should be empirically based but are not. In addition, psychology majors have the skills to be particularly critical of the law's attributions of causal relationships. Thus a behavioral science background adds a richness of thought to legal studies through the empirical perspective that the student cannot obtain in law school.

Psychology majors have a special insight as well into areas of substantive law. Mental health law, criminal law, and family law all involve areas where the relevant evidence is based on psychology. Without studying psychology, one's critical understanding of the specific legal arguments in these areas may be superficial. "An enormous range of legal issues requires information from the social and behavioral sciences for its intelligent resolutions" (ABA, 1980, p. 119).

The late legal scholar Karl N. Llewellyn (Vanderbilt, 1981, p. 31) listed the skills he felt a student should acquire through prelegal education.

• To read and write well

• To use a library

• To evaluate opinion and evidence both qualitatively and quantitatively

• To size up people

Although these skills were outlined in 1931, their relevance for legal study has not changed. They are integral parts of the psychology major, as well. Ideally, reading, writing, using the library, and evaluating qualitatively develop out of liberal education in general. Undergraduate psychology focuses more specifically on quantitative evaluation and the "sizing up" of people.

In addition to the above skills, the ability to analyze factual situations in a logical and concise manner is essential for legal studies. Students who have opportunities to write research results in APA style receive excellent training in writing a step-by-step analysis. In fact, more exposure to research-oriented courses and experiences as an undergraduate should improve one's abilities to write, analyze systematically, and evaluate quantitatively.

Additional relevance to legal practice

In the same ways the psychology major prepares students for legal study it also prepares them for legal practice. Vanderbilt (1981, p. 18) describes the lawyer's job as dealing with the interaction of rules of law, facts, and persons. Consider how similar this is to a description of the psychology major as the study of theory (rules of law), empirical results (facts), and individual differences (persons). The analogy is a very close one.

One final skill acquirable through the psychology major that is essential in the practice of law is counseling. The ability to put oneself

in another person's frame of reference is of the utmost importance in interviewing clients and witnesses and in negotiation and arbitration. Although it is possible to take such a course in law school, it will be at the expense of more substantive courses, and probably not taught by anyone trained in counseling, much less by a psychologist. Counseling skills do not help the student get through law school, but are extremely useful in dealing with clients in the years beyond.

Recommendations

For the psychology major who is considering a career in law there are only a few specific recommendations I would make for courses to take within the major itself. It is important to take several experimental psychology and statistics courses, if they are available, and to obtain as much research and writing experience as possible. A course in counseling is very useful in the practice of law. A course in social psychology will alert the student to aspects of the legal system such as jury dynamics, eyewitness testimony, and plea bargaining in which new psychological discoveries are rapidly being made. Courses that give a knowledge of abnormal behavior, psychological tests, and mental health institutions are important because these subjects crop up frequently in substantive legal issues, and a psychology major will be expected to be able to deal with them.

In choosing courses to supplement the major, students should carefully read Appendix B, The Statement on Prelegal Education, in Law Schools and Professional Education by the American Bar Association (1980). The ABA recommends that prelegal studies educate the student for: (a) comprehension and expression in words, (b) critical understanding of human institutions and values, and 8c) creative power in thinking. To accomplish these goals several course areas are suggested as possibilities, with a note that they are not necessarily the best courses to take.

Drawing heavily on the ABA suggestions, I recommend the following courses to supplement the psychology major. Some of these may be general distribution or specific requirements at a particular college or university.

• Writing and public speaking courses
It is important in many careers, if not most, to write and speak well. In law it is essential.

• Argumentation and debate
This course will help students understand

the importance of being able to frame arguments, to back up these arguments with evidence, and to think under pressure.

- Western political thought and the history of Western civilization
  These courses will enable the student to put legal thought and our legal system into a broad historical perspective.

- Philosophy courses in logic and ethics
  These are fundamental to legal thought.

- Introductory physics and biology
  A well-educated person should be in touch with developments in science and technology. These basic courses will make it possible to read the more serious popular literature and interview some technical witnesses. The rigorous thinking involved in science courses is also important.

- American politics and international relations
  These put the judicial system into a context of current political structures.

- Introduction to micro- and macroeconomics
  Economic issues pervade nearly every area of law. Along with economics, statistics courses are also important, but psychology majors will have had these in the major.

- Basic accounting
  This is fundamental to most courses dealing with business law.

- Any computer language course will help the student master computerized legal research

The student should also appreciate how difficult it is to apply old legal theories to the problems presented by the new technologies.

The courses in economics, accounting, computers, and statistics form the foundation for further study in areas of business. They add marketability to the undergraduate major in psychology, even for students going into human services areas.

Many schools offer law courses: criminal law, constitutional law, family law, business law. Because broad education is so important in studying law, it is probably a waste of time to take courses that will be repeated in law school. One such course, however, would be beneficial for the student who is not familiar with the format of judicial opinions and wishes an additional indication of whether the study of law is of interest.

References

American Bar Association. (1980). *Law schools and professional education. Chicago: Author.*

Astin, A. W. (1984). Prelaw students—A national profile. *Journal of Legal Education, 34,* 73–85.

Swenson, E. V. (1983). Incorporating law into the undergraduate psychology curriculum. *Teaching of Psychology, 10,* 119–120.

Vanderbilt, III, A. T. (1981), *Law school: Briefing for a legal education.* New York: Penguin.

PART 6

Issues of interest to specific groups

Chapter 29

Career issues and problems for women

Patricia W. Lunneborg, University of Washington

The special worries of psychology majors as they settle uneasily in the Undergraduate Advisory Office at the University of Washington to talk about careers guided the choice of topics for this chapter.

A lifespan approach is vital

Job interviewers very often ask, "What do you see yourself doing 5 years from now? 10 years from now?" They want to know whether the candidate has a long-range outlook and well-thought out and realistic career goals. To be able to answer these questions is good enough motivation for adopting a lifespan approach to a career, but here are two more from a long list of compelling reasons.

Experts in career development are clear about the importance of challenge in one's first job after graduation. The consequences over a lifetime of settling for less than a challenging first job are horrendous. Female psychology baccalaureates should not panic and be tempted by a first job offer, unless they can explain to their college advisers how it really is an invaluable opportunity.

Many women in psychology plan to interrupt their careers for childrearing. There are all kinds of patterns for doing this, but the patterns found to lead to greater personal satisfaction and greater career success involve postponing marriage and childrearing as long as possible.

Personal and social barriers to career development

A common personal barrier among women because of sex-role socialization is math anxiety. Perhaps even worse is mechanical reasoning terror. As a consequence, the required statistics course in psychology is dreaded, postponed, and not enjoyed. Ditto the college mathematics necessary to enter many graduate fields.

Female psychology majors bring along with them another potential problem. They have an overwhelming interest in social service occupations and very low interest in technical occupations. Thus, female graduates compete with one another for scarce and low-paying social service and education positions, while male graduates seek employment in broader areas. Men apply psychology more often in technical jobs such as computer programmer, systems analyst, and human factors engineer.

As for economic barriers, one can safely say that every salary study has found that among psychology graduates at all levels, women earn less than men. Psychology is no different from the rest of the work world as far as the earnings gap is concerned. Within psychology one finds the same disproportionate lack of women at higher-level occupations. For example, in higher education, female psychologists continue to be concentrated in the lower, untenured, instructor and assistant professor ranks, men in the higher, tenured professorial ranks. And as a result of their overriding interest in helping others, the areas within psychology to which women gravitate are counseling, clinical, developmental, and educational psychology, while they are underrepresented in physiological, experimental, industrial, and measurement psychology.

Strategies for overcoming these barriers

Here is a list of supplementary courses with which every woman should graduate:

- business administration, management, marketing, law, finance

- technical writing, business communications

- accounting, statistics, mathematics

- computer programming, data processing, and

- public speaking.

Women cannot fall back on the excuse of sex-discrimination in hiring if they lack qualifications.

Students can further boost their self-confidence by using all available resources: assertiveness training at the counseling center, a math anxiety workshop, noncredit time management course, a political organization in need of fund-raising chair, the student chapter of a professional organization in search of new members. Working steadily on overcoming socialized barriers to career development is as important as any academic course.

A way to handle women's traditional channeling into education and social service jobs is for them to seriously consider the jobs male psychology baccalaureates apply for in science, technology, and sales. Science and technology will involve no more curriculum shifting than the courses listed above, and selling is learned on the job.

Female baccalaureates are already turning from social service to organizational careers because, quite simply, the bulk of jobs for all college graduates exist in business. However, two powerful tendencies to beware of are the shunting of women to low, dead end, clerical positions and the lack of promotions for women. Overcoming these tendencies requires assertiveness, mentors and sponsors, a supportive network of other women, and visibility—visible achievements, visible leadership.

A student can demonstrate leadership by taking responsibility within some college organization and coordinating and completing that group's projects. The best extracurricular activities for women are those that develop teamwork and leadership skills.

What can women do about the earnings gap? Get an advanced degree. A graduate degree means more money, prestige, freedom to quit and move on, promotions, and respect. There are many advanced degrees besides those in psychology that are appropriate for psychology majors. In the past, fewer women than men have gone on to graduate school in psychology. One reason is that women tend to underestimate their abilities and have lower self-confidence. Male psychology majors are not more intelligent than female majors: however, when you believe you can accomplish more, you do.

Finally, the areas of greatest opportunity for women going on to graduate school within psychology are those areas where women are underrepresented. To compete in these areas, women must take courses and do research that will be attractive to selection committees in animal experimental, quantitative, industrial, sensation and perception, and physiological psychology.

Knowing the world of work in relation to themselves

Some self-knowledge is necessary to face the world of work and prepare résumés, research companies and organizations, and sell oneself in interviews. Ask students if they know their

- strongest and weakest vocational interests

- top work values, both intrinsic, such as self-expression and recognition, and extrinsic, such as salary and a desk of their own

- transferable job skills gained from college courses

- transferable high-level skills from lowly part-time, summer jobs

- personality traits that are work strengths, and

- environmental needs at work such as commuting distance and support staff.

How many women make a habit of browsing around their campus Placement Center? Most centers have workshops and classes devoted to self-knowledge, as well as means for practicing interviews.

A plan of action

What employers want to be especially sure of in women is that they do not have a short term orientation, that is, I plan to do such and such until I get married, or until my husband finishes school, or until I have children. If they need help in setting immediate, short-term, intermediate, long-range, and far-future goals, the adviser should provide it.

You can help students by asking them the following questions for sometime in the future, perhaps 5 years from now.

• Where will you be geographically?

• What are your most likely work activities?

• What will your living arrangement be?

• How much income per year will you be making?

• What will be your major source of day-to-day satisfaction?

Author's Notes

This chapter is a miniversion of *To Work—A Guide for Women College Graduates* written by P. W. Lunneborg and V. M. Wilson and published by Prentice-Hall.

Chapter 30

Women in psychology: Who are they, and where are they going?

Diana M. Zuckerman, U.S. House of Representatives, Subcommittee on Human Resources and Intergovernmental Relations, Washington, DC

For many years, university researchers have depended on their female students' willingness to participate in psychology experiments. Young women enrolled in psychology courses have been used to study perception, achievement motivation, conformity, attitude change, cognitive ability, self-esteem— everything possible, it seems, except the abilities, values, and other traits that are unique to them as future female psychologists.

The number of women in psychology graduate programs, like those in other professional fields, has escalated dramatically during the last 20 years. At some colleges, careers in male-dominated fields such as medicine, law, and journalism have replaced teaching and other traditional careers as women's most popular career choices. Although the number of women who aspire to careers in psychology remains modest compared to many other professions, the proportion of students obtaining degrees in psychology who are women has increased substantially for every subfield. Between 1920 and 1972, approximately one fifth of psychology graduate students were women, ranging from less than 5% in industrial and organizational psychology to almost half of the students in developmental psychology (Vetter & Babco, 1984). In contrast, almost half of the students in most psychology graduate programs are now women, and women represent one third of the students in industrial/organizational psychology and two thirds of the students in developmental psychology. These statistics are presented in Table 30-1. This trend follows the increase of women among baccalaureates in psychology; in 1973–1974 the proportion of female baccalaureates exceeded 50% for the first time, and by 1981–1982 nearly two thirds of the bachelor's degrees in psychology were awarded to women (Vetter & Babco, 1984).

Ironically, very little research has been conducted to determine what type of men and women are attracted to careers in psychology. Although many studies have focused on women's changing aspirations during the past decade, there are no published studies on the women who become psychologists. However, in 1981 I conducted a study of 9,000 college students, which included a small number of senior-year women who planned to become psychologists. This chapter will describe the results of a substudy, which compared women who aspire to careers in psychology with those aspiring to careers in other professions, in terms of their family backgrounds, career motivations, self-concepts and self-esteem, and experiences with stress. I will also discuss the role of women who have already completed their degrees in psychology.

The study

Questionnaires were mailed to 1200 second-semester senior women from the class of 1981 at seven very selective liberal arts colleges. Students who did not complete the questionnaire were urged to do so in follow-up letters, phone calls, or personal reminders by dormitory counselors. Two thirds of the women who received questionnaires completed them.

In this chapter, I will discuss only the 428 women who comprised the following career categories: students aspiring to careers in psychology ($n = 24$), careers in business ($n = 99$), careers in writing and communications ($n = 85$), and careers in science ($n = 38$); students who planned to attain doctorates in other fields ($n = 99$); students who majored in psychology or sociology who aspired to careers in law ($n = 24$) or medicine ($n = 25$); and

Table 30-1. Doctorates Awarded in Psychology from 1920 to 1973 and in 1983 by Subfield of Doctorate and Sex

Subfield	1920–1972			1983		
	Total	Women	% W	Total	Women	% W
Psychology subtotal	26,383	5,530	21.0	3,307	1,572	47.5
Clinical Psychology	6,764	1,533	22.7	1,209	572	47.3
Counseling	1,270	272	21.4	432	199	46.1
Developmental Psychology[1]	941	439	46.7	219	148	67.6
Educational Psychology	1,629	376	23.1	153	74	48.4
School Psychology[2]	393	111	28.2	121	72	59.5
Exper. Comparative Physiological Psy.[3]	3,076	415	13.5			
Experimental Psychology[3]	3,042	513	16.9	209	81	38.8
Comparative Psychology[3]	173	25	14.5	11	4	36.4
Physiological Psychology[3]	888	152	17.1	94	27	28.7
Human Engineering[4]	34	0	0.0			
Industrial & Organizational Pers. Psych.[5]	775	38	4.9	90	30	33.3
Personality Psychology[2]	447	112	25.1	32	9	28.1
Psychometrics	344	44	12.8	10	8	80.0
Social Psychology	1,945	423	21.7	191	103	53.9
Cognitive Psychology[6]				65	31	47.7
Quantitative Psychology[6]				14	4	28.6
Psychology, General[7]	4,100	941	23.0	287	130	45.3
Psychology, Other[7]	562	136	24.2	170	80	47.1

Note: 1 = "Developmental" and "Gerontological" until 1983; 2 = added in 1960; 3 = Experimental, Comparative, and Physiological Psychology were broken out into three separate fields in 1962; 4 = dropped in 1962, included now with Psychology, Other; 5 = "Industrial and Personnel" until 1983; 6 = added in 1983; 7 = subfields were not specified until FY1958. Except for a few cases in earlier years, all doctorates were included in the "general" classification of their respective fields. Adapted from Vetter and Babco (1984) by permission.

students who were completely undecided about a career ($n = 38$).

The questionnaires took approximately 30 minutes to complete and focused on life goals, family background, career motivations, experiences with and responses to stress, self-esteem, and self-concepts.

Goals

Two questions assessed goals: (a) the highest degree that the woman planned to attain, and (b) the career she wanted to pursue.

Family background

The questionnaire contained questions about age, race, marital status, religious upbringing, birth order, number of siblings, type of high school attended (coed vs. single sex; public vs. private), parents' countries of origin, parents' educational attainment and occupations, mother's employment status (homemaker vs. work force) when the respondent was growing up, and parents' current marital status.

Career values

The questionnaire included 17 questions regarding the importance of materialistic, altruistic, and other considerations when selecting a career. Students rated each item on a 4-point scale ranging from *not important* to *essential*. The items were factor analyzed and four patterns of values emerged: helping (the opportunity to help others, work with people, work for social change, and express one's own values); prestige and security (desire for high income, status, a secure and stable future, and concern about the availability of jobs); challenge and autonomy (the desire for intellectual challenge, freedom from supervision, and the opportunity to be creative and exercise initiative); and fewer demands (interest in a job with low pressure and stress, fewer training requirements, reasonable work hours, and a flexible time schedule).

Stress

I asked students to measure how stressful each of the following areas had been in their life during the last month: school work, family, intimate relationships, friends, living conditions, money, physical health, and mental health. Students rated each area of stress on a 10-point scale or stated that the area was *not applicable* to their situation.

I assessed responses to stress by the Habits of Nervous Tension scale, which was developed by Thomas (1971). This scale consists of a checklist of 26 possible responses to stress, such as loss of appetite, nausea, or insomnia. Responses were analyzed in terms of three stress reaction patterns: depression, anxiety, and expressed anger.

Self-esteem and self-concepts

Self-acceptance was assessed by the Rosenberg Self-Esteem scale (Rosenberg, 1968). The Rosenberg scale consists of 10 statements, such as, "On the whole, I am satisfied with myself," or "All in all, I am inclined to feel that I am a failure." For each statement, the student responded on a 4-point scale ranging from *strongly agree* to *strongly disagree.*

Interpersonal self-confidence was assessed by the Texas Social Behavior Inventory (Helmreich & Stapp, 1974). This inventory consists of 16 statements, such as, "Other people look up to me," or "I am not likely to speak to people until they speak to me." For each statement, the student responds on a 5-point scale ranging from *very characteristic of me* to *not at all characteristic of me.*

I measured self-concepts by 23 questions describing abilities and personality traits. For each item, students rated themselves on that trait on a 5-point scale ranging from *among the highest 10%* at their school to *among the lowest 10%* at their school. When factor analyzed, these descriptions produced eight self-concepts: achievement-oriented (persevering and driven to achieve); artistic/creative (artistic ability and originality); attractive (physically attractive and popular with the opposite sex); interpersonally oriented (cheerful, understanding, and popular with members of the same sex); independent (self-sufficient and able to cope with stress); leadership and public speaking ability; math and science ability; and scholarly (intellectual curiosity and academic ability).

Because of the small number of future female psychologists and the very uneven number of women in the different career groups, multivariate statistical methods could not be used. Instead, chi-square analyses and *t* tests were used to compare future psychologists with women in other career groups.

Results

Family background

Before comparing the future psychologists to their classmates, it is important to describe what all the women were like. Students' descriptions of their parents' educational attainment show that most of the women in all the career groups enjoyed high socioeconomic status. More than half of the fathers and almost one third of the mothers have graduate degrees. Virtually all of the students are single; 86% are white, 5% are Asian, and 5% are Black. Most describe their religious background as Protestant (36%) or Catholic (27%); 17% are Jewish, and 12% report no religious upbringing. Almost one fourth have at least one foreign-born parent. Two thirds have mothers who are currently employed, and 75% report that their mothers were employed when they were growing up.

The women who want to become psychologists do not significantly differ from their classmates on any of the family background traits that were measured, except birth order. Only 13% of the future psychologists are last-born children, compared to 32% of their classmates ($x^2 = 4.16$. $p < .05$). This difference is accounted for by the larger proportion of middle-born children among future female psychologists (46%, compared to 27% of their classmates).

Career values

Most of the students in the study express considerable interest in finding a career that is interesting and intellectually challenging, where they can help people, work with people, and express their creativity and ethical standards. In contrast, high income, status, low-stress work environments, and shorter training requirements are much less important to them.

However, the women who aspire to careers in psychology describe their career motivations differently than the other students. Compared to most of their classmates, future psychologists are more motivated by the desire to be helpful. They rate the helping motivations as significantly more important than students who aspire to careers in business ($p < .0001$), science ($p < .0001$), writing and communications ($p < .001$), and other doctoral level fields ($p < .001$), as well as the students who are undecided about a career ($p + .001$). They rate the prestige and security motivations as marginally more important than students aspiring to doctorates in other fields ($p < .09$) and significantly less important than do students aspiring to careers in business ($p < .01$). Future psychologists do not differ significantly from their classmates on whether they are interested in less demanding jobs or jobs that offer greater challenge and autonomy. In addition, the future psychologists rate their motivations as rather similar to those women who aspire to careers in law or medicine, whether or not the latter majored in psychology.

Stress

Most of the students report moderate or high stress in the areas of life that were included in the questionnaire. The women who want to be psychologists are highest of all career groups on the stress that they report from intimate relationships. Their score of 6.9 (on a scale ranging from 1–10) is significantly higher than future businesswomen (5.7, $p < .05$) and writers (5.5, $p < .05$), and marginally higher than future scientists (5.4, $p < .07$) and women aspiring to doctorates in other fields (5.7, $p < .06$). They also report moderate stress related to school work (6.5). This is not as high as future lawyers (8.0, $p < .05$), but is comparable to students aspiring to doctorates in other fields (7.3), future scientists (6.5), businesswomen (6.4), physicians (6.3), and women who are undecided (6.6).

On the Habits of Nervous Tension scale, future psychologists report somewhat different responses to stress than do their classmates. They are most likely to report symptoms of anxiety than future physicians ($p < .01$) or future businesswomen ($p < .06$).

Self-concepts and self-esteem

The women who want to be psychologists do not differ from other students in terms of their feelings of self-acceptance, as measured by the Rosenberg scale or their interpersonal self-confidence, as measured by the Texas social behavior inventory. However, they do differ in their other self-descriptions. The women who want to be psychologists rate themselves higher than any of the other career groups on their interpersonal-orientation (cheerful, popular with women, and greater understanding of others). They are significantly higher on this self-concept than future scientists ($p < .001$), students aspiring to doctorates in other fields ($p < .05$), and students who are undecided about their career goals ($p < .01$) and marginally higher than future lawyers ($p < .08$). They rate themselves significantly lower on math and science ability than the future physicians ($p < .001$) and significantly lower on leadership and public speaking ability than future businesswomen ($p < .02$) and future lawyers ($p < .05$). Future psychologists rate themselves similarly to their classmates on the five other self-concepts (achievement-oriented, artistic and creative, attractive, scholarly, and self-sufficient and able to cope with stress).

Implications for psychology

The number of women who aspire to careers in psychology in this sample was unexpectedly small, given that a large proportion of students major in psychology at the seven colleges participating in the study. This modest number of future female psychologists makes it difficult to interpret the results of the study, because the sample is too small to analyze with more precise and sophisticated statistical analyses. Therefore, the results should be interpreted with caution.

This survey implies that women from these colleges are not especially attracted to careers in psychology. Of the approximately 3% of the women in the sample who hope to enter the field, some will probably not be accepted into graduate schools and others will not finish their graduate degrees. Of course, some women interested in other careers may later decide to become psychologists, but it seems likely that fewer than 24 women from this sample will actually become psychologists. I do not know whether or not the small number of women from these colleges who aspire to careers in psychology reflects a national trend. However, these colleges are of particular importance because 6 of the 7 schools ranked in the top 25 colleges and universities, in terms of the numbers and percentage of alumnae who obtained doctorates in the social sciences between 1920–1973 (Tidball & Kistiakowsky, 1976).

Of course, the apparent declining interest in psychology among these alumnae may reflect changes in the kinds of students these schools attract, or the decline could be seen as an appropriate response to the scarcity of academic jobs in the field. When we look at the statistics for the country as a whole, we see an almost steady decrease in the number of bachelor's degrees in psychology, from 52,256 in 1973–1974 to 41,031 in 1981–1982 (Vetter & Babco, 1984). However, the number of women receiving these degrees has been maintained at approximately 26,500 each year since 1973–1974. Moreover, the number of master's degrees and doctorates has remained stable during those years for both men and women. These results suggest that in the coming years there may be less competition for graduate programs, although not necessarily less competition for jobs.

The results indicate that future female psychologists do not differ greatly from their classmates in terms of family background and generally positive feelings about themselves. However, there are some very dramatic and interesting differences in self-concepts, career values, and experiences with stress. The women who aspire to careers in psychology are more altruistic and people-oriented and report somewhat greater concerns with stress in their intimate relationships. Compared to most of their classmates, they describe themselves as more cheerful, understanding, and popular with women. They also report lower math and science ability than premedical students, and lower leadership and public speaking ability than future businesswomen and lawyers. Compared to future businesswomen and lawyers, future psychologists are more likely to report that they respond to stress with symptoms of anxiety. However, this latter difference could reflect either stronger anxiety reactions or greater awareness of anxiety.

Although the women who want to be psychologists are in many ways very similar to their classmates, there is a consistent pattern indicating that future psychologists tend to emphasize interpersonal relationships in their values, self-concepts, and worries. In these respects they are quite similar to students majoring in the social sciences who aspire to medical or law careers and consistently different from students aspiring to scientific careers or doctorates in other fields. In future research, it would be interesting to study whether middle-born birth order has influenced these interpersonal attitudes, skills, and concerns.

Despite the competition they will face in gaining acceptance into graduate programs and finding jobs and the stresses they will experience in their careers, future female psychologists do not see themselves as especially academically gifted, self-sufficient, or able to cope with stress. However, the women in this study who aspire to careers in psychology are being compared primarily to women who aspire to other high-status professions.

Overall, it is discouraging that so few women aspire to careers in psychology, but encouraging that the women who want to be psychologists report altruistic values and a positive self-concept in terms of their abilities to interact well with others. In most respects, they are not noticeably more emotionally distressed than their classmates, despite some of the negative stereotypes of psychologists. In addition, the self-described traits of future female psychologists seem quite appropriate for their chosen profession.

The future

What kinds of jobs await these women? The most recent available statistics show that women are still a minority in psychology, especially in faculty positions and higher paying jobs. In a study of members of the APA conducted in 1979, 91% of the men and 75% of the women holding doctorates in psychology were employed full time in the labor force (Russo, Olmedo, Stapp, & Fulcher, 1981). In addition, 84% of the men and 63% of the women with master's degrees were employed full time (Russo et al., 1981). These employment statistics apparently do not reflect choice; the women are more likely to be looking for jobs than the men. Minority women are more likely to be employed full time than are white women. There are similar differences among men from different ethnic groups.

Women who are employed tend to work in somewhat different settings than the men (Russo et al., 1981). At the doctoral level, women are more likely to work in schools and other educational settings that do not include colleges and universities, whereas men are more likely to work in business or government settings. At the master's degree level, women are more likely to teach at universities than men, but are again less likely to work in business or government.

Since half of all APA doctoral members obtained their degrees in the 1970s, the difference in postdoctoral work experiences of the men and women was only 2.3 years. As expected, differences in years of postgraduate experience led to income differences between the male and female psychologists. However, even when one takes into account the number of years since graduation and the types of employment settings, the men earn more than the women. This is true among those with master's degrees as well as those with doctorates. The gap between men's and women's salaries was greater than the gap between white and Black psychologists' salaries. However, among minorities, the female psychologists earn more than the male psychologists.

In academia, women are especially underrepresented in faculties of graduate departments in psychology: Only 23% of these faculty were women in 1983–1984 (Vetter & Babco, 1984). In all programs, women are less likely to be tenured, more likely to have lower academic rank, and more likely to have part-time appointments (Russo et al., 1981).

These sex differences in income and faculty positions are similar to those found in other fields, but that is scant comfort for those women who are the victims of discrimination in their employment as psychologists. The rapid entry of women into the field of psychology during the last decade has not yet been felt at all academic and professional levels. It is likely that sex differences will narrow as more women enter the positions where they make the decisions regarding salary and tenure for other psychologists.

References

Helmreich, R., & Stapp, J. (1974). Short forms of the Texas social behavior inventory (TSBI), an objective measure of self-esteem. *Bulletin of the Psychonomic Society, 4,* 473–475.

Rosenberg, M. (1968). *Society and the adolescent self-image.* Princeton, NJ: Princeton University.

Russo, N. F., Olmedo, E. L., Stapp, J., & Fulcher, R. (1981). Women and minorities in psychology. *American Psychologist, 36,* 1315–1363.

Thomas, C. B. (1971). Suicide among us: II. Habits of nervous tension as potential predictors. *Johns Hopkins Medical Journal, 129,* 190–201.

Tidball, M. E., & Kistiakowsky, V. (1976). Baccalaureate origins of American scientists and scholars. *Science, 193,* 646–652.

Vetter, B. M., & Babco, E. L. (1984). Professional women and minorities: A manpower data resource service (5th ed.). Washington, DC: Scientific Manpower Commission.

Chapter 31

Becoming a psychologist: A challenge for American Indian students

Damian A. McShane, Utah State University

As American Indian and Alaska Native communities have taken more responsibility for educational matters, the number of American Indian and Native students graduating from high school has increased. These numbers have been large enough on or near certain reservations that more American Indian students are attending universities than ever before. In fact, some of the larger tribes have established their own colleges: Navajo, Navajo Community College; Sioux, Sinte Gleske (first four-year accredited Indian college) and Oglalla Community College; South and Eastern Tribes, Haskel Junior College. Others have created special programs in nearby public institutions, for example, Ojibwa at the state universities of Minnesota and Mount Scenario College. Many American Indian students going on to the university seek programs relevant to critical community needs such as teaching, nursing, and social services. Recently, more American Indian students have been entering undergraduate programs in psychology.

Why become a psychologist?

While many young American Indians may come into contact with American Indian teachers, nurses, social workers, or even lawyers, there are few American Indian psychologists available to students examining possible career choices. However, job opportunities on the American Indian reservation and in urban areas are increasingly available to qualified American Indian applicants who have been trained in psychology. Counselors in alcohol-related programs, diagnosticians in school systems, and therapists for mental health programs are in demand by the Indian Health Service, Bureau of Indian Affairs, tribal organizations, and public institutions serving American Indian populations. Not only are direct service delivery personnel recruited, but there is an unmet need for adequately trained American Indian administrators for these psychologically oriented programs. American Indians working in related areas may become aware of these opportunities and go back to college to obtain more relevant training, or students perceive the possibilities available by going on to secure training in psychology. Not all students who enter university-based training programs in psychology succeed; in fact, many American Indian students fail to finish.

Why American Indian students fail to complete training in psychology

American Indian students in a special field-based psychology program at Utah State University made the following comments on a survey (McShane, 1988) designed to capture some difficult aspects of their experiences trying to complete the program.

What were your reasons for dropping out?

"I dropped out due to the difficulty my husband had in accepting my career."

"Money is the main factor."

What problems did you have?

"Snow, one of our classmates had an accident coming to class."

"Certification requirements different in Arizona and New Mexico."

"Release time was most difficult. I have a full-time teaching contract."

"To Chuska from Shonto [where class was held] about 300 miles one way."

"If I am with my family, I have to think of them first."

"I was afraid to be away too long; my wife might divorce me."

"Troubles with tribal scholarship."

"Harassment at community level for an educated person."

"I have temporarily dropped out to have a baby and to recuperate my financial situation."

"I was a single parent at the time. . . . Great distances I had to travel created a financial strain. . . . There were times when I had to borrow gas money to make it to class."

"I would like to complete this program sometime in the future when my children grow up."

The difficulties faced by American Indian students at the university level are often the same, although exacerbated, as those they experienced during earlier periods of schooling. These difficulties tend to occur in relation to the following areas: values, identity, aspirations and motivations, orientation to change, academic preparation, individual and group interpersonal relationships.

American Indian students with the greatest difficulty coping with the challenges of college often have no unified value system. This may have resulted from having had no realistic models for growing up well or from the lack of personal contact with helpful adults (perhaps, for example, because of family break-up). The young American Indian may have had little experience fulfilling responsible roles (versus dependent roles). Usually this results in value confusion (not value conflict). For instance, achievement may be viewed as a way of standing above one's peers or group and, thus, be seen as undesirable. On the other hand, achievement may be important because it is the way to become competent enough to do something useful in the world, for your community, family, and self. Not having a consistent value system often results in spending significant emotional energy developing one, which distracts from the personal resources being applied toward academic achievement. In fact, the ability to organize and direct one's energies is essential to success in college.

American Indian students experiencing trouble in school often wonder how well friends and family like them, whether the skills they have or are acquiring are important to parents and peers, and they may end up doubting their self-worth. Such students may not have a detailed knowledge of their community's history and culture, or they may not have a clear geographical center or place called home. These questions typically are only symptoms of low self-esteem, which undermine the confidence and energy needed to succeed in college.

Merely wanting a higher-paying job or the status that comes with a degree is not sufficient motivation to last the duration of the training period. Often clear and attainable adult roles and patterns, which can represent detailed, desireable and realistic goals for young students, are not readily available. While it may be easy for the American Indian student to perceive needs of the community by observing the effects of alcoholism, developmental disabilities, divorce, and foster placement of children within the reservation or urban neighborhood, it is much more difficult to find American Indian adults effectively resolving these problems. Therefore, unrealistic expectations exist of what a certain role (e.g., psychologist) involves, as well what it takes to achieve such a role. On the other hand, occupational aspirations may be lower than the capabilities of a particular student warrants; unfortunately attainable goals may not be even attempted in such a case.

A particular relational attitude, orientation to change, is especially critical to the success or failure of American Indian students. Enmeshed in relations between two disparate cultures, American Indian students are pressured to assimilate (relinquish cultural identity and move into the larger society), to integrate (maintain cultural integrity while becoming a part of the larger society), to reject (by withdrawing from contact or influence, or by resisting actively or passively), or to experience marginality (a combination of cultural loss, deculturalization, and exclusion from participation in a dominant society). These bewildering forces significantly impact the relationship between aspirations and the educational system, in many cases detrimentally. For example, many American Indian students have gone back home to participate in traditional activities or ceremonies (e.g., ricing, naming ceremonies, seasonal religious ceremonies) during critical times in the academic year (e.g., first two weeks of semester, mid-term week). Other students have become embroiled in tribal political issues to such a degree that their studies have suffered.

In spite of good role models, clear goals, good adult support, and positive attitudes, an American Indian student simply may not have the academic preparation to enable success in college. Appropriate writing, language, and mathematical skills are particularly important to finishing training in psychology. This may be the case especially for those students who are bilingual.

And finally, American Indian students often come to universities from communal settings with prominent ideological, rather than technical, goals. While the importance of reciprocity in family and tribal subgroup relations on the reservation cannot be overemphasized, the interpersonal aspects of college life often take a back seat to the technical skills of acquiring facts and information, manipulating symbols and words in quite abstract ways outside the context of social life, and communicating with individuals who are not only strangers, but whose status and interpersonal relationship to the American Indian student are undefined (in social terms). This isolation from interwoven familial and group life can create a serious sense of alienation, damaging mental health and well-being.

How American Indian students can succeed in obtaining training in psychology

American Indian students involved in our psychology training program provided the following comments when surveyed.

What are your reasons for completing the program?

"To help all young Navajo children, especially those with specific behavior disorders or handicapping conditions. To give me the strength which I may share with others (strength = professional information). To complete the goal I set (one of my weakest areas)."

"I would like to eventually become a child psychologist."

"My life depends on it. There is a great need for Sioux diagnosticians to serve our Sioux students; I intend to fill that need."

"I feel there is a definite need for Indian psychologists who can work with other Indians to provide better services for the children, the schools, and the communities."

In order to discuss academic success by American Indian students in any area, the concepts of competency and community value must be explored. For any group, these two important criteria are central to securing resources to serve the needs of a community. The first, competency, relates to qualities in a resource person which permit the greatest effectiveness of effort through the application of skill and knowledge. A community tries to select for the highest level of competency, thus hoping for the greatest benefit to the community. The second concept, community value, relates to the relationships between people within a community which characterize the quality of communal life, such as familiarity, acceptance, trust, respect, reliance, dependence, reciprocity, and commitment. While competency creates a product needed by a group, community value is the process which reflects the heart or meaning in community.

Most individuals seek both; that is, a person tries to be as competent as possible, while belonging to a defined community and securing all the rich benefits true community carries in the character of its reciprocal relationships. However, competency does not always come with community membership. This is especially the case in smaller communities where the human resource pool is not large, and individuals need to journey outside the group to obtain skills and technical knowledge, while temporarily losing a sense of community relatedness or value. This is the situation in which American Indian students find themselves. What can the American Indian do in this situation? Based upon the experiences of Indian students who have successfully completed university training in psychology, the following points are most important.

The student must develop a clear value framework. Although there are many points of conflict between tribal cultural norms and the expectations of the larger society, there are also points of harmony between the two. These points of congruence in value systems need to be emphasized by the student. The student needs to come to grips with issues of competition versus cooperation, public performance and public discussion of making mistakes, time deadlines, direct and indirect handling of differences of opinion, reacting to constructive criticism, and so on. It is most helpful if a student has had extensive experience in making explicit value choices in social contexts that offer a welter of confusing possibilities and someone with whom to clarify the nature and consequences of those value decisions. Culturally appropriate character ideals facilitate resolving value confusion.

Central to the success of previous students has been a clear and strong sense of identity. This has included an accurate and in-depth understanding of community history and culture, a sense of home being located at some specific geographical center, and a perception of the current and future needs and directions important to the tribal community and the student's potential place in that future.

The student needs some useful analytic tools for academic success. Concrete experience examining and practicing logical and deductive thinking processes will help the student learn the "rules of the school game" as practiced by non-American Indian classmates and instructors.

Clear educational and occupational aspirations can be facilitated by spending time with an individual doing what it is the student would like to be trained to do. Whether it be helping a school psychologist working with handicapped children, an alcohol counselor running an after-care resource program, or a mental health counselor facilitating a support group, observing, examining, and discussing specific role, skill, and training requirements with such a functioning professional will help the student refine his or her career and academic expectations.

Once at the university, it is absolutely critical for the American Indian student to secure a mentor relationship with an advanced student or teacher in the student's area of study. This "personal teacher" not only becomes the model which guides the student's actions but also the ally upon whom the student can rely to prevent and resolve crises. Often, advisers are assigned randomly to incoming students. As students experience a variety of teachers and university staff, an individual with whom the student is most comfortable or who would be an especially good role model usually can be identified. Whether the adviser and mentor roles are supplied by the same person, it is very important for the American Indian student to secure this mentor/ally/guide/elder/personal teacher and cultivate the relationship.

As early as possible it is also extremely important for the American Indian student to join groups at the university, which will provide interpersonal and professional relationships of a reciprocal nature somewhat analagous to tribal life. The psychology club,

student associations (American Indian and other), well-defined sports, and social groups are all possibilities. While creating an interpersonal home away from home, it is important for the American Indian student to consciously plan periodic visits home, in such a way that they do not interfere with school, and meet personal needs to restore family and tribal group relationships. This planning should also include ways of creating expectations for peers and family consistent with a planned schedule, rather than leaving the student in the position of being expected to respond to a variety of crises at home whenever they occur. Frequent contact (again, preferably systematically periodic), which communicates a detailed and accurate picture of the university experience to family and friends, will help them to understand the student's experience and maintain the interpersonal ties that exist, rather than letting them lapse and causing the student to become alienated from the community. This may occur through telephone calls, letters, visits back home, visits from people from home to the university, and visits from school friends to students' families and friends. Volunteer or paid work in psychologically related areas in the tribal community during school breaks can facilitate keeping in touch and expanding understanding of the student's development.

Students who have been successful in completing a program of study have been able to adapt and change to a variety of situations or circumstances into which they are thrust. Whether it be long distance travel, losing a romantic attachment, death or illness in the family, or financial hardship, American Indian students who succeed are those who have the strongest commitment to a specific goal. They are able to clarify potentially conflicting values such as maintaining present orientation versus developing future orientation, learning the old ways versus seeking to move up the ladder of success, maintaining anonymity versus individual visibility in excellence, tending toward harmony versus mastery. Especially important attitudes and behaviors surrounding the need to be humble and/or submissive versus the need to be aggressive can be resolved by learning how to be respectfully assertive. Students from other backgrounds can be very open to learning from American Indian students more about the ethic of sharing. Indeed, some American Indian students have initiated cooperative study groups, which have challenged the belief that being ruggedly and individually competitive is necessary in order to secure academic success. And other students have learned to be selective concerning the particular issues and the extent to which political action takes a priority over academic preparation. It is, as always, important for the American Indian student to have balance within and without.

Finally, there is a great need for trained American Indian psychologists; many job openings (in all parts of the country) have gone unfilled because of the lack of qualified applicants. As the Code for Long Life and Wisdom, a set of educational objectives formalized for one tribal education system, suggests, it is imperative to produce those individuals trained at the highest levels

> to sing
>> to dance
>>> to lead
>>>> to dream
>>>>> to bear the brunt of conflict
>>>>>> to teach
>>>>>>> to hunt and provide, and
>>>>>>>> to heal.

References

McShane, D. (1988). *Successful and unsuccessful American Indian psychology students.* Unpublished manuscript.

Chapter 32

Asian Americans and psychology

Richard M. Suinn, Colorado State University

Why specifically address Asian Americans about majoring in psychology? One good reason is that the field is wide open and waiting with open arms. Of over 35,000 members of the APA with a doctorate degree, only 1% (or about 378 persons) were Asian American. Considering the inclination of Asian Americans to flock to and become successful in the sciences and professions, this underrepresentation is somewhat surprising on the surface.

On the other hand, perhaps my own history is explanatory. After a successful academic high school education, with an obvious expectation that I would attend college, I enrolled in our local university. Beyond knowing that I was a natural for further academic studies, I really did not have any strong inclination towards a major and had not received any vocational counseling. Possibly, everyone assumed that I was as self-sufficient in career planning as I had been in other aspects of my life; however, being bright and competent did not guarantee being sophisticated in vocational choice.

Science was my immediate, though not well-considered, choice. My first year's "decisions" included declaring a medical technology major on my admission application, changing to physics on the day of freshman orientation (despite my feeling alienated in my high school physics course), then to chemistry by the start of classes. One semester's worth of chemistry was enough for me to know that I had best look elsewhere.

So what was going on? First, I believe that my selection of science, including the early medical science choice, reflected family standards. There was no explicit pressure to become a doctor, but I knew that my parents would be pleased with a medical science degree. Additionally, I think there was a sense that majoring in another field would mean wasting my intellectual aptitude on unchallenging ventures. The standard was to achieve the highest levels; society and family defined science as representing such levels.

I see the bunching up of Asian American students in the engineering and science majors today as due to a number of factors. Many are following their aptitudes for mathematics, or physics, or engineering; a number have been encouraged by earlier successes in science fairs and have given less attention to their equal competencies in less reinforced skills. Some are responding to the stereotype that Asian American students are scholarly and are less outgoing. Possibly there is still the desire to succeed and to accept society's definition of what fields are considered valuable and worthwhile. Where parents have themselves been in business or nonscientific occupations, their hopes for their children to reach further levels of achievement may be a factor.

Why a psychology major?

Having reviewed the various reasons that affect career selection, why consider psychology? In my case, I realized that intellectual curiosity can be channeled into curiosity about humans. The interest in orderliness that was the attraction to chemistry formulas fit some of the course content of psychology as well, such as the paradigms of Hullian learning, and the psychometric methods and concepts underlying psychological test construction. Possibly a major event for me was becoming free from the need to choose a field that was worthwhile, valuable, or respectable as defined by society. The clincher was that psychology *is* a science with specialties ranging from the applied science to theory construction and even to mathematical and statistical developments. In addition, the topic of study is always the human being; the principles that are developed are relevant to people. At the same time, there is an important role for students who are less interested in relating to people and more interested in the laboratory or computer simulations.

Should students become psychology majors? If they are beyond the simplistic level of only wanting to help people; are able to take on the basic science content, which eventually will prove to be relevant to their interest in people, but may not be immediately evident; are willing to balance off a need for an orderly, predictable approach along with a tolerance for some ambiguity associated with human behavior; are willing to invest not only years of undergraduate training, but also of graduate education in working toward a goal; and want the satisfaction of understanding human behavior from a more wholistic and dynamic perspective than is offered by other sciences, then the answer is yes. While other scientists examine humans from a narrower focus (e.g., physicians focus on physical factors), psychologists must be exposed to a broader perspective, as they study physical, social, and environmental factors. In a textbook on abnormal psychology, the reader finds information about human physiology and brain anatomy, about biochemical factors, about child development, about cultural and societal variables, about the role of the environment, about genetics and endocrinology, about religion and philosophy, and about psychological factors in abnormal behavior.

The role of ethnicity

Let us return to some of the implications of my earlier comments. If students choose a psychology major, they will need to deal with a variety of issues. Assuming that their family retains some Asian cultural orientation, then they may be faced with their family's feeling that they are in a marginal field. In some Asian languages, there is no exact word for *psychology;* in many Asian countries, psychology is still struggling for recognition. Students may need to be prepared to share their knowledge with parents, aunts and uncles, and grandparents in terms that communicate well to their standards. In some instances, the scholarliness of the field conveys reassurance that it is intellectually appropriate. In others, the various graduate specialties enable an appreciation of the job opportunities. In yet other instances, the growing body of knowledge directly relevant to psychology and topics of concern to ethnic minority people provides a contact point. In some cases, the presence of a faculty member who is Asian American conveys a certain reassurance that the field is a valid one. However, in the final analysis, students need to be prepared, if their family expresses concern, to evaluate their own reasons for selecting psychology. If they have chosen psychology for the right reasons, they must be patient and understanding of family concerns. Their interest is stirred by their desire for the best life possible for their son or daughter.

On the other hand, perhaps the student selected psychology inappropriately. Although some psychologists, particularly those who choose counseling, clinical, or school psychology, do work with people in a helping relationship, not all persons who want to help should select psychology. Social workers help, attorneys help, nurses help, day-care center personnel help, teachers help, ministers help. One of the most psychologically skilled helpers whom I know and who daily faces unpredictable human trauma is a funeral home director! Occasionally, students consider psychology as a major because news publicity makes the field seem unusually attractive. Because of my work with various Olympic athletes, I am often contacted by persons whose goal is to provide psychological services to professional and Olympic teams and who want to know where to go to school. My stock answer is to suggest that the caller be absolutely committed to a career in some other area of psychology (to support themselves) during the years in private practice in which not a single athlete or team is willing to pay for your services. Which brings me to the original point: Students should utilize all of their personal and local resources in helping them decide about their major. They must examine their aptitudes and experiences, as they reflect how they voluntarily spend time; their abilities; their strengths and limitations; their finances available for education; how their interests match those of others in psychology; and what life goals they consider important, and how much time and effort they are willing to spend. Encourage students to talk to psychologists employed in various fields, make an appointment with a faculty member, and seek the guidance of the counseling center and its career planning services.

On being an Asian American student

Studies of ethnic minority persons have recognized the importance of identity. Asian Americans will not escape this, even though they may not be fully aware of the issue. As they look different from the majority culture, eventually they will have to confront this difference for themselves. Some Asian Americans elect to have their primary identity as an Asian, to the degree that their friends, food selection, and personal standards reflect an Asian background and value system. Others choose a purely Western orientation with Western values coming first and foremost in actions and decisions. In some cases, the biculturalism is more descriptive—an ability to exist in both orientations, depending upon the activities or issues. Such a person may feel more kinship with other Asians and Asian values, but also accept certain Western standards and aspirations. None of these approaches to identity are without gratifications and conflict. Students may be faced with making decisions in college in terms of their identity.

As more universities accept that ethnic minorities contribute important diversity to their campuses and view such diversity as part of an educational experience, students' minority status can become a source of visibility. Although they may not feel Asian or different, or may wish to go unnoticed, they may occasionally find their ethnicity identified, such as in a sociology course on culture. Interested faculty members may assume that Asian students are experts in not only Asian values, but also Asian philosophy and Asian history, as well as Asian cooking secrets, martial arts, and language. If students are personally comfortable with their ethnicity, then such interest would be relatively easy to handle in an honest, straightforward manner; if students are knowledgable about Asian affairs, then they can share their knowledge; if they are not, then they can redirect the discussion by pointing out the stereotypes that assume such expertise, and how they feel about being viewed in this manner. If students have not resolved their identity, then the experience might become a valuable stimulus for introspection.

My experience in serving on a committee distributing scholarships to ethnic minorities is that Asian American students tend to shy away from viewing themselves as minorities. The term may connote negative perceptions that Asian Americans wish to avoid, such as poverty, being underprivileged, being militant, or being foreign. As a result, I have had to take extra efforts to encourage, or almost to incite, Asian American students to even apply for their share of the funds. Interestingly enough, when the APA was forming the Board of Ethnic Minority Affairs—of which I eventually became chairperson—some minority psychologists objected to the title "minority" because of its connotations. Over the years, I think I have become less sensitive to, and more knowledgeable about, the appropriateness of the term to describe the experiences of Asian Americans. We *are* physically different in appearance; others *do* react to these differences; there *are* stereotypes, some of which are intentionally derogatory; there *has* been evidence of overt prejudice. But being labeled as an ethnic minority does not simply mean negative associations; Asians do have a separate cultural history that can be identified within the United States; we do have our own special values; and there can exist a certain camaraderie and empathy when families and friends celebrate traditions together. Thus, Asian Americans fit the two definitions of ethnic minority: the one which emphasizes being a group with features physically distinctive from the dominant culture and maintaining certain unique cultural mores or traditions; as well as the definition which emphasizes being a subgroup that has experienced discrimination.

In some settings, including admissions to graduate training or applications for scholarships, the special status as an ethnic minority may be important. How do students deal with this? What they are facing may be the mixed issue of personal identity, personal values and commitments, or personal philosophy. If they are bicultural or Asian in identity, then they would permit themselves to be recognized in this way. If they feel they are only secondarily an Asian but believe that they can serve as a model to others by doing well with a scholarship or succeeding in training, then they may feel comfortable in the circumstance. On the other hand, if their personal philosophy is to refuse any special treatment, or they believe that their personal characteristics should not influence decisions, then they might have no interest in such opportunities. I personally believe that limited resources (such as scholarships) or specialized training programs (such as those in cross-cultural psychology) should require the student applicants to prove their unique ethnic-identity via activities. Yet, I also know that in many settings, Asian Americans do not receive their rightful share of services, financial support, or training simply because of a failure to apply or a distorted sense of pride at not being needy or a minority.

Ethnicity in psychology

Until recently, the study of ethnicity did not receive the acceptance it rightfully deserved. However, several events are important to note. First, professional journals and conferences have now accepted research, symposia, and workshops on ethnicity as a variable influencing human performance and achievement. Second, volumes are now appearing on conceptualizing and designing cross-cultural or culturally sensitive counseling and psychotherapy. Third, university courses now exist which are devoted to minority content and research, and treat it as a legitimate, scientific subject rather than a social advocacy issue. Fourth, the APA membership formally recognized the importance of ethnicity by forming the Board of Ethnic Minority Affairs and Division 45, Society for the Psychological Study of Ethnic Minority Issues, which takes leadership in such matters as identifying ethnic minority resource persons, developing ideas for education and training, initiating further scientific research endeavors, and promoting culturally sensitive delivery systems. The membership has elected two minority persons to presidency of the APA. Fifth, in addition to participating in the efforts of the APA, Asian American psychologists have also organized their own professional association, the Asian American Psychological Association. And finally, the National Institute of Mental Health sponsored the National Asian American Psychology Training Conference, in recognition of the importance and needs of Asian American psychologists.

Planning their future

In the event that students wish to become significantly involved in the future as psychologists in ethnicity studies, there are many avenues for their interest regardless of the specialty they elect within psychology. If they eventually specialize in experimental psychology dealing with cognitions or information processing, then they might study the influence of bilingualism on later concept formation or decision making among Asian Americans. Or, if they select work in developmental psychology, they might examine the role of family approaches to discipline as they relate to performance of Asian American children. An interest in clinical psychology could draw a student's attention to the ways in which different cultures provide coping resources or the effects of folk treatment approaches for abnormal behaviors.

How can students best prepare for such future studies? They should use all their family contacts available to have a personalized Asian American experience. Recommend that they find out how their parents' generation perceives and thinks about life, what values are involved in decisions, how decisions are made. Suggest that students engage in those aspects of tradition that offer another perspective, such as an Asian church. By observing the familial environment with fresh eyes, students may find activities that represent culture and meanings previously overlooked. Encourage them to seek out and compare reactions of Asian Americans and non-Asians to the same events, looking not to evaluate but to learn about similarities and differences. Further, oral histories can provide students with an intriguing source of information that may not be found in books.

On campus, Asian American students should take advantage of Asian American student services or Asian American student organizations. Student services are not only for students in academic or financial trouble, but can be a locus for persons sharing similar ethnic characteristics. In addition, student services can be a resource for more information, such as arranging for visits from Asian touring performance groups, for special speakers, or for involvement with research projects. Non-Asian faculty and students who are doing things may stimulate students' own growth and identity. The person who teaches Asian literature, philosophy, or geography may be a great source of insights, even though he or she might not be Asian. Persons of other ethnic backgrounds might discuss their own thoughts or beliefs which can raise topics equally important to Asian Americans.

Students should find out who has written on subjects of interest to them by talking to the faculty. As they start to identify common themes, conflicts, or issues that psychologists are studying related to Asian Americans, they should seek to identify recurring names of experts, especially Asian American psychologists.

As part of students' "field experience," they can help plan activities or locate resources for an Asian Awareness Week, including defining the goals to be met by this endeavor. Volunteering to do a special studies research project with a faculty member who is sympathetic and interested in Asian American ethnicity, such as a survey of Asian students' majors as they match that of their parents or siblings, is rewarding.

If the student lives in a community with a large Asian influence, encourage volunteer work that places the student in contact with people, for instance in nursing homes, crisis centers, or Asian American counseling centers. Case conferences, training presentations, or any public speeches on Asian psychology sponsored by the community agency benefits the undergraduate.

Courses offering a scientific foundation from different viewpoints, such as sociology, anthropology, psychology (of course), literature, philosophy, and perhaps even political science broaden the student's preparation for a career in psychology. Exposure to conversational language classes are valuable for the monolingual Asian American student. An Asian American graduate student can advise the undergraduate about what mistakes to avoid and what opportunities to take advantage of before graduation.

Do not be afraid to have students establish links with major organizations. Encourage students to write to be on the mailing list of groups such as the American Psychological Association's Board of Ethnic Minority Affairs or Division 45. Suggest that they become student members of the Asian American Psychological Association and attend meetings when near their location.

And finally, students must retain a balance. Ethnic psychology does not exist in a vacuum. By itself, it can be too narrow a focus even if a university specialized only in minority psychology curricula. First, students must learn all about the basic foundation material of psychology, then they can expand their horizons to include material on ethnicity.

Chapter 33

Why should Black undergraduate students major in psychology?

James M. Jones, American Psychological Association, Washington, DC

The simple answer is that they are needed. The world needs them. And, it is an interesting, challenging, and highly regarded profession. Consider the following:

- Over 60% of all Black babies born in the United States are born to mothers who are teenagers.

- Over 40% of all prison inmates are Black.

- Among corporate managers in the major U.S. corporations, Blacks are 28% more likely to leave their jobs during a given year.

- Melanin, a substance responsible for pigment coloration which is prominent among Blacks, is also a precursor to serotonin, a drug used to treat schizophrenia.

- It has been argued that race is no longer as significant as economic class as a determinant of opportunities for Black Americans. It is also argued that there is no distinctive Black culture apart from the culture of poverty.

- It has recently been shown that Black students on predominantly Black college campuses perform better than their Black counterparts on predominantly White campuses.

- It has been demonstrated that Black adolescents who adopt a militant coping style in confronting racism in the United States experience greater stress than those who choose to either fit in or withdraw from racial issues.

Each and every one of these issues and concerns is the legitimate concern of psychology as a science, profession, and discipline committed to promoting human welfare. Although I have couched these important issues in a somewhat negative framework to emphasize the need for Black psychologists, the basic goal of psychology is to contribute to our understanding of human thought and behavior. The thought and behavior of Black people is a legitimate and important concern of psychology, one that has not been sufficiently or adequately addressed to date.

What is Black psychology?

Generally, psychology concerns the thought and behavior of people and attempts to explain why certain behaviors occur and others do not. Psychology tries to describe processes of thinking, language development, socialization of values, and attitudes. A goal of psychology is to understand why some people experience mental and emotional anguish that results in behaviors that are personally destructive at worst, and simply dysfunctional and unproductive at best. In applying the discipline to Black people, Blacks have been painted in not very flattering strokes. No matter what area of human thought, behavior, emotion, values, and expectations we consider, psychology has a way of demonstrating Black people's deficiencies. In fact, I have had students tell me that it is foolish to major in psychology as it is psychology that supplies the rationale for racism!

In recent years the number of Black psychologists who have earned doctoral degrees has grown significantly. Over the past 3 years, an average of 333 Black students have earned degrees in psychology. What most of these

Black psychologists have done is focus their attention on issues of concern to Black people from a perspective that assumes a positive basis for Black existence that can be described and demonstrated within the general framework of psychology.

This position begins with the general premise that racism is a fact of American life and is responsible for many of the issues and concerns raised at the beginning of this chapter. Further, its proponents assert that contrary to popular opinion, it is necessary and appropriate to recognize that Black people come from an African heritage—a culture with values, traditions, symbols, and beliefs that influenced Black's current existence. Thus, Black psychology is committed to learning the variety of negative consequences of an oppressive existence in a racist society, as well as the positive consequences of that experience. Sorting out the truth and its consequences will advance the humanity of all Americans. Finally, Black psychology advances the idea that certain features of the African and European interaction have produced a significant, talented, intelligent culture of people known variously as Afro or African American people. To be Black in a multiracial and multiethnic society is to understand the dynamics of race, class, and culture. Black psychology is a disciplined inquiry into these dynamics.

Majoring in psychology

What is involved in a psychology major, what can you do with it, and what jobs are available? A psychologist is by definition one who has earned a doctoral degree. Thus, the first decision students need to make is whether to seek a doctoral degree. To do so, students need to maintain a 3.0 grade point average and, more importantly, to gain experience of two kinds. The first is experience in research. The doctoral degree (the PhD, particularly) is a research-based degree requiring some original research. Students can assist in running subjects, coding data, interviewing, and so on, and thereby gain exposure to research and develop a relationship with a faculty member, which is closer than one typically established in classes. This is particularly important when students need letters of reference. Second, any sort of counseling experience (dormitory, summer camp, mental health clinic, etc.) is useful, especially in application areas, such as clinical and counseling. The point is to gain experience beyond the classroom—either research or practice—that are relevant to psychology.

Course work in statistics, history of psychology, and systems and methods is important for the basic knowledge in psychology and provides a background for the Graduate Record Examinations (GRE). Furthermore, encourage the department to create a course in Black psychology. Several books are available for such a course, including a sourcebook of such course syllabi available from the Association of Black Psychologists in Washington, DC.[1]

Students should take the GRE in the spring of their junior year. This will give them an indication of their rating, and, if needed, they can then take preparatory courses over the summer. The GRE can be repeated in October of the senior year so that scores will be available early in the graduate school application process. Schools vary widely in whether and how they use the GRE for Black students. My advice is to take no chances. High GRE scores will never hurt!

Graduate Study in Psychology and Associated Fields, published by the APA each spring for the following academic year, lists all the graduate programs in the country and includes information about the qualifications of entering students, the programs in which they give degrees, and financial aid. This guide assists students in narrowing their selection of schools to a region of the country, the type of program that interests them, and the level of qualifications that fit their undergraduate record. Students should select about five programs, write for information, study it carefully, and apply early.

Encourage students to apply for financial aid; they should expect that their doctoral study will be supported financially, as it is easier to get support for doctoral than master's study. Several fellowship programs for minority students in doctoral programs exist, including the Ford Foundation, the National Science Foundation, as well as the American Psychological Association Minority Fellowships and the Committee on Institutional Cooperation Graduate Fellowships for Minorities (for a limited group of schools). In addition, the U.S. Department of Education has funded several psychology departments for minority training stipends through its Graduate and Professional Opportunities Program (now the Patricia Robert Harris fellowship), as has the National Institute of Mental Health through minority-oriented training grants. In addition, each university's psychology department has its own source of support, including research and teaching assistantships and fellowships. Finally, there are also student loans at favorable payback schedules and interest rates.

Taken together, students should be able to find funding for their doctoral study. If the student is committed to becoming a psychologist, a program exists; the important part is to match the student and the program.

Does this mean that if a student is not interested in obtaining a PhD, he or she shouldn't major in psychology? The answer is *no*. There are many interesting and important jobs for baccalaureates in personnel offices, mental health and day-care centers, school settings, and so on, but they are not "professional" jobs. It is also possible to gain employment in private industry, which usually involves taking a management training position.

Career choices

The psychology major will be useful if the student decides to go on for a master's or doctoral degree or go to law school, medical school, business school, or into a management training position.

Students considering a career as a psychologist must examine how they want to spend their adult working life; the mix of a career in which they can both help others and feel fulfilled and creative; and what life styles and associated economic requirements they envision. A career in psychology permits them to fulfill each of the above if they are creative, hard working, motivated, and plan intelligently and effectively.

A brief chronology of my own development provides a description of the wide range of experiences and opportunities available through psychology. I began by running rats in the research laboratory of my undergraduate professor. Although it was interesting, rat-running wasn't my idea of a career. I worked at the Franklin Institute of Philadelphia as an engineering psychologist (with only a BA), where I conducted multidimensional scaling studies of radar controllers and designed simulated decision-making games based on the Vietnam War. I received a master's degree and studied how the value of coins influenced the psychophysical judgments of their size (dimes were overestimated, and pennies were underestimated). I entered a doctoral program with the express purpose of becoming a Black psychologist and studying the problems of racism and the development of Black people in America; however, I studied attitude change and the psychology of humor. I took an academic job, where I continued studying the physiological correlates of laughter and humor, racial differences in performance of Black and White athletes, the minority content of public television programs, wrote a book on prejudice and racism, and another on a Black National Football League player. After working in a private consulting firm and conducting program research for the federal government, I moved to the APA where I became an administrator and program manager of the Minority Fellowship Training Grant and conducted a major investigation of the turnover of minority managers in major U.S. corporations. Once again, I am a professor of psychology in an academic department.

My résumé illustrates the wide range of activities possible within the field of psychology. The psychologist has many options; he or she can address the problems of Black people directly as a researcher, a therapist or counselor, a school psychologist, a teacher or professor, a consultant, or a program administrator. The largest incomes come to psychologists who are in industry or government and those who establish private psychotherapy practices. Industrial and organizational positions are popular because they both provide a forum for studying major problems of Blacks in corporations, and they pay well. Most Black psychologists combine these activities, taking academic teaching appointments, establishing small private practices, and consulting as well as conducting research. The limitation is only one's energy, imagination, and time; however, the psychologist must be well trained and have a marketable skill. The degree alone will not do it! As students plan their careers, they must identify skills that have market value: psychotherapy skills, computer and research design, group training, statistics, survey methodology, interviewing techniques, and so on. These are tangible skills that will both assist in gaining employment and increase one's options in the marketplace. Moreover, such skills enable students to fulfill their goals, whatever they may be.

Finally, another aspect of a career as a psychologist should be noted. Psychology is a profession and a science and is organized to promote itself in the service of human welfare. The Association of Black Psychologists was founded in 1969 and continues to provide an opportunity to become directly involved in issues of relevance to and critical importance to the Black community. The association has organized testimony and expert witness presentation on issues of testing and jury selection, and Black child development and abuse. Through regional associations and annual conventions the psychologist maintains contact with the Black community and Black psychology colleagues.

There is also representation of Black and other ethnic group concerns within the APA. The Board of Ethnic Minority Affairs (BEMA) represents the policy issues that affect ethnic minority citizens as well as psychologists. One's interest and concern with Black psychological issues will also gain support through APA's National Policy Studies, which organizes testimony on issues that affect the psychological community and the concerns of organized psychology.

In sum, the profession of psychology welcomes an individual not only as a practicing psychologist (teacher, researcher, etc.), but as a member of national associations which help to organize the psychologist's expertise and concerns.

There are important problems of Black life and culture in this society, and indeed in the world, that need Black psychologists to address them. There are people who need help. The undergraduate psychology major is the first step. Encourage students to do well, to set up mentoring relationships with faculty and others, to prepare for graduate study, to gain admission to a program of their choice and receive adequate financial support. Students should select a training program that confers tangible skills and point themselves toward a career with flexibility, foresight, and energy.

Footnotes

1. Contact Dr. Ruth King, National Liaison, 821 Kennedy St., N.W., Washington, DC 20011.

Chapter 34

Hispanics in psychology

Richard C. Cervantes, University of California, Los Angeles

The field of psychology, both as a science and as a profession, is young. About 100 years ago, the importance of examining mental processes, as related to physical illness, gained acceptance and recognition. Since the early work of many European psychologists, the field of psychology has grown rapidly and now has an influence on many aspects of human life, ranging from health care to industry. Psychology, as a profession and science, is here to stay!

The application of psychology continues to expand. Vast numbers of psychologists, both those with PhDs as well as those with bachelor's degrees, find themselves working in areas that seem to have little relationship to psychology. In addition to the traditional roles of health and human service providers (e.g., clinical psychology) and university professors, psychologists now work in such diverse areas as engineering, aerospace (e.g., artificial intelligence), business and industry, and the legal system. Psychology has a growing influence in areas that previously had no reason to consider hiring a psychologist. It is fascinating to imagine what role psychology will have in society by the year 2000. Indeed, psychology offers an ever-expanding range of career opportunities for those who find they have an interest and aptitude for entering this field.

Students may ask themselves, "How can I determine whether or not I have an aptitude for psychology?" The best way to find an answer to this question is to expose themselves to people who teach, study, or work in areas directly related to psychology. A good start is to enroll in psychology courses which sound interesting. Many undergraduates gravitate to psychology after taking related courses in major areas of study. For example, it is not uncommon to see undergraduates majoring in

psychology along with a minor in business administration, biology, or premedicine. While an introductory psychology class is often required for undergraduates, a host of other elective psychology courses may help answer any questions regarding one's aptitude and interest in the field.

Why Hispanic psychology?

Although Hispanics represent one of the many cultural minority groups in the United States, recent statistics from the Bureau of Census reveal a picture of an emerging population with growing needs.

- Hispanics are united by a common Spanish language and cultural heritage but are diverse in terms of geography, country of origin, race, class, and circumstances surrounding their entry into the United States.

- There are more than 14 million Hispanics (Mexican American, Puerto Rican, Cuban, or Central American) now living in the United States, approximately 6.4% of the total U.S. population. Hispanics have tripled in numbers over the past 3 decades.

- The median age of Hispanics in the United States is substantially lower than that of the general population, 23 years as compared to 30 years. Nearly 58% of all Hispanics are under the age of 34.

- Because of the lower average age of Hispanic females, the birth rate is also very high.

- Since the 1960s, Hispanics have become the dominant immigrant group in the United

States, now representing 42% of all immigrants entering the country. This percentage does not include estimates of undocumented immigrants.

- By the year 2000, Hispanics will be the largest of all minority group populations, comprising about one-fourth of the total population.

These figures reveal a young, diverse, and rapidly growing population. Many researchers sense that the social, political, and economic impact of this growth in the Hispanic population is already apparent. As with any growing population, increased social and economic demands require a greater understanding of the characteristics of this population, and this is where psychology has its place. The Hispanic psychology major has an added opportunity of becoming involved in the progress of Hispanics either at the individual level (e.g., providing mental health services) or at the community level (e.g., conducting research which aims to improve public policy).

Stapp, Zucker, and VandenBos (1985) suggest that less than 2% of all psychologists are Hispanic. This creates a tremendous need to train young Hispanics to enter the field of psychology. In fact, one of the primary problems in the practice of psychology and in Hispanic psychological research is the lack of people in the field who are well acquainted with Hispanic culture. Acasta, Yamamoto, and Evans (1982) suggest that many Hispanics prefer not to go to community mental health agencies because of the lack of trained bilingual-bicultural therapists. This underutilization of mental health facilities is extremely detrimental, as many mental illnesses go untreated. In California alone, where the Hispanic population is close to 5 million, training new Hispanic psychologists lags far behind, leaving a tremendous gap between the mental health needs of this community and the number of qualified professionals.

In addition to the lack of qualified mental health professionals who treat mental illness (e.g., clinical psychologists), another grossly underrepresented area of psychology is school psychology. Given the number of school-aged Hispanic children, problems arise when language and other cultural characteristics are mistaken for learning deficits. These otherwise normal children face the stigma of being labeled inferior because their language and culture are different from that of other students. Many of them are placed in special learning-disabled classes which often hamper their later achievement and academic success.

The need for qualified Hispanic bilingual and bicultural school psychologists is immense.

Many researchers argue that the present educational system does not foster success among Hispanic children. This may be most evident in the very high number of Hispanics who never finish high school. Certainly this is an issue that needs further research so that the exact nature of the problem can be understood. Again, these culturally relevant educational issues are best addressed by Hispanic psychologists who are sensitive to the problems.

Many other research opportunities for Hispanic psychologists are available. In addition to conducting mainstream psychological research, the Hispanic psychologist has the additional opportunity to conduct cross-cultural research. Hispanic psychologists are beginning to uncover the influence of Hispanic culture in such areas as psychotherapy, bilingualism, education, stress-related disorders, cognition, and a host of other factors which traditionally have not been addressed in psychological research. Research is needed which helps identify differences found within the culture. For example, one area of psychological research which holds promise is that of investigating the process of immigration as related to mental health. What effects does changing one's country of residence have on mental health? What are the effects of prejudice and discrimination on new immigrants? Are there mental health problems that are specific to Central American refugees who are not voluntary immigrants?

As you can see, from a psychological research perspective there are many questions that would be best addressed by researchers familiar with Hispanic culture. The need for Hispanic researchers and service providers will continue to expand with the tremendous growth in the Hispanic population which is projected to continue at least until the year 2000.

Strategies for Hispanic psychology undergraduates

Developing a strategy for success early in the undergraduate curriculum is important. This strategy building is, however, contingent on the decision about graduate school. For many who decide that the bachelor's degree is sufficient, certain strategies can help improve one's marketability following graduation. Crucial to improving one's marketability is a well-rounded curriculum. Potential employers seek out the psychology major as these students tend to be more people-oriented. While this may provide some advantage following graduation, a psychology degree complemented by another related area of study is preferred. Many students choose to minor in other more traditional areas, such as business administration or biochemistry. This gives the graduate the advantage when it comes time for job interviews. Hispanic students should not be fooled into thinking that affirmative action employers will hire them because they are a minority.

The best advise for students choosing graduate school is to be well prepared. Strategies for this preparation are varied, but all include doing something that gives them an advantage. While many graduate programs express some desire to recruit minority students, candidates should not assume that this is the case. Rather, they should rely on their own merits, which include a good GPA and involvement in actual field experience or research. Part-time positions in a human service setting (e.g., nursing home or mental health clinic) often serve the dual purpose of exposing the student to the general area or profession and enhancing his or her qualifications for graduate school. Similarly, working or volunteering to do some research allows the student to gauge his or her interest in psychological research and improves his or her graduate school application. Research experience can often be gained by working with a psychology professor who is involved in research which interests the student. A Hispanic professor who can not only share with the student mutual research interests but can serve as a guide by sharing experiences as a Hispanic student in psychology is optimal.

While there are many paths to the successful completion of undergraduate and graduate education, few Hispanics have chosen to become professional psychologists. A career in psychology is a challenge that requires diligence and hard work, but one that is rewarding in terms of personal achievement and the contribution one can make to improving the lives of many Hispanics through research and service activities.

References

Acosta, F. X., Yamamoto, J., & Evans, L. A. (1982). *Effective psychotherapy for low-income and minority patients.* New York: Plenum Press.

Stapp, J., Zucker, A. M., & VandenBos, G. R. (1985). Census of psychological personnel. *American Psychologist, 40* (12), 1317–1351.

Chapter 35

Reentry of women and men in psychology

Patricia W. Lunneborg, University of Washington

Between 1972 and 1982 the increase in enrollment of college students between the ages of 18–24 was 23%, while the increase among students 25–34 years old was 70% and among students age 35 and over, 77% (Grant & Snyder, 1983). In psychology these increases in enrollment among older students are probably greater, as psychology meshes with a primary motivation of returning students—self-improvement. Career is also a major motivator; some reentry students need college to advance or change careers, while others are entering the job market for the first time (Reehling, 1980).

While *mature* or *older* have been applied to students from ages 25 to 85, this chapter is aimed at the middle range, people in their 40s.

Problems to overcome before the bachelor's degree

The quantitative deficit

Returning students of both sexes typically have a verbal advantage over younger students (better vocabulary and reading comprehension), but they are at a disadvantage in quantitatively based courses. (How many jobs afford much practice of the mathematics learned in high school 25 years ago?) One common way of coping with this quantitative deficit is to avoid a major and courses that rely on mathematics. This may be one reason why reentry students choose majors in the humanities and social sciences in overwhelming numbers.

The psychology major is very attractive to older students except for the statistics course.

Many returning students put off taking statistics until the last possible minute, thus denying themselves statistical knowledge that would make all their other psychology courses easier.

A better way of coping is to take mathematics courses as soon after reentry as possible. Academic advisers can recommend remedial courses, help locate tutors, suggest study partners, advertise math-anxiety workshops on departmental bulletin boards, and encourage students. Students who take remedial work in mathematics open new possibilities for themselves in terms of college courses, graduate programs, and jobs. The statistics course is no longer a hurdle, and a master's degree becomes a real possibility.

Self-defeating sense of urgency

Many reentry students have a need to get their bachelor's degree yesterday. They feel an urgency to finish as soon as possible as if life is passing them by while they sojourn in college. As a result they may sign up for more courses than anyone can handle or ignore prerequisites and get in over their heads. Older students need to be reminded that it takes them just as long as younger students to study adequately, to grasp psychology, to acquire research experience, and to complete fieldwork.

Readjusting the old life

Reentry students typically adjust too slowly to returning to school. They take a long time to acknowledge all the adjustments in their old life that must take place. Spouses and children may not be much help; they may not want anything to change except that Mom or Dad is also going to college. As a result, the first year back at school may be painful for families until the many radical arrangements that must be made are finally set in place, such as spending far less time with family members and friends. If a reentry student tries to hold on to an old job and go to school, the results can be disastrous.

A new base for self-esteem

Going back to school can be a real blow to an older student's self-esteem. Can I still learn? What if I fail? Why are the instructors so young? How can I compete with those kids? What if they make fun of me? A new self, a new identity as a psychology major is necessary for eventual success as a job hunter—a job hunter with a new employment objective written on one's résumé, new skills and knowledge, and new goals for life.

Academic advisers can put older students in touch with one another by organizing a conversation hour devoted to reentry. Mail invitations to older students, advertise the meeting through posters and announcements read in classes, and make it attractive by holding it at noon (never late in the day or evening) and by offering refreshments. Feature a successful reentry speaker. Use the meeting to form a support network of older psychology students, drawing up a list of addresses and phone numbers, and offering clerical assistance to whomever can be drafted to keep it going. There is no better way to build self-esteem than to share one's successes with people who understand and applaud and reveal one's failures to people who will laugh with you, not at you.

Problems to overcome after the bachelor's degree

An entry-level job at ridiculous pay

Older students are no different from younger students when they start out in a new field. They will be asked to start at the bottom with a low salary. Many cannot tolerate this idea and go back to their old, not-related-to-psychology jobs at better-than-entry salaries. But overcoming personal resistance to starting at the bottom can be worth it. Eventually the experience and skills acquired before going back to school can be added to the psychology degree to lead to earlier promotions than a younger, less experienced graduate experiences.

One can settle for a long (one year or more) job hunt that includes gimmicky but successful tactics. For example, an older graduate who had been a secretary for 15 years wrote a letter of recommendation for a person qualified for management, based on business experience and college training, and closed by saying the person was herself. This letter secured a job which led rapidly to manager of personnel (Berman, 1980).

I'm too old for graduate school

Graduate programs are not biased against older students; some even prefer them. The problem to overcome is that sense of urgency that says one can't afford to spend any more time in college. If an older student desires to function at the master's or doctoral level in psychology and in all the important ways (grades, GRE scores, research experience) is qualified, she or he should go for that degree.

I can't move

Reentry students of both sexes are often adamant about the fact that they cannot relocate for further education or employment because of family. Often the family has not been consulted. If opportunities are better in other parts of the country, serious family discussion regarding the possibilities for everyone's growth and advancement for everyone are important.

All psychology majors no matter what their ages need to apply to graduate programs across the country (a) to guarantee they will be accepted somewhere, and (b) more importantly, to insure they will be accepted at a place that matches their interests and values. One can wait for a lifetime to be accepted at a local program, when the individual could have studied 1,000 miles away and returned home in 4 years employed as a PhD psychologist. Even more tragic is attending a local program that is mismatched with one's goals and personality.

What psychology departments can do

Psychology departments can take the lead by recognizing that not all students are aged 18–22, live near campus, have no non-academic responsibilities, are financed by their parents, and have adequate study skills and unlimited time to study (Hooper & March, 1980).

Departmental advisers can provide individualized counseling for reentry psychology majors, which assumes they received little or no orientation to campus resources. Advisers can emphasize social support from peers, employment on campus if they must work, remedial courses, tutoring, study skills, and the importance of working closely with a faculty member by lending teaching or research assistance. Departmental advisers who track reentry baccalaureate's success in the job market will have a file of role models for current students—role models whom students can visit in the workplace for informational interviews or who can visit campus to speak to reentry students in career workshops.

Psychology faculty need to be aware that although reentry students look more mature, they will not necessarily behave more maturely than younger students. For example, they may not ask questions for fear of appearing ignorant; not use student health services, although they have paid for them; not use the tutoring center because of the stigma; not take remedial mathematics because it would prolong their studies; not seek help soon enough when failing a class; and not seek a graduate degree although qualified, because of other responsibilities and lack of family support.

Far more than younger students, our reentry majors need encouraging comments on excellent final exams such as, "I hope you're planning on getting a PhD!"; "Let me know when you need a letter of recommendation for graduate school!"; or "Psychology needs you. How can I help?"

References

Berman, E. (1980). *Re-entering: Successful back-to-work strategies for women seeking a fresh start.* New York: Crown.

Grant, W. V., & Snyder, T. B. (1983). *Digest of education statistics, 1983–84.* Washington, DC: National Center for Education Statistics.

Hooper, J. O., & March, G. B. (1980). The female single parent in the university. *Journal of College Student Personnel, 21,* 141–146.

Reehling, J. E. (1980). They are returning: But, are they staying? *Journal of College Student Personnel, 21,* 491–497.

Chapter 36

Resources

This chapter contains valuable resource information for the adviser and for the bachelor's candidate in psychology. The materials include a list of organizations and societies with descriptions and addresses and a bibliography of publications with useful information on selecting a career in psychology and choosing a college and obtaining financial aid.

Organizations

The American Psychological Association

The American Psychological Association (APA) is a society of scientists, teachers, and professionals organized by charter to advance psychology as a science and as a means of promoting the public welfare. Its membership in 1987 was more than 60,000. The Association publishes scientific and professional journals and holds an annual convention to promote communication and exchange of new knowledge among psychologists. Many APA boards and committees devote their attention to a wide variety of concerns, ranging from the social and ethical responsibilities of psychologists to their education and training.

The national efforts of APA are greatly facilitated by regional, state, and local associations of psychologists. State psychological associations are particularly active in representing psychologists' professional and scientific interests to state legislators and other policymakers. The addresses and the offices of these associations may be obtained by writing to the Governance Services Office, APA, 1200 17th Street, NW, Washington, DC 20036.

Divisions of the APA

The numerous interests of psychologists are represented within the APA by 47 divisions. Psychologists who belong to the APA usually join one or more divisions. Most divisions publish a journal, a newsletter, or both. Information about divisions and their publications may be obtained from the division secretaries, whose addresses are listed each November in *American Psychologist,* a journal published by APA. Addresses of division secretaries and newsletter editors are also available from the Governance Services Office, APA, 1200 17th Street, NW, Washington, DC 20036.

1. General Psychology
2. Teaching of Psychology
3. Experimental Psychology
5. Evaluation and Measurement
6. Physiological and Comparative Psychology
7. Developmental Psychology
8. Personality and Social Psychology
9. Society for the Psychological Study of Social Issues
10. Psychology and the Arts
12. Clinical Psychology
13. Consulting Psychology
14. Society for Industrial and Organizational Psychology
15. Educational Psychology
16. School Psychology
17. Counseling Psychology
18. Psychologists in Public Service
19. Military Psychology
20. Adult Development and Aging
21. Applied Experimental and Engineering Psychologists
22. Rehabilitation Psychology
23. Consumer Psychology

24. Theoretical and Philosophical Psychology
25. Experimental Analysis of Behavior
26. History of Psychology
27. Community Psychology
28. Psychopharmacology
29. Psychotherapy
30. Psychological Hypnosis
31. State Psychological Association Affairs
32. Humanistic Psychology
33. Mental Retardation
34. Population and Environmental Psychology
35. Psychology of Women
36. Psychologists Interested in Religious Issues
37. Child, Youth, and Family Services
38. Health Psychology
39. Psychoanalysis
40. Clinical Neuropsychology
41. Psychology and Law
42. Psychologists in Independent Practice
43. Family Psychology
44. Society for the Psychological Study of Lesbian and Gay Issues
45. Society for the Psychological Study of Ethnic Minority Issues
46. Media Psychology
47. Exercise and Sport Psychology

Other APA sources of information

APA Membership Directory: Biographical, geographical, and divisional membership listing of APA Fellows, Members, and Associates. Published every 4 years.

APA Membership Register: Lists names, addresses, and states as Fellow, Member, or Associate in APA and its divisions. Published in years when the Directory is not.

APA Monitor: A monthly newspaper containing news about the field of psychology, APA, and behavioral science legislation.

Psychology Today: A monthly magazine for the general public containing articles and news about psychology and behavioral sciences.

PASAR: APA also operates the Psychological Abstracts Search and Retrieval (PASAR) system. PASAR provides a computer-generated bibliography consisting of citations and abstracts from the PsycINFO database and the PsycALERT File, tailored to the individual researcher's requirements.

Honor Societies

Psi Chi

Psi Chi, the National Honor Society in Psychology, recognizes excellence in scholarship by graduate and undergraduate students in psychology. It provides the opportunity for early involvement and recognition in psychology. Membership is through chapters located at accredited colleges and universities that have met Psi Chi's standards. To join, undergraduates must rank in the upper 35% of their class and have completed a specified number of credits in psychology. Graduate students must have at least a "B" average. A registration fee pays for lifetime membership. The Psi Chi Newsletter is published quarterly. For further information, contact Psi Chi, PO Box 180500, Chattanooga, TN 37405-7500, (615) 756-2004.

Psi Beta

Psi Beta is the honor society in psychology for students who attend 2-year colleges. Psi Beta teaches students, before they transfer to a 4-year institution, that honor societies and related activities are important to their development as psychology students. For further information, contact Psi Beta, PO Box 180500, Chattanooga, TN 37405-7500, (615) 756-2004.

Special group organizations

Women

• APA Committee on Women in Psychology
• Association for Women in Psychology

For the name of the person to whom to write at these two organizations, write or call the Women's Program, APA, 1200 17th Street, NW, Washington, DC 20036.

Minorities

• Minority Fellowship Program

Funded jointly by the National Institute of Mental Health and the APA, the Minority Fellowship Program awards fellowships to individuals of ethnic minority background for graduate study in psychology leading to the doctorate. The program also advises students, faculty, and administrators on behavioral science and mental health issues related to ethnic minority populations. For more information, write or call the Minority Fellowship Program, APA, 1200 17th Street, NW, Washington, DC 20036.

Other resources

- APA Board of Ethnic Minority Affairs
- Association of Asian-American Psychologists
- Association of Black Psychologists
- National Coalition of Hispanic Mental Health and Human Services Organizations
- National Hispanic Psychological Association

For information about these organizations, write or call the Ethnic Minority Affairs Office, APA, 1200 17th Street, NW, Washington, DC 20036.

People with handicaps

- APA Committee on Psychology and Handicaps

For information, write or call the Office of Social and Ethical Responsibility in Psychology, APA, 1200 17th Street, NW, Washington, DC 20036.

Lesbians and Gays

- APA Committee on Gay Concerns
- Association of Lesbian and Gay Psychologists

For information about these organizations, write or call the Office of Social and Ethical Responsibility in Psychology, APA, 1200 17th Street, NW, Washington, DC 20036.

Organizations for fields related to psychology

There are many careers in fields related to psychology. The following organizations can provide you with information about the careers suggested by their names.

American Anthropological Association
1333 H Street, NW
Washington, DC 20009
(202) 232–8800

American Association for the Advancement of Science
1515 Massachusetts Avenue, NW
Washington, DC 20005
(202) 326–6400

American Council on Education
One Dupont Circle
Washington, DC 20036
(202) 939–9300

American Medical Association
535 North Dearborn Street
Chicago, IL 60610
(312) 645–5000

American Orthopsychiatric Association
19 W. 44th Street, Suite 1616
New York, NY 10036
(212) 354–5770

American Association for Counseling and Development
5999 Stevenson Avenue
Alexandria, VA 22304
(703) 823–9800

American Psychiatric Association
1400 K Street, NW
Washington, DC 20005
(202) 682–6000

American Sociological Association
1722 N Street, NW
Washington, DC 20036
(202) 833–3410

Commission on Professionals in Science and Technology
1500 Massachusetts Avenue, NW
Suite 831
Washington, DC 20005
(202) 223–6995

National Academy of Sciences
National Research Council
2101 Constitution Avenue, NW
Washington, DC 20418
(202) 334–2000

National Mental Health Association
1021 Prince Street
Alexandria, VA 22314
(703) 684–7722

National Association of Social Workers
7981 Eastern Avenue
Silver Spring, MD 20910
(301) 565–0333

National Education Association
1202 16th Street, NW
Washington, DC 20036
(202) 833–4000

National Institute of Mental Health (Publication inquiries)
5600 Fishers Lane
Rockville, MD 20857
(301) 443–4515

Publications

Books and booklets on careers in psychology

Items published by the APA or its divisions are available from the APA, 1200 17th Street, NW, Washington, DC 20036, unless otherwise noted.

American Association of State Psychology Boards. (Undated). *Entry requirements for professional practice of psychology: A guide for students and faculty.* New York: Author

American Psychological Association. (Rev. biannually). *Graduate study in psychology and associated fields.* Washington, DC: Author.

American Psychological Association. (1983). *Psychology as a health care profession.* Washington, DC: Author. (Revision underway)

American Psychological Association, Division of Consulting Psychology. (1980) *Consulting psychology.* Washington, DC: Author. (Available from APA Division of Consulting Psychology, 631 A Street, SE, Washington, DC 20003)

American Psychological Association, Division of Military Psychology. (Undated.) *Military psychology: An overview.* Washington, DC: Author.

American Psychological Association, Division of Industrial and Organizational Psychology. (Undated). *A career in industrial-organizational psychology.* Washington, DC: Author.

American Psychological Association, Division of School Psychology, (Undated). *The school psychologist.* Washington, DC: Author.

Basmajin, J. V. (1983). *Biofeedback: Principles in practice for clinicians.* Baltimore: Williams & Wilkins.

Bloomquist, D. W. (1981). *A guide to preparing a psychology student handbook.* Washington, DC: American Psychological Association.

Careers, Inc. (1982). *Psychologist, school.* Largo, FL: Author. (Address: PO Box 135, Largo, FL 34294-0135)

Careers, Inc. (1983). *Psychologist, clinical.* Largo, FL: Author.

Careers, Inc. (1983). *Counselor, school.* Largo, FL: Author.

Careers, Inc. (1984). *Psychologist.* Largo, FL: Author.

Catalyst National Headquarters. (1975). *Psychology* (Career Opportunities Series No. C-19). New York: Author. (Address: 14 East 60th Street, New York, NY 10022)

Catalyst National Headquarters. (1975). *Psychology* (Education Opportunities Series No. E-19). New York: Author.

Chronical Guidance Publications. (1982). *Psychologists* (Occupational Brief No. 144). Moravia, NY: Author. (Address: PO Box 1190, Moravia, NY 13118-1190)

Figler, H. (1975). *PATH: A career workbook for liberal arts students.* Cranston, RI: Carroll Press.

Fretz, B. R., & Stang, D. J. (1980). *Preparing for graduate study: Not for seniors only!* Washington, DC: American Psychological Association.

Fuller, G. D. (1977). *Biofeedback: Clinical applications in behavioral medicine.* Englewood Cliffs, NJ: Prentice-Hall.

Gould, C. A. (1983). *Consider your options: Business opportunities for liberal arts graduates.* Washington, DC: Association of American Colleges.

Hatch, J. P., Fisher, J. G., & Rugh, J. D. (1987). *Biofeedback: Studies in clinical efficacy.* New York: Plenum Press.

Kantowitz, B. H., & Sorkin, R. D. (1983). *Human factors: Understanding people-system relationships.* New York: Wiley.

Moore, C. G. (1976). *The career game.* New York: Ballantine.

Olton, D. S., & Noonberg, A. R. (1980). *Biofeedback: Clinical applications in behavioral medicine.* Englewood Cliffs, NJ: Prentice-Hall.

Parsons, H. M. (1976). Psychology for engineering and technology. In P. J. Woods (Ed.). *Career opportunities for psychologists: Expanding and emerging areas* (pp. 180–193). Washington, DC: American Psychological Association.

Parsons, H. M. (1984). Engineering psychology. In R. J. Corsini (Ed.), *Encyclopedia of psychology* (pp. 436–440). New York: Wiley.

Rudman, J. (1980). *Psychologist* (Career Examination Series No. C–627). Syosset, NY: National Learning Corp.

Sanders, M. S., & McCormick, E. J. (1987). *Human factors in engineering and design* (6th ed.). New York: McGraw-Hill.

Super, D. E., & Super, C. M. (1982). *Opportunities in psychology* (4th ed.). Skokie, IL: National Textbook.

Waterman, D., Candy, B., & Peper, E. (1978). *Relaxation: A bibliography.* Denver: Biofeedback Society of America.

Wickens, C. D. (1984). *Engineering psychology and human performance.* Columbus, OH: Charles E. Merrill.

Woods, P. J. (Ed.). (1979). *The psychology major: Training and employment strategies.* Washington, DC: American Psychological Association.

Woods, P. J. (Ed.) with Wilkinson, C. (1987). *Is psychology the major for you?* Washington, DC: American Psychological Association.

Choosing a college and getting financial aid

There are many publications that list undergraduate programs at colleges and universities. A sample are listed below. They are available in bookstores and many public libraries.

Brownstein, S. C., & Weiner, M. (1984). *Compact guide to colleges* (4th ed.). Woodbury, NY: Barron's.

Cass J., & Birnbaum, M. (1983). *Comparative guide to American colleges* (11th ed.). New York: Harper & Row.

The College Board. (1984). *The college handbook: 1984–85.* New York: Author.

The College Board. (1984). *The college cost book: 1984–85.* New York: Author.

Feingold, S. N., & Feingold, M. (1982). *Scholarships, fellowships, and loans* (Vol. 7). Arlington, MA: Bellman.

Kesslar, O. (1983). *Financial aids for higher education* (11th ed.). Dubuque, IA: William C. Brown.

Lehman, A. E., & Suber, E. A. (Eds.). (1987). *Guide to four-year colleges 1988* (18th ed.). Princeton: Peterson's Guides.

Lovejoy, C. E. (1983). *Lovejoy's college guide.* New York: Simon & Schuster.

Macmillan. (1983). *The college blue book* (Vols. 1–3). New York: Author.

National Academy of Sciences. (1980). *A selected list of fellowship opportunities and aids to advanced education for United States citizens and foreign nationals.* Washington, DC: National Science Foundation.

APPENDIXES

Appendix A

Titles of jobs in human services for students with a bachelor's degree in psychology

Michael J. Zeller, Mankato State University

The following is a list of job titles which were compiled from actual job descriptions available from a variety of sources over one year. The search revealed over 300 jobs whose descriptions and qualifications of acceptable candidates would include undergraduates with formal training at the bachelor's level in psychology. Some require experience in addition to the BA. This list might be used to broaden students' perspectives on the kinds of jobs which are likely to be available in human services and to make students aware of specific titles of jobs when they begin their job search.

activity director
addiction counselor
administrative program assistant
admissions market analyst
admissions—public relations director
admissions recruiter
admissions representative
adolescent care technician
adolescent chemical dependency counselor
advertising trainee
adviser-educator
affirmative action officer
agency representative
airline reservations clerk
alcohol counselor
alcoholism counselor
alcoholism unit manager
area administrator
arena and sports facility instructor
assistant residence manager
assistant youth coordinator
association manager
behavior analyst
camp staff director
caretaker
case tracking specialist
case worker
center supervisor
chemical dependency advocate
chemical dependency coordinator
chemical dependency counselor
chemical dependency secretary

chemical dependency technician
child care counselor
child care worker
child development worker
child protection worker
circulation manager
clerical worker
collection assistant
collector
college admissions representative
community activist
community correctional service worker
community outreach coordinator
community organizer
community service coordinator
community worker
compliance officer
consultant
cottage treatment team
counselor
counselor aid
counselor (drug)
counselor/therapist
county personnel officer
crime prevention coordinator
customer relations
customer service trainee
daily living aid
day-care aid
demonstration coordinator
deputy juvenile probation officer
developmental reading instructor
development officer
director of activity and recreation
director of alumni relations
director of day-care center
director of displaced homemakers
director of human services
director of Indian education
director of planned parenthood
director of planning
director of security
director of youth service bureau
driving instructor
drug counselor

early childhood specialist
education prevention specialist
education daytime coordinator
educational coordinator
educational representative
educational salesperson
educational textbook representative
employee assistance program specialist
employee counselor
employment counselor
employment representative
executive director
export order coordinator
field representative
foster home parent
grants coordinator
group home coordinator
group home counselor
group home parents
group leader
group worker
head of alumni affairs
head of fund raising
host/hostess
houseparents
human relations director
human services technician
infant stimulation teacher
information specialist
information referral specialist
inservice director
instructor
instructor, handicapped adult program
insurance agent
interviewer
investigator
juvenile justice planner
juvenile prevention program coordinator
juvenile specialist
living unit assistant
loading dock superintendent
management trainee
marketing manager
mental retardation professional
mental retardation unit manager
neighborhood outreach worker
occupational information developer
park and recreation director
patient service representative
personnel analyst
personnel coordinator

personnel generalist
planner-assistant
planner-evaluator
private school representative
private tutor
probation officer
professional worker
program consultant
program coordinator
program director
project learning instructor
police training coordinator
public information officer
rehabilitation aid
relief houseparents
research analyst/planner
research assistant
research trainee
residence counselor
resident aid
resident caretaker
residential assistant
residential director
residential service coordinator
residential supervisor
resource developer
retain manager
salesperson
secretary
security officer
service adviser
social security adjudicator
social security interviewer
social service director
social services supervisor
social studies teacher
social worker
social worker coordinator
statistical assistant
student activities adviser
supervisor
support service manager
task force coordinator
temporary admissions clerk
textbook coordinator
trainer
trainer-coordinator
veteran's adviser
volunteer coordinator
work activity program director
youth worker

Appendix B

Guidelines for preparing a student advisement handbook

One of the most useful resources for advising is a student handbook providing possible psychology majors with a well-prepared handbook of basic information about obtaining a psychology degree and going on to work or further study. Such a handbook (a) saves the adviser time by allowing him or her to concentrate on students' questions and concerns that go beyond general information and (b) gives the student a source of information he or she can refer to when advisers are not available. There is no standard student handbook—the resources and requirements of each department and school vary too much. However, there are components that should be included in such handbooks.[1]

Keys to Successful Preparation

• Information should be easy to find and be written in a how-to format.

• The handbook should be attractively prepared, make use of headlines and subheads, and be easy and economical to update.

• Do not duplicate information that is available from another source; that is, concentrate on what is unique to your program and use publications such as *Is Psychology the Major for You?*, *Careers in Psychology*, *Ethical Principles for Psychologists*, and similar publications to provide general information about psychology and being a psychologist.

What to include

• Table of contents

• Resource list—what materials are available and their location in department or school library, or how to obtain them

• Psychology faculty description—number, names, and areas of specialization

• List of courses in other departments that are psychology-related

Explain how the psychology department and these other departments relate to each other in preparation for courses and degrees.

• Student activities
  Organizations—on campus and off-campus
  Research opportunities
    Ethical principles in research
    Funding sources for undergraduates
  Writing activities
    Research reports
    Term papers
    Field experience

• On-campus resources
  Counseling centers
  Placement centers
  Libraries (department, school)

• Graduate school information as applicable
  Preparation required
  Recommended reading
  Relationship and value of bachelor's, master's, and doctorate degrees
  Required entrance exams
  Information on successful graduate acceptances and list of schools students have entered

• Information on honor codes, ethical codes, plagarism, and so forth

• Sources of information on psychology

• Information on American Psychological Association (APA) and APA divisions, Psi Chi

Each year, before the school session begins, the student handbook and other resources should be reviewed and updated. New publications (both books and journal articles) should be added to the department library.

Footnotes

1. Portions of the guidelines were adopted from *A Guide to Preparing a Psychology Student Handbook* by Douglas W. Bloomquist, copies of which can be obtained from the Educational Affairs Office, American Psychological Association, 1200 17th Street, NW, Washington, DC 20036.

Your Responses to *Is Psychology for Them?*

Dear Reader:

We invite your comments or suggestions concerning this title. Did you find the information helpful? What else would you like to have discussed? Please write your comments below and send them to:

American Psychological Association
1400 North Uhle Street, Room 700
Arlington, VA 22201
Attn.: Separate Publications

Name: _____

Address: _____

_____

_____

Phone: _____

Please do not remove. A photocopy may be used.